THE LIFESTYLE

A Look at the Erotic Rites of Swingers

TERRY GOULD

FIREFLY BOOKS

A FIREFLY BOOK

Published by Firefly Books Ltd. 2000

Second Printing, 2001

U.S. Cataloguing in Publication Data

Gould, Terry, 1949–
The lifestyle: a look at the erotic rites of swingers/Terry Gould.–
1ˢᵗ ed. [392] p. : cm.
Originally published: Canada: Random House Canada, 1999.
Published by arrangement with Random House Canada,
a division of Random House of Canada Limited.

Includes bibliographic references and index.
Summary: An examination of the "swinger" sub-culture in North America.
ISBN 1-55209-482-0
1. Group sex. 2. Sex customs. I. Title.
306.77/097 –dc21   2000
CIP

First published in the United States in 2000 by
Firefly Books (U.S.) Inc.
P.O. Box 1338, Ellicott Station
Buffalo, New York
14205

Cover design: CS Richardson
Cover image: Detail taken from *The Worship of Venus*
by Peter Paul Rubens, Kunsthistorisches Museum, Vienna
Interior design: Sun Ngo

Printed and bound in the United States of America

To my wife Leslie

Table of Contents

We ought not to view it as something special, as depraved or in some magical way better than other kinds of behavior. We ought to see it simply as a kind of behavior some disapprove of and others value, studying the process by which either or both perspectives are built up and maintained.

HOWARD BECKER, *Outsiders*

CHAPTER ONE

Welcome to the Lifestyle

Do not do unto others what you don't want others to do unto you.

HILLEL

Tribal rituals of spouse exchange. Neolithic hordes dancing naked upon the heath. Whole cities pouring into the streets in libidinous revelry.

Throughout human history these practices have been used as a means to extend kinship ties, as celebrations of fertility, or as an annual blowing off of steam. Erotic rites were common in Canaan when God made His covenant with Abraham. As late as the 1940s "extra-mateship liaison" was an approved custom in 39 percent of cultures studied throughout the world—from the Himalayas to the South Seas and from the Arctic to the Amazon. Today we know that there is a deeper, unconscious motivation behind the rituals. They combine the two biological imperatives that paradoxically have governed the sex lives of humans for eons: the drive to seek long-term partners for raising children, and the equally powerful drive for genetic and sexual variety.

Of course, many of us do not accept shared eroticism between couples as a normal part of life. Sensual play between more than two people is often seen as coercive, compulsive, or even evil. That belief is the chief reason one of the great stories of our time has remained truly untold.

This book breaks the lock on denial. It tells the story of "the lifestyle," a subculture that is now thriving worldwide, one in which millions of middle-class, married couples openly express their erotic fantasies with others. Accompany your own spouse to a lifestyle event and you will change your mind about the boundaries of behavior for pair-bonded humans.

Acting within strict rules of etiquette, lifestyle couples participate to varying degrees in everything from sexual costume parties to multipartner sex as a form of social recreation within
marriage. Every ball they attend revives the time-honored tradition of the rustic bacchanal.

The lifestyle has grown so quickly in recent years that,
wherever you live, you won't have trouble finding it. It is not
an underground movement or a cult. It is a public, grass-roots,
heterosexual orientation among mainstream couples who
claim to have overcome the kind of loneliness, jealousy, and
shame adulterous marrieds endure. Lifestyle "playcouples"
belong to three hundred formally affiliated clubs in two dozen
countries, and to thousands of unaffiliated clubs. They have
their own travel industry that flies them to a dozen vacation
spots catering to their tastes. Hundreds of magazines and
thousands of Web sites, news groups, and chat rooms keep
them connected. Large lifestyle conventions are held eleven
times a year in eight U.S. states, sometimes monopolizing
entire resorts. The three-day Lifestyles '96 convention in San
Diego drew thirty-five hundred people from 437 cities in seven
countries. One-third of the participants had postgraduate
degrees; almost a third voted Republican; 40 percent considered themselves practicing Protestants, Catholics or Jews.
Public figures with towering positions in society, pro-sex
feminists, and even evangelical Christians attended the convention as "lifestylers."

But where did this term "lifestyle" come from? Aren't
the couples who say they are "in the lifestyle" talking about
swinging—the free and easy sharing of spouses at parties?
Lifestylers will patiently tell you that some of their number
don't go that far. They adopted their global name in the 1980s
because more and more "straight" couples were attending
their events and they wanted to be freed from the snappy terms
that made them into media fast food. A lifestyle party quite

often does not culminate in sexual intercourse among couples; roughly 10 percent of the people who attend just like being in an atmosphere where such an interchange is conceivable. Lifestylers believe they live in a certain *style* that melds responsible family values—matrimony, children, emotional monogamy—with the erotic cultivation of their marriages through the practice of rites they celebrate as fun and natural.

It's that simple. And it's that complicated.

Even the most avid proponents of the subculture admit the behavior of playcouples can sometimes appear pornographic —a threat to civil society—especially when strobe-lit in a camera's flash or summed up by the bug-eyed mainstream press as a shocking exposé of swingers running rampant. Lifestylers have been described as "uncivilized," "dangerous," "smelly," "repellent," "tacky," and "revolting," labeled as "deviates" and zoomorphized as lizards and hippos. Never comfortable with the chaos of sex, city police forces and government agencies regularly investigate lifestyle clubs: they infiltrate dances and threaten to withdraw the liquor licenses of the hotels that host them; they raid private homes and charge participants with public lewdness; and they sometimes wind up arresting themselves since a number of male and female police officers are lifestyle members.

Despite this harassment by morality squads, most studies show lifestylers to be "absolutely not deviant" and "quite normal psychologically." They also note the behavior of swingers "does not involve a victim." The movement has a California-based overseeing body, called the Lifestyles Organization, or LSO, that certifies clubs as ethical, nondiscriminatory, and law-abiding. The lifestyle's out-of-the-closet spokespeople, who come from the ranks of social workers and business managers, doctors and mortgage brokers, insist their millions of compatriots behave in a safe and consensual fashion. On LSO's board of directors sits an executive from Mensa and a former chair of the sociology department at the University of California at Riverside. They broaden the discussion of the lifestyle by claiming that when examined in the cool light of the latest research on the biological, evolutionary, and emotional roots of human sexuality, the lives of many playcouples force us to re-ask some of the most crucial questions of human history. Why, for instance, has the word "morals" always referred almost entirely to sexual matters? Why has sexual self-sacrifice always been seen as morally superior to sexual indulgence? And why has religion always been so angrily focused on controlling our sex lives, from the time God sent down fire and brimstone to exterminate homosexuals and orgiasts to the Rev. Billy Graham's remark that "if God doesn't do to America what he did to Sodom and Gomorrah, He owes them an apology"?

For average citizens, however, it comes down to this question: Can you dress for the harem or the beach, go to a party with your spouse of ten years, enjoy a night of bacchic sexuality, and still be a good, happily married parent?

You can if you're in the lifestyle. At least according to lifestylers.

———

Although the lifestyle's tradition of sharing spouses has remained unchanged since the subculture's public emergence after World War II, the media's reporting of the practice has gone through various incarnations. Back in the 1950s it was dubbed "wife swapping" in the male-centered press, which alleged that otherwise straight suburban husbands were having their wives throw house keys into a hat to see who would retire with whom for the evening. In the sexually revolutionary sixties wife swapping progressed to a more democratically arranged swinging. Millions watched the 1969 film *Bob & Carol & Ted & Alice* enlivened by the crowded engagements of

California couples who were treated as adventurous and hip in some press outlets, although their real-life counterparts in the heartland were usually declared "bizarre" and "sick." The seventies saw couples warned away from swinging because of the herpes virus and in the eighties they were informed they could die of AIDS if they participated. By the end of the Reagan era swinging was supposedly over, a relic, like LSD and Charles Manson, of the darker side of the best-forgotten past. In their 1989 book *Burning Desires*, journalists Steve Chapple and David Talbot surveyed the coupling patterns of Americans and declared spouse sharing belly up, doused by "a wave of sexual terror." AIDS-terrified swing clubs were closing and those dwindling deviants who hung on seemed to belong in a Fellini film. Swingers had changed their name but they couldn't change the new realities of sex. A Lifestyles convention of die-hards in Las Vegas exhibited mounds of "wilted flesh pushed towards dangerous extremes in the service of pleasure." Hip young people were repulsed. "There was no doubt about it: swinging was no longer cool."

That was the way the lifestyle appeared to me back in 1989, when I was assigned by a Vancouver magazine to produce a feature article on the local swing-club scene. For years my writing had focused on the dark world of organized crime and so I approached the assignment as an investigation of the dark world of organized sex. I infiltrated one dance and one orgy put on by a group of mostly working-class souls in a club called the Vancouver Circles and then rang the warning bell of disease and degeneracy in my article. At a quick glance I concluded that these people needed a dip in the gene pool. Their group sex violated every romantic notion I'd been brought up to believe in and contravened every religious doctrine designed to free the mind from the body so as to promote unselfish behavior. At the same time, they seemed to tear to shreds the warnings about promiscuity issued by health organizations throughout the world. The only things I found intriguing about swingers was that they didn't need to numb themselves with booze to have sex in their unusual way, and they insisted they were just behaving like the movie stars of their day. They even used the term "heterophobia" to describe their treatment in the press.

Not surprisingly, swingers were repugnant to the feminists I talked to, who disbelieved that dancing in see-through lingerie and sharing spouses could be a woman's fantasy, and who were therefore convinced that the wives in Vancouver Circles had to have been coerced into participating. They were disgusting to the moral majority who lived around the Legion-type halls where they held their dances and who saw them as harbingers of the apocalypse and falling real-estate prices. And they were thought of as pathological freaks by the academic liberals I interviewed, who assessed swingers as probably trying to escape their problems in ways that could be equated with addictive drug use.

And yet something odd happened after the publication of my scathingly condemnatory article. I got more telephone calls from curious readers—both male and female—than I'd had for all my articles on the Chinese Mafia, Sikh terrorists and gun-running Nazis combined. Here is a partial transcript of a typical call I received from a woman.

CALLER: Is this the same Terry Gould who wrote "A Dangerous State of Affairs"?

GOULD: The very same.

CALLER: I couldn't believe my eyes. I had no idea that the health department or police would even allow that kind of thing.

GOULD: Well, it's apparently not against the law.

CALLER: It should be.... My husband and I were sickened. Either the women must be lesbians or

I don't know what their husbands have done
to them. Are most of the women lesbians?

GOULD: I guess you'd say some are bisexual.

CALLER: So this is their outlet then....Okay, I'm sorry
to take your time. But just—I thought something should be written more on the subject.
Are you permitted to give me a telephone number for this so-called swing club?

One way or another, most of the people who called me got
around to asking that question, and I doubted it was because
they intended to picket the Vancouver Circles club, which
actually saw an increase in membership. Who knows but
maybe these callers were among the 20 percent of women and
40 percent of men under forty-four who (according to a
National Health and Social Life Survey) consider that "watching others do sexual things" is "appealing." That was certainly
one of the biggest fascinations for the lifestyle couples I'd met.
Perhaps my female callers were among the 10 percent of
women who admitted to pollsters that they found sex with a
stranger appealing, or the 9 percent who considered group sex
in the same favorable way?

What I certainly noticed over the next few years was that
the lifestyle movement began to take off. The personals ads in
newspapers were filled with couples seeking other couples; a
thirteen-acre lifestyle resort with "twelve thousand square feet
of party space" was doing a thriving international business just
across the border in Washington State; and new clubs were
sprouting up all over North America. Pretty soon I found my
own article in good company: GQ, Marie Claire, Details, and
even the thoroughly hedonistic Penthouse all published sarcas-
tic and sanctimonious assessments of swingers. One article in
Esquire, titled "Deviates in Love," broke the news that "at this
very moment, all across America, millions of others are doing

the same thing." If millions were doing it, I began to think, why were they called deviates? Why were public voices still denigrating them in ways one would never accept if they were gays or lesbians—on whose behalf feminists, liberals, and arts-funding agencies were now adopting a vigorous defence. Watching a number of government-backed documentary films about gays (the Canadian Broadcasting Corporation's *Coming Out*), lesbians (the National Film Board's *Forbidden Fantasies*), and voguing drag queens (the National Endowment for the Arts-supported *Paris is Burning*), I began to ponder in a new light the couples who were drawn to this avowedly heteroerotic subculture. I also became suspicious that those publications that condemned lifestylers for their organized licentiousness were actually capitalizing on the vicarious needs of their readers. Had I hurt some vulnerable people simply by denying them the same dignified treatment afforded other "fringe groups" in society who were now recognized as victims of sexual intolerance?

Then, in 1993, I met an articulate couple in the lifestyle whose seeming normalcy contradicted everything printed about swingers in the popular press. I was at a party for a prominent Vancouver author when I overheard a woman joking to her husband about moving the whole staid crowd down to New Horizons—the thirteen-acre swing club in Washington. That got my attention. I introduced myself, and, after assuring the pair we were off-the-record, I learned that they'd been in the lifestyle for five years in the States and had then moved smoothly into the swing scene here in British Columbia. When I told them I couldn't picture them at the Vancouver Circles parties I'd attended, they informed me that in many of the clubs in which they'd been members there were people they couldn't relate to at all, but maintained that, as in any group, "you have to pick and choose your friends." Much of the time, they said, they didn't even swing. They just enjoyed being in a close-knit crowd of married people where the boundary between friendship and sex was a titillating line to be openly approached, not a wall to sneak around in deceit. They also offered an interesting explanation for the variety of mainstream opposition to their behavior: married couples, they said, both treasure and are terrified of the adulterously wild genies in their bottled bodies (ergo the term "heterophobia") and would rather sneak the cork open in secrecy than have a fling in the open. "Men and women who cheat on their partners are addicted to dangerous romance," the woman told me. "In the lifestyle we've grown out of that immaturity. Straight people think we spoil all the fun. Actually, we don't threaten morality—we threaten immorality."

At that moment, looking at this couple against a backdrop of academics and writers (some of whom I knew to be adulterous), I began to believe there might be a broader dimension to their lifestyle—a "true movement," the couple claimed, about which the world had an incomplete understanding.

They gave me a contact number for a Vancouver association called New Faces New Friends—a "Cadillac club," they called it, as opposed to the "low rent" Vancouver Circles club I'd written about. New Faces New Friends was so discreetly run that I'd never heard of it, but it had become so profitable in the last three years that its owners, known to the world as Jim and Linda, were in the process of purchasing a mansion in the suburbs as the first step to opening a ten-acre lifestyle resort. (The resort is currently called Paradise Ranch and it packs in more than a hundred people on many weekends. It has an Olympic-size pool, a glassed-in dance floor lit by swirling strobe lights, dining facilities, "straight" recreation areas for neophyte couples, and softly lit rooms lined with beds separated by translucent muslin.)

When I met Jim and Linda a few weeks after the author's party, I found them to be attractive, perceptive, and disarmingly straightforward; like William Masters and Virginia Johnson they had seen just about every human behavior there was to see when inhibitions are cast off. They said they made sure their 250-couple organization retained its cultured panache by conducting lengthy interviews with all prospective members. These were rigorous affairs in which couples were assessed for any hint that one partner might be coercing the other into joining. "Women drive the lifestyle movement," Linda told me emphatically. "We would never accept any couple in which the wife was not as interested in exploring the lifestyle as the husband. If I even suspect otherwise, I tell them both, 'Go home and think again.'"

"I hate when jerks call the lifestyle wife swapping," Jim averred. "I hate that term and what it implies. By that I mean a woman being forced into something because her husband says, 'Look honey, let's go.' To me that's abuse. That's opposite to what the lifestyle is all about."

In fact, there was no *single* lifestyle, Jim and Linda told me, and they were particularly resentful of the received wisdom that their subculture was populated only by groping orgiasts. A certain percentage of their clients came to parties merely to express the usual voyeuristic and exhibitionist fantasies that are part and parcel of erotic parades. Others practiced "soft swinging," which only permitted nudity, massage, and some sexual touching. Some drew the line at having "side-by-side" sex with another couple, with no spouse exchange. "Open swingers" practiced spouse exchange with a couple in the same room. "Closed swingers" enjoyed the circumscribed thrill of adjourning to separate rooms to make love with exchanged partners. None of which is to say that on a roaring night I might not see wives involved in lesbian daisy chains three links long, and other couples group-chambering the way I had seen the busy bodies at Vancouver Circles enjoying themselves. Basically, it seemed from their rundown, couples

set their own parameters and accepted and respected the parameters of others.

The lifestyle was also not about dying of a dark disease,
Jim said, a pointed concern given the number of different
people to which some couples made love. While Jim didn't
patrol the many bedrooms on his premises with a flashlight,
he did have a safe-sex rule, and his PR brochure stated, "Com-
plimentary condoms are available and placed in several convenient locations in the house and we encourage you to practice
safe sex at all times."

Jim gave me permission to attend parties so long as I kept
things on a first-name basis. (Couples at lifestyle gatherings
generally identify themselves as, say, "Jack and Jill"; in these
pages I've sometimes modified that to "John and Jody.") A few
weeks later, New Faces New Friends held a "Ladies' Lingerie
Night" in a ballroom at a suburban hotel that was quite posh.
I showed up to find middle-aged career women wearing practically nothing. There was one woman in a fishnet outfit and
no underwear, another in underwear and no outfit, yet another
dressed as a bikinied version of Dracula. At ten o'clock many
of the ladies lined up for a beauty contest. One by one these
executives, teachers, and real-estate agents strode across the
dance floor, stopped in the spotlight and assumed grandly
self-parodying poses, then ran off to embrace their laughing
husbands and friends. Dracula won a gift certificate from a
lingerie shop.

I watched this amazing display from a table where I was
sitting beside a stunning woman anomalously attired in jeans
and an old sweat shirt. I turned to her and told her I was a
writer and that I was thinking of exploring the lifestyle in
depth. Maybe I would make a documentary. Maybe I would
write a serious book.

"Oh I think that is marvelous," Ellie said, in accented
English. "It is time. Now is the time." When I asked her why

she was a lifestyler, she replied: "The reason is simple. I do not like to lie."

"One thing in life that is lied about most is sex," her husband Jerard said. "You look around here. What do you notice? Very many women almost naked—better than naked, very sexy, no?" He gestured at the dance floor, now packed with intermingling couples. "These men, they are acting very civilized. No groping, even when they dance close. See? Now, imagine if any of these ladies, they go to a disco dressed like this?"

"There's no understanding, no matter what you wear—none," added Ellie. "Just young brutes, old brutes. Men proving themselves. Sex and anger—sex and jealousy."

Another couple, Murray and Cara, pulled back chairs and sat down at our table. "You do find a percentage of bi-women," Murray said when I asked him about the lesbian component in the lifestyle. "It's a mode of expression."

I then posed what in my own mind was The Big Question: How did they handle jealousy? Why were they not plagued with stabs of hate and angry recriminations that a single wayward kiss at a normal party would elicit from a spouse? I told them I was married for twenty-two years and that if I ever caught my wife cheating on me my entire world would be upended.

"Who's talking about cheating?" Murray laughed. "Watching her is one of my biggest pleasures in this lifestyle."

"I enjoy the pleasure of Murray when he's enjoying sex with a woman," Cara said. "I do get a vicarious thrill. But that doesn't violate our devotion. And Murray knows that my pleasure with someone—be it a man or a woman—doesn't lessen my devotion to him."

Again and again I would hear that refrain in the ballroom. In the lifestyle, they all said, veteran playcouples become connoisseurs at transforming their own spouse into an alluring fantasy figure. Once they learned that their relationship was not threatened by comarital sex acts—acts that very rarely became extramarital affairs—a husband or wife found observing their partner with another was an enormous aphrodisiac. And they often watched each other with their eyes locked in love. After parties they had sex as if they'd just met.

"You see," Ellie said, "straight people, they cheat on each other all the time. Tremendous percentages. They lie. They sneak. But the erotic act is part of our marriage. It is not an act of cheating, but play. Flirtation, it's between us—as a couple—and someone else. Jerry is always there, he is there. We do not cheat, we do not lie."

Cara kissed Murray's forehead. "I always save the last dance for him."

None of this is to say that after expanding my circle of acquaintances in New Faces New Friends I did not encounter marriages that had rearranged themselves in the club, that people were not hurt, or that I didn't learn of swinging "dropouts." I tracked down one such exile from the subculture, a Vancouver professional who told me that he regretted the day he introduced his common-law wife to the erotic exchanges at Jim and Linda's. He said they were not part of any "depressing, anonymous, look-for-a-space-and-jump-in crowd." They had in fact set up a series of sensitive, lasting friendships with intellectual couples in which several dinner dates or camping trips would go by without sex. The difference, of course, was that if sex did come up, it was not forbidden. He and his partner had an understanding whereby they "shared the excitement as part of our relationship." But after a year of pick-and-choose fun at the club, his woman experienced a flaming session with the mythical man of her dreams, and was lost to him for good. "It was a devastating shock," he told me, pointing out that he had somehow deluded himself regarding the possibility of an unexpected, heartfelt detonation occurring during sex. "It would be wrong to say that this is not a charged and dangerous atmosphere to become involved in. I'd hate to see you advocating it."

Not long after he offered me this warning, however, he was back on the margins of the lifestyle, attending parties on special occasions. And not long after that I learned that his former common-law wife had dumped her swinging lover and then taken up with a straight married man.

———

Was the lifestyle delusional, then? Compulsive? A fetish? How much of my previous thinking about it was accurate? Were swingers—as I'd claimed in "A Dangerous State of Affairs"— risking their health while distracting themselves from lives they cannot endure?

When my 1989 magazine article first appeared, Dr. Frank Darknell, a professor of sociology at the University of California, Sacramento, phoned me up to tell me that he was troubled by the same things about the lifestyle that troubled me. The year before, this austere, strait-laced Ph.D. had begun a study of swingers and the historical and prehistorical background of open sexuality and spouse sharing out of which the modern lifestyle was born. He'd found that this sexual culture was actually old hat in aboriginal North America until the missionaries arrived and put an end to it. In the nineteenth century, partner sharing was picked up by communards and free-love radicals. Artists and secret societies embraced it in the 1920s, and eventually it evolved into the open sexuality of the left-wing beatniks and the swing parties of otherwise conservative suburbanites. But his preliminary research confirmed that there had never been a time when the practice had not been assessed as grossly outlandish by the vast majority of North Americans, some of whom now saw AIDS as a divine justification for their condemnations.

When Darknell and I said good-bye on the phone in 1989 we agreed that I'd probably hit the nail on the head with my article: modern swingers could be involved in a risky and never-satisfied search for sensation. Then, after setting up a database of swinger publications, Darknell attended the August '89 Lifestyles convention in Las Vegas where he met and interviewed many participants. After this sojourn among thousands of suburbanite swingers Darknell arrived at an opinion at variance to the one he had expressed in our first conversation, and similar to the self-conscious caution and confusion I now had about leaping to eviscerating judgments. From what he could see, he told me years later, swingers were not maladjusted perverts hellbent on self-destruction. "They were well-mannered and decent to each other," he said. "Really, they're folks you wouldn't question, except that they seemed to enjoy behaving that way with one another, running around to all these seminars on swinging and going to the parties. They didn't rob banks, their fantasies don't include anything that's illegal—like involving children and that sort of thing—and it looked very consensual."

I told him that the swingers I had met claimed that women drove the lifestyle movement.

"Well, you know," he replied, "there's a point at which that becomes true, once they become involved. Their husbands get them into it, of course, but then they find things about it they really like—being the glamorous queen bee and that sort of thing. The women were on all these committees arranging events and the like—they were quite enthusiastic."

I reminded him that back in 1989 we had both been concerned that HIV/AIDS could explode in the swinging community the way it had in the gay community but that, despite the million or so couples who had been going to clubs for years, I'd heard of very few cases of HIV-infected swingers in North America. Darknell had also heard of only a few cases and attributed the lack of an outbreak of the disease in the subculture to various "co-factors." His opinion was that while HIV/AIDS could spread in swing clubs, the co-factors were probable explanations for why it hadn't.

Contrary to the lifestyle's "anything goes" attitude toward adult sexual fantasies, bisexual contact between men is taboo behavior in swing clubs, as is drug use. In 1986, after the Centers for Disease Control reported in its journal that two female members of swing clubs in Minnesota tested positive for HIV after having anal intercourse with bisexual men, "Greek" between swinging men and women became frowned upon as well. These days, statistically, we know that the rate of transmission of HIV is roughly one in two thousand per act of unprotected vaginal intercourse if neither partner has another STD, and ten times that if one partner does have a venereal disease. One poll of attendees at the Lifestyles '96 convention would eventually show that 92 percent of 312 respondents believed swingers "should" be using condoms, and that 77 percent had had HIV tests. Thus, many lifestylers (not all) probably use condoms. In addition, the screening process at almost all clubs helps keep members to middle-class couples who probably maintain their health in typically bourgeois fashion, running to the doctor at the slightest sign of venereal disease. To say the least, the statistics regarding the heterosexual transmission of HIV are not a sanction of free-wheeling partner exchange, and almost all health experts agree that people should be using protection when having sex outside of marriage, straight or swinger. (I concur with this view.) That has not kept millions of straights—nor, I can tell you, some lifestylers—from going ahead and having unprotected sex anyway.*

---

* In 1998, Dr. Norman Scherzer, a Clinical Associate Professor at the University of Medicine and Dentistry in New Jersey and a lecturer on human sexuality and STDs

When Darknell returned from the 1989 Lifestyles Convention he collated his preliminary findings and submitted them to his university for a research grant that would enable him to complete his study. He was turned down, for reasons he felt in part could have had to do with the general distaste in officialdom for what they saw as "wife swapping." "I talked to John Money," Darknell told me, referring to the Johns Hopkins University sexologist, "and he predicted I'd never get the grant, not for an ethological study on the sex practices of swingers. So be it.

"Basically," he went on, "what I found was that the main concern of swingers wasn't health but whether to come out of the closet. Swingers justify themselves in exactly the same way homosexuals do, and I suppose we have to respect their right to do so. They don't want to get fired from their jobs if they're exposed, or have their clubs shut down. But if they come out they risk that."

———

In May 1993, when I got in touch with the Lifestyles Organization in Anaheim, I learned that eliminating the threat of a backlash was one of the main concerns of the lifestyle's international overseeing body. Lifestylers in California were now declaring

---

at Rutgers University, informed me that the co-factors Darknell cited probably account for why he, too, has not heard of an outbreak of HIV at swing clubs. Scherzer has scrutinized the sexual practices of swingers since the early 1990s and lectures at Lifestyles conventions on the risks of having unprotected sex. The CDC has not published any studies of swing clubs since the 1986 article about the Minnesota clubs, and Patricia Fleming, Chief of the Surveillance Branch of the CDC's HIV/AIDS Division, told me at the 1996 Aids Conference in Vancouver that her division had not received any reports of outbreaks of HIV among heterosexuals identified as swing-club members since the HIV-positive tests in Minnesota were published. It is possible, of course, that among those heterosexuals who have tested HIV-positive there are some who have simply not announced themselves as swing-club members.

themselves a political force, and LSO formed campaign central. It was headed by a goateed, former aerospace engineer, Dr. Robert McGinley, a sixty-year-old counseling psychologist who was at the time almost universally described in the media as a reckless libertarian and shrewd businessman.

McGinley invited me to attend his annual convention at Las Vegas's Riviera Hotel in August and I decided to spend the $350 for the three-day gathering. It coincided nicely with my research for a story I was working on at the time. I was looking for a Vancouver gangleader named Steven Wong whom the RCMP heroin squad believed had staged his own death and cremation in order to escape drug trafficking charges. I appreciated the irony that, in his own criminal way, Wong considered himself a swinger. Though short and dumpy, he had many gorgeous girlfriends who were attracted by his flashy and dangerous lifestyle. The number one woman in Wong's harem happened to have been connected through marriage to a couple of big shareholders in a luxury Las Vegas casino. The marble tower constantly entertained a mix of high-rolling racketeers who looked out for one another. I thought it might be possible to attend the swing convention and also discover some rounder who had seen the disappeared desperado after his supposed death.

The convention was a couples-only affair and so I asked my wife to come along. Not being a stranger to people who inhabited subcultures Leslie agreed to join me. By day she may have been an executive director of a communications firm, but by night she sketched nudes at a bohemian studio where many of her companions were in the gay or lesbian lifestyle. She is, in all facets of her life, no shrinking violet. When I first met Leslie in 1970 she worked as New York City's only female cab driver. Twenty years later columnist Allan Fotheringham, Leslie's friend and client, nicknamed her "Ms. Giotti," partly because she has the same accent as the New York Mafia boss, partly because she possesses what he calls "da attitude." Over-all, Leslie and I weren't just husband and wife: we were best friends, cooperative colleagues, business partners, and good lovers. On the morning of August 17, 1993, when I told her in the airport that I was a pretty lucky guy, she punnishly summed up her willingness to travel where perhaps other wives wouldn't: "If you wrote about cannibals and needed me for cover, I'd go—just so long as I didn't have to eat anybody."

That afternoon Leslie and I entered a social whirl of three thousand wheatfield North Americans dressed like the stars who all expressed their relief at being in a virtual city-state ruled by the norms of playcouples. Throughout the event the throngs of middle-class swingers were reassured that they weren't aberrant by nonswingers sanctioned by straight society. Luis De La Cruz, for instance, headed the Erotic Arts Exhibit at the convention and was the facilities director of the Music Center of Los Angeles County and the curator of the Newport Harbor Art Museum. The convention's keynote speaker was Stan Dale, winner of the Mahatma Gandhi Peace Medallion. Forty seminars were delivered by ten Ph.D.s and other experts on everything from "Sexuality and Spirituality" and "Exotic Playcouple Travel" to an "AIDS Update" by Dr. Norman Scherzer, the Rutgers University expert on STDs.

Most fascinating of all, I encountered a whole clutch of people who were living their lives as out-of-the-closet swingers. Their parents knew, their friends knew, in some cases their kids and grandkids knew. One couple, Frank and Jennifer Lomas, a former bank broker and a business manager, had left high-paying positions to work at LSO because they wanted to be surrounded all the time by people like themselves. They were a gentle, interracial couple in their late thirties, unabashed advocates of partner sharing, and they had not been treated kindly by studio audiences on TV talk shows, who'd shouted them down with catcalls such as "We hope you die of AIDS!"

"Most swingers will tell you they're not in it for an orgy," said Frank, son of an Air Force sergeant-major, after he and Jennifer had delivered a convention seminar called "Social Games for Fun, Laughter and Intimacy." "Some are like that, but everyone else is in it for the social interaction and the erotic acceptance. You wind up with a trusting fellowship," he added, using a phrase that perhaps came from his occasional attendance at his local black Baptist Church.

I had been reading about some of the economic origins of spouse exchange, and so I asked Jennifer about her relationships with swingers outside of parties. It turned out she and Frank were part of a tight-knit group of thirty couples who cooperated in every way, like a tribe. They had an investment club, a camping club, and a ski club. "When people stop the sexual control, it's such a relief to them," Jennifer told me. "You can be married twenty or thirty years, and you can go to a lifestyle party with your partner and have the security of your relationship throughout. You can do that right into old age. I think that holds a lot of appeal for women—it's why you see them running the show here."

Whether or not women actually "ran the show," there is no question that at the theme dances Leslie and I attended hundreds of middle-aged ladies displayed their sexuality to men in a way that made us both wonder how the world had gone on as it had for five thousand years. By the night of the grand finale Erotic Costume Ball I understood that these people had tilted their lives 23 degrees sideways and believed they were now properly aligned with the natural axis of the earth. I heard people say things like: "The minority knows more about the majority than the majority knows about the minority." And this, from a European woman dressed as Marlene Dietrich: "When you're forty the lifestyle is permitted; when you're sixty it's recommended; and when you're eighty it's compulsory."

On the morning after the erotic costume ball I stepped out

into the solar furnace of Las Vegas Boulevard and took a walk south. Behind me, on one end of the strip, the attendees at the organized sex convention were waiting for limos to take them to the airport. At the other end of the strip the attendees at the ongoing organized crime "convention" were in full swing. I thought of what Ellie had told me at the New Faces New Friends dance regarding her opinion of the straight world: "Just young brutes, old brutes. Men proving themselves. Sex and anger—sex and jealousy." As a journalist, as a man, I was standing between two worlds back then. For so long I had been surrounded by criminal brutes who used force and violence to demonstrate their attractiveness to women, and, on the other side of the law, men who fought the good fight against them—but perhaps for not entirely different reasons. At some level, I believed, every male understood that one of the rewards of living dangerously was being considered attractive by women. The equation is one of the biological mysteries of life. Lawmen, lawyers, gangsters, and journalists were particularly well placed to demonstrate to women that they were hunters able to provide resources and excitement. And yet here in Las Vegas (of all places), and at New Faces New Friends, and even at Vancouver Circles, the swinging men I'd met didn't need, or want, to pose as dangerous risk takers to make themselves more attractive to women. Swinging women didn't need, or want, them to do so. The exhibition of strength and assets was not necessary for the acquisition of partners in their world. I had the feeling I had been witnessing something profound in the swing world—tacky as it was to most people. It was a way of living that my previous reporting experience had not prepared me to write about at all. I wanted to explain it rather than just expose it.

It would be another three years before I left what swingers call "the real world" and entered their world full time. I knew it was a risky career move. "People will think you did it for the

sex," a straight friend of mine told me. "Just to give yourself an
excuse to swing." I accepted that as a logical suspicion about a
man in his mid forties. Indeed, when the crowd was attractive,
as it was at Lifestyles conventions, I did like looking at couples
who wore sexy clothing. Sometimes, like many men, I did like
"watching others do sexual things." But, as at a nude beach,
that novelty soon wore thin. Once I'd been to a few lifestyle
parties in a row, I could concentrate on the dynamics of the
behavior rather than the visual aspects of it. For me, and for
Leslie, the experience of being in a room filled with lifestyle
couples was sometimes erotic, sometimes uncomfortable, and
sometimes just plain funny. Generally, it was like going to the
circus without wanting to run away and join it.

It was the *behavior* of these everyday people who had
broadened their sexual practices into an all-encompassing lifestyle that fascinated me. And it was the denial that what they
did was explainable that motivated me. The news had been
spread far and wide that the gay lifestyle had been reasoned
through by geneticists, anthropologists, biologists, and ethi-
cists. But there was a virtual blackout on the news that the
swinging lifestyle had also been reasoned through by experts in
those same fields. In place of this news there was scolding. I
wanted to explain the scolding too.

In the end, I know that I did not write this book "for the
sex." I spent months on my own among willing, beautiful
swinging women, and I never cheated on Leslie once.

CHAPTER TWO

The Hero of Suburbia

Just look at our evolution as a nation and you'll
see where the playcouple fits in naturally.

ROBERT MCGINLEY

There's a tale the president of the Life-styles Organization likes to relate about the moment he realized he would spend the rest of his days publicly fighting for swingers' rights. I first heard this tale when I arrived at LSO headquarters in the summer of 1996 and found Robert McGinley on the phone with a couple of members of Dallas' Inner Circles club recently arrested in a raid that had also netted a house full of their white-collar friends, including a Drug Enforcement Administration agent and his partner. When McGinley got off the phone, he turned to me and began to tell his "pebble story." He said he'd named the story after an incident in a children's novel in which an Etruscan warrior, vowing to avenge the devastation of a town, picks up a pebble and carries it with him as a reminder of the change in his consciousness.

McGinley's pebble story takes place in 1966 in Washington, D.C., outside the headquarters of the Department of the Air Force. The compactly built and bearded thirty-three-year-old was then an aerospace engineer employed by the Bendix Corporation to design and test some of the most sophisticated electronics systems in America's aircraft arsenal. He was a civilian, but in his line of work he needed a security clearance, subject to military regulations—which included a code that oversaw the sex lives of all uniformed personnel. The week before, McGinley had been summoned to Washington from his office on California's Travis Air Force Base, where the top-secret SR-71 spy plane was being tested. The charge against Tech-Rep McGinley was sexual deviance.

Walking beside McGinley on the road to his epiphany was a senior bureaucrat named Cronin, the head of an investigation team that monitored the sexuality of soldiers. Without legal warrant, the Air Force had been intercepting McGinley's private mail and then turning it over to Cronin's team, which had been working its way through a web of sexual intrigue that spidered out from almost every military base in the country. One of the strands they pulled from that web led to the hapless McGinley, then in the middle of a divorce from his fundamentalist Christian wife. Some months before, McGinley happened to have answered an ad placed by a sergeant's wife in a swinger magazine. Her erotic reply to him, and his reply to her, had brought him to this moment.

Overhead, a Huey chopper was hovering so that McGinley and Cronin had to shout to make themselves heard as they approached the building where McGinley was, in effect, going to be court-martialed for the crime of composing steamy prose. He was terrified of ruin. He had five children to support, debts to pay, and he was totally dependent on his security clearance. If he lost that clearance he was afraid he'd never get a job in his field again. He'd be fixing television sets.

"I said to Cronin, 'Sir, I swear, it never occurred to me that if I wrote a letter to a swinging lady I would become a security risk.'"

Cronin, six feet tall to McGinley's five-foot-five, and with eyes that never lost focus from a point one yard in front of his hat brim, informed McGinley that his team had some fifty thousand cases of swingers under investigation. The government had reached the "trigger point" when it came to this threat and they were going to remove it by court-martialing and discharging all involved.

"God I was naive," McGinley remembered—in fact, never forgot for a second. "I said: 'Why? Were there any swingers who were Communists?' Because Communists in those days were traitors. Cronin said, 'No, but swinging leads to black-mail by Communists, ruined lives, marriage breakups, suicides, and lost jobs.'

"So I sat there at the hearing, and heard them say the same thing over and over again—how swingers ruined themselves. And when they told me they were revoking my clearance and I began to collapse inside, it hit me. Swinging didn't cause what I was feeling. *They* caused what I was feeling by doing this to me.

"*That* was the pebble! That turned my whole life around. I thought of the fifty thousand people going through what I was going through, for what? And I said under my breath, 'You bastards. You have picked the wrong guy to do this to.'"

———————

As I would learn, it was one of the ironies of McGinley's life that the Department of the Air Force, which rejected him and launched his career as a swinging activist, unwittingly worshipped the memories of America's first modern spouse sharers. According to two doctors of sexology named Joan and Dwight Dixon, who have been in the lifestyle since the sixties and writing on sexuality in journals for two decades, the original spouse sharers were none other than World War II fighter pilots. The marital exchanges that Cronin had been determined to wipe out because they supposedly led to marriage breakups and ruined lives first emerged as an Air Force ritual that united families into a clan and provided an insurance policy for wives.

As Joan and Dwight explained to me later that summer, pilots, unlike infantrymen, were relatively well-paid officers. During the war years they often brought their spouses to live near their bases across the U.S. "There was a special brotherhood among those pilots," Joan said, which was reinforced not only by their elite military status but by their fatality rate (the highest of any branch of service), which would claim one out of every three in combat. It was the pilots who first defied the officer tradition of keeping their wives monogamously at home while they philandered about town. It was the pilots and their wives who invented the term "key club," which was unknown in the forties, became widely known in the fifties and sixties, and then was forgotten until the 1997 film about suburban swingers, *The Ice Storm*. It remains unconfirmed whether airmen actually threw keys in a hat, their wives then randomly choosing one and making love with the owner. Nevertheless, if actual key parties did occur among World War II pilots, the process would have been less random than you'd think. On a combat air base, pilots and their wives were all part of an exclusive caste—with every pilot carrying a set of genes that was probably in the top 1 percent of the nation. They were often extraordinarily attractive men, both as physical specimens and as the kind of risk takers who signal success everywhere they go. The women who married them were risk takers too: they fell for these wild warriors who might very well die within the year.

At first it struck me as odd that the most aggressive and competitive warriors on the planet were also among the least possessive when it came to their wives having sex with other men. But the culture of contemporary swinging to which pilots and their wives gave birth apparently served purposes that went beyond the sexual. They shared each other as a kind of tribal bonding ritual, with a tacit understanding that the two-thirds of the husbands who survived would look after the widows. For North Americans, it marked the start of a whole new, "co-marital" way of experiencing adultery.

When the war was over one of the veterans, whose last name was Leidy and whose first name has disappeared into the mists of swinging history, became a traveling salesman, packing around with him a list of known swingers that came to be called the Leidy List. The Leidy List grew longer with every town the salesman visited, and everywhere he stopped he left copies of the list with swingers. This was probably the original swingers' magazine, with a few details about each couple next to their first names, plus a contact phone number or post office box. Spouse sharing had never really ended on the air bases, however, and in the late 1940s military installations from Maine to Texas and California to Washington had thriving swing clubs that still bore the code word "key" in their names —probably as a metaphor, since, *The Ice Storm* notwithstanding, no academics have ever been able to verify the rumor that swingers drew lots at parties. By the end of the Korean War these "key clubs" had spread from the air bases to the surrounding suburbs among straight, white-collar professionals, and the growth of these clubs was paralleled by the emergence of group sex among the first beatniks of the era. In 1953, the sex statistician Alfred Kinsey made a brief reference to the phenomenon in his book *Sexual Behavior in the Human Female*. Kinsey reported that of the thousands of adulterous histories he and his co-authors had accumulated, "there is a not inconsiderable group of cases in the sample in which the husbands had encouraged their wives to engage in extramarital activities." The motivations of the couples were varied, including the desire of the husband "to find an excuse for his own extramarital activity," but Kinsey concluded his few lines on swinging by restating his primary finding: "It should, however, be emphasized again that most of the husbands who accepted or encouraged their wives' extra-marital activity had done so in an honest attempt to give them the opportunity for additional sexual satisfaction." To Kinsey, "This represented a notable break with the centuries-old cultural tradition."

Kinsey's reference to spouse sharing went almost unnoticed, however, as it was overwhelmed by his exhaustive revelations of other secret sexual behaviors. It was not until 1957 that the story broke in the media—or the fringe media, at least—and was picked up by the mainstream press soon after. Everett Meyers, the New York editor of a semipornographic men's magazine called *MR.*, published a short article on "wife swapping," set between photos of bosomy, half-naked females that were the usual fare of his trade. He had no idea of the impact the story would have. Sales for that issue were so overwhelming that Meyers realized he had hit something like a pressurized stratum of oil. He began to publish a monthly column of letters from readers telling their own suburban tales of orgies with the neighbors. *MR.* prospered and other girlie magazines copied Meyers, adding a twist that would become the staple of the swing world. It was the swinger ad, usually accompanied by the crude swinger photograph, which generally went something like this (at its best): "Attractive white couple, he thirty-seven and fit, she thirty-four with hourglass figure, interested in meeting other couples and bi women for romantic evenings of pleasure. Will answer all."

By 1960, twenty magazines devoted exclusively to swinging ads were selling out on the stands of North America. That led to the first big swing parties, which were advertised in these magazines at twenty-five dollars a couple (big bucks for then), and some of which were attended by hundreds of respectable married pairs. Naturally enough, the wives at these events objected to the term "wife swapping," and, in any case, the public flirtations and hotel-room orgies that took place at these events involved something far more than "swapping." No one knows who came up with the term swinging, though it probably has its ties to the music vernacular of the forties, which in turn probably derives from the freedom of movement which the dances of that era exemplified: it sure captured the loose-limbed freedom of the swingers' gatherings that quickly spread across North America. By the time Robert McGinley opened a club called WideWorld in 1969, everybody knew what swinging was.

———————

"Okay, here's what we're about," Robert McGinley announced, standing directly beneath a model of the *Enola Gay*, the B-29 that dropped the first atomic bomb. "LSO is now mainstreaming the lifestyle. We're showing society how acceptable being a playcouple is. Now I realize certain segments of society may not be too happy with that, but we've come a long way."

McGinley was lecturing me and another writer named David Alexander in the fluorescent-lit board room of the Lifestyles Organization, whose headquarters sit midway between Disneyland and Knott's Berry Farm in Orange County. On a green chalkboard the short, barrel-chested CEO had listed eight LSO companies that circled the globe both physically and electronically and accounted for more than $1.5 million in annual revenue, the employment of fourteen people, and the five thousand square feet of office space around us. According to the figures on the board, LSO, Ltd. had grown by a factor of five since the bad old 1980s when swinging had been declared a public health threat and its so-called "King," McGinley, had been labeled "willfully ignorant," "dangerous," and "irresponsible" in the liberal media. Three hundred swing clubs now belonged to the North American Swing Club Association (NASCA), the trade organization McGinley had founded in 1980. There were three million swingers in the U.S. and Canada and in a month thirty-five hundred of them would be converging for the 1996 Lifestyles convention, scheduled to take over the forty-six-acre Town and Country Resort in San Diego just after the delegates to the Republican National Convention left the premises. Certain Republican bigwigs pushing "family values" held reservations for both conventions.

"I'd say swingers are already pretty mainstream," observed Alexander, writing down McGinley's chalkboard notes. Alexander, the editor of a magazine called *The Humanist*, published by the International Humanist and Ethical Union, was a fifty-year-old nonswinger who occasionally attended LSO's Friday-night dances with his artist wife and their academic friends. He was also the author of the best-selling *Star Trek Creator: The Authorized Biography of Gene Roddenberry*. The combination of Alexander's reputation as a popular writer and an editor led McGinley to ask for his help in designing a Lifestyles Internet magazine. McGinley told me he wanted LSO's magazine to be of a caliber that mainstream, straight couples would never expect to be associated with swinging. In fact, he wanted the magazine to follow *The Humanist*'s editorial mandate to present "a nontheistic, secular, and naturalistic approach to philosophy, science and broad areas of personal and social concern." To be sure, there would be articles on sexuality, marriage, as well as tactfully described swing parties.

"Playcouples are mainstream, of course," McGinley said now, "but most people don't know that. Millions of honest citizens—doctors, lawyers, teachers—they've got to stay in the closet because of how they're perceived."

"They're different-colored chickens and they're afraid they'll be pecked to death by the other chickens," Alexander said.

"That's *got* to stop," McGinley replied. "That's what my life has been about for thirty years. That's what the playcouple philosophy is about."

The two-paragraph playcouple philosophy, posted on McGinley's Playcouple Website, opened with the suggestion that people were naturally non-monogamous: "Adult men and women are sexual beings and they have relationships." Unfortunately, McGinley pointed out, "the religious and political right wing proselytize that open sexual expression is sinful and worthy of condemnation, while the political left wing seeks to inhibit and restrict sincere and honest expression." Defying both political wings, however, playcouples shared erotic fantasies, traveled exotic paths, and placed "the highest value on the intimacy they share with each other and those around them." The word swinging was not mentioned in the playcouple philosophy, although a click of the mouse on the Website gave you a tour of swing clubs on five continents, including McGinley's Club WideWorld, the most successful and longest-running swing club in North America. It was just down the sun-scorched suburban block from us, and every weekend it hosted dozens of playcouples in a Japanese-style mansion featuring a California-size pool and patio, a hot tub, a glass-walled bedroom that bordered the living room, and numerous mini-boudoirs down the hall. "We want to raise the consciousness level of people so that playcouples can come out of the closet if they so choose," McGinley said. "There is no reason anyone should feel they have to be ashamed or afraid, or that they risk anything. These are men and women who are fully enjoying their life and sexuality," he went on, paraphrasing more of the playcouple philosophy in the emphatic manner he'd used in hundreds of TV and radio interviews over the years. "We have every right to the enjoyment that this lifestyle affords us—without interference from religion or neighbors or the boss or government or the media."

A voice paged him on the intercom: "Bob McGinley! *Cosmopolitan*'s on line three." As usual at this time of year, he was receiving a flood of calls from editors, TV producers, and reporters wanting to attend his convention.

"Excuse me, guys, that's their British edition, I gotta take it," McGinley said. "I'm not paying thirty bucks to return an editor's call to England just so she can shaft me. The Brits are as bad as our guys." He was referring to a British edition of *Elle* that had published an article the previous year amply illustrated with bikinied playcouples whom the writer had appraised as society's "walking wounded." A couple of years before that the British edition of *Marie Claire* had featured five large photos of naked swingers, and then scolded them for using "their bodies as sex objects, toys to enjoy." *GQ*—"our guys"—labeled McGinley's conventioneers "sweaty, smelly and uncivilized." One Florida TV station had even played McGinley's jovial comments about swinging over shots of a graveyard.

McGinley headed out of the board room to his adjoining office, which was decorated not with *Marie Claire*'s portraits of naked swingers but with framed photographs of fighter air-craft cruising through clouds. In fact, from the front door facing the busy corner of La Palma and Magnolia to the back door where McGinley sometimes parked his beat-up 1979 Mercedes, there was almost nothing in the modern offices that indicated LSO catered to the needs of couples who practiced open eroticism. McGinley *always* expected cameras, and he wanted any reporter coming through the door to be shocked that there was nothing pornographic about the business end of the lifestyle—it reflected the nonsalacious everyday lives of the people LSO served. That was the reason why the swing-ing employees McGinley hired for the front office were all white-collar folks both in their straight world credentials and in their conservative dress and demeanor. Jenny Friend, director of research, had one master's degree in education and another in science; seeing her in her business suit, you wouldn't have had a clue what she did on weekends. Dr. Steve Mason, LSO's director of publicity, was the Southern California program chair of Mensa and a onetime psychology professor at Penn State. Joyce, the company's iron-willed operations manager (affectionately called General Joyce by the LSO staff), was a high-profile activist for various civic enterprises throughout Southern California (although, because of this, she never gave TV interviews and never used her last name around reporters). One swinging travel agent for Lifestyles Tours and Travel was the wife of an Orange County police detective, another was a churchgoing Christian. Like Frank and Jennifer Lomas, who had recently left the company to resume their career tracks in the straight business world, they all fit McGinley's belief that most swingers were ordinary people. And now that so many millions of these garden-variety folks were in the lifestyle, McGinley expected an official backlash. He had a sense that his "mainstreaming" of the playcouple lifestyle had reached the trigger point as far as the government was concerned. Ultimately, that was why he wanted help from Alexander, who had recently devoted an entire issue of *The Humanist* to documenting the threats posed to the U.S. Bill of Rights by both the angry folks on the religious right and the kindly inquisitors on the politically correct left.

McGinley came back in the boardroom laughing. "Every year they tear us apart and every year they phone me up all nice and sweet to ask if they can come back and tear us apart again. Funny thing is, a few of them wind up having a fabulous time at the convention and *still* write the story they decided to write before they showed up."

"I'm personally having a little difficulty differentiating between the *New York Times* and the *National Enquirer* these days," Alexander commented dryly.

"The *New York Times* hasn't phoned me yet, but if I'm right they'll be on that line wondering what the hell has happened to society. Biggest concern I have," McGinley added, turning to me, "is that some Cronin-type bureaucrat will come down on us because they think the press is behind them. However, I'm taking steps to deal with that."

———

The LSO chief has a plan. He is moving forward on all fronts and making headway at gathering the most stable element in the world behind his playcouple philosophy: the suburban middle class. It takes only a married couple, a house, and willing friends to make a lifestyle club; it takes a businessman with a mission and an engineer's mind to link them together.

If you asked most swingers about McGinley's plan, they'd be unaware of it. They would tell you they were part of a populist subculture that acknowledged no leader. Indeed, most couples in the lifestyle have never even heard of Robert McGinley, or, if they have attended a Lifestyles convention, only vaguely know him as its impresario. But if you asked the owners of the clubs and resorts where swingers gathered for their opinion of McGinley, they'd speak of him deferentially. They'd explain that he'd succeeded in gathering so many hundreds of facilities under one umbrella that the lifestyle was now thriving, and that he was the subculture's most important defender.

"If there's one thing I'm going to work for till the day I keel it's the freedom for couples to openly express their dreams without guilt or public backlash," McGinley told me over a dinner of buffalo burgers across the strip from Lifestyles headquarters. He sipped his extra-large root beer and stared out across the avenue at his two-storey office building, which, with its terra cotta eaves and sunproof windows, looked like a suburban bank. The side streets that ran perpendicular to his headquarters were all lined with small homes fronted by neatly trimmed lawns, replicas of the houses lining the block on which Club WideWorld stood, as well as the homes of its patrons. "My whole life's message is this," he said. "You can be a middle-class, mature couple, responsibly married yet free to responsibly enjoy your dreams."

Middle class; responsibly married; free to enjoy a dream; and—by implication of the word "mature"—middle-aged. If there were four characteristics that expressed the core of suburban life in North America since World War II, McGinley had just stated them. In the articles I'd read through in McGinley's library, most journalists disparaged swingers for fitting this suburbanite profile—for resembling "the Florida mall crowd," in the words of *Elle*. For much of my life I'd shared that prejudice against suburbanites. It had been taught to me by my New York City parents, reinforced by my peers, and I'd been tested on it in college sociology courses, where I'd studied books on 1950s-era North American culture: *The Lonely Crowd, The Man in the Gray Flannel Suit, The Organization Man*. Suburbanites were conformists and philistines who were doing materially well but who were always hungering for something just out of their reach. McGinley, on the other hand, is the only Ph.D. I've ever met who proudly professes a respect for suburbanites. He hates bourgeois bashers and values suburban values. That McGinley is so sympathetic to the mall crowd has been attributed to the fact that they form the core of his clientele, but he told me the media has him wrong. His respect for the bourgeoisie is sincere: McGinley is loyal to his kind. After all, he hadn't just grown up in the suburbs; he'd grown up where the suburbs were invented.

A few months after Pearl Harbor, when McGinley was nine, his parents bought a plot in a brown field twenty miles south of L.A. that was then being developed into what McGinley called "the first multiple-house, suburban tract development in the country—a thirty-six-dollar-a-month decent neighborhood where working people could afford a house, a yard, a garage, and live like the rich." The values and fantasies that were bred in those newly paved lanes of Lakewood, so close to Hollywood and so far from the stars, would be bred in ten thousand other suburban developments built after the war. In the drive-in theaters these good neighbors went to, suburban values like hard work, raising a family, and spousal loyalty were promoted side by side with fantasies of being effortlessly rich and sexually promiscuous. But it was understood by the suburbanites that it was forbidden (indeed impossible) to combine their fantasies with their values. Most suburbanites wound up in church on Sunday where preachers praised North American values and damned North American fantasies. It would become Bob McGinley's life's work to bring the values and the fantasies together, but not until he was past thirty. For all the years beforehand McGinley accepted the message of damnation as the true one.

His mother Mabel, step-daughter of a preacher, and his father Dan, a laborer in the Long Beach shipyards, raised Bob as a Nazarene Christian—a fundamentalist Protestant sect founded on the principle that worshippers should strive to attain the "sinless perfection" of the original Nazarene, Jesus Christ. All forms of nonprocreative sex led one away from the perfection. Nevertheless, Bob maintained he was a "sexually normal" adolescent for the years he attended Woodrow Wilson High School—the same years Kinsey began publishing his revelations about the secret ways Americans were tapping into their fantasies and the first nude pin-ups began appearing in men's magazines. "By 'normal' I mean that, for then, I was acceptably prudish," Bob told me. "Christian attitudes about sex were generally accepted across America as the right ones for a young man to have. You didn't talk about sex and you didn't question that the thoughts and desires that American culture provoked were naughty. You just looked at Jane Russell on a bale of hay in a movie and you wondered, Oh my God, is there anyone else in the world who wants to do with her what I want to do? I must be the only one—better not tell anyone." The man the vice president of Penthouse International would one day call "the Christopher Columbus of sexuality" became the leader of a Boy Scout troop at fifteen, and at seventeen the leader of a Sea Scout troop. Wearing his uniform, sporting merit badges and chastely sipping soda pop after Sunday school with the girls in their tartan skirts, young

McGinley would have made a good subject for a Norman Rockwell painting.

One of the girls he sat with at the fountain was an evangelical Baptist named Bonnie, a pretty seventeen-year-old too immersed in Bible study to finish high school. The bond between Bonnie and Bob was a religious one, and because of that it became permissibly romantic. They kissed under a laurel tree one evening and that was enough to convince them both they were in love. Bob married Bonnie the day he graduated from high school. That night he had a prim experience of sexual intercourse, missionary style. "When you don't know what you're missing, you don't know what you're missing," Bob said.

The Korean War was still on and he joined the Naval Air Force Reserve, which tested his aptitude, found his IQ to be just below that of a fighter pilot's, and enrolled him in electronics school. Watching the jets screaming above his head gave Bob a thrill and so he specialized in aerospace electronic engineering. He didn't drink, he didn't smoke, he didn't curse, he voted for Eisenhower, and fathered five children in a row as the government trained him to be a Cold War technician. In 1957, the year *MR.* broke the story about swinging, Bob went to work for Bendix as a civilian organization man: he joined the lonely crowd, wore a gray suit, bought a house in Anaheim and took the wife and kids to church every Sunday and to Disneyland every season.

"Tell you a funny story that happened in 1960 on Edwards Air Force Base, show you how ignorant I was," Bob said. "There was a tech sergeant on the base attached to my office, and he invited me and Bonnie for dinner. So he and his wife— who was a very attractive person by the way—they asked us if we'd like to join the base's key club. I had no idea what a key club was. I thought they were talking about a club where you had to be an elite person to get the key to the door, and I've always been opposed to elite organizations. I was raised to treat the guy who delivered groceries the same as the doctor who delivered babies, I was dead against prejudging someone based on their station in life. So I jumped in and said, 'Absolutely not! Who the hell do you think you guys are trying to get us to join a key club?' And I started lecturing them both that we would never attend any key club in our life! They, in turn, thought I was talking about swinging, and that I was attacking them for being swingers. They were mortified. 'Oops, wrong couple.' It didn't dawn on me what they'd been talking about until a couple of years later."

During those two years, Bob's Christian faith and his marriage began to collapse in tandem. He was turning thirty, a time of reassessment in most men's lives. Bob's belief in religion had always been based on the unquestioning acceptance of the Bible's stories about miracles. For years, however, McGinley had been manipulating the properties of the physical world to produce machines that performed seemingly miraculous functions, but without violating the laws of physics. The miracles in the Bible violated those laws, offering no explanation of how they came to be. If the laws of physics were set by God, McGinley wondered, what was the mathematical formula God was using to violate the laws? Was it a different formula for each miracle? Rereading the Bible, Bob discovered that almost all the miracles either punished people because they were enjoying sex or rewarded people who swore off sex.

"Sex was at the heart of it. That was one of the most significant realizations of my life," he told me. "It was not just a self-serving deduction, it was actually frightening. I basically sat bolt upright and saw the Bible as a sex manual written by people who didn't want other people to have sex except in the way they wanted people to have it: married and in the missionary position. When you open that lid of your mind, there's no putting it back again. It was very confusing for me. I entered a period of spiritual and emotional crisis. I had five kids, I wasn't about to have an affair, but with my new awareness I had a great appetite for sexual experience—oral sex, whatever. At the same time, my desires were offensive to Bonnie. We began to fight, and then we had no sex at all. So much for experience."

He was shipped to Japan as an instructor for Bendix and was assigned to train fighter pilots in the landing systems he'd helped develop. Bonnie came along with the kids and kept up her Bible study with the Christian wives. For two years, Bob progressed in the other direction. "For a man casting about spiritually and sexually, Japan was like the promised land. The formal acceptance of pleasure as a part of life, God not being this angry person who hated you for wanting pleasure—all that was a revelation to me." He experienced sex with a geisha—the first time he'd enjoyed what would later be called "total body pleasure." He also heard lots of talk about key clubs by the pilots and now he knew what they meant. He returned home with Bonnie in 1965 to find skirts were shorter and the Pill was on the market. The music was entirely different than when he'd left, full of sexual allusion and throbbing experimentation, and the words "sexual revolution" were beginning to be used in the media. He became absolutely convinced that he'd been denying a normal part of his life, and made a 180-degree turn from his Christian faith. He read *Playboy* at home, grew a beard, and stopped off at strip shows with his colleagues. "Bonnie was raging against everything that was happening at that time in California, and I was totally open to it," he said. "Not the drugs, of course, but the free thought, the freedom of thought. She began to openly hate me, accused me of having an affair, which actually I wasn't although I was close. She's not a bad person, but she had a temper. One day I just said, 'This is it. The end.'" Bonnie agreed: she filed for divorce, and Bob immediately took the fateful step of answering the swinging wife's ad.

He kept the ensuing troubles with the Air Force over his correspondence a complete secret from Bonnie, and stayed at home right up until their divorce came through in 1966, just after he lost his security clearance. "I thought about fighting her on the custody issue, but in those days the woman always got custody of the kids. We arranged I'd see them on weekends, and actually, when they got old enough, some of them began moving in with me. Now three of them work for LSO on and off, but none are swingers. They're just free thinkers."

Rather than fix television sets Bob sold real estate in the lucrative Southern California market, put some money together and drove up to San Francisco to launch an appeal of the Air Force decision. He stayed on a few weeks to attend meetings of the newly formed Sexual Freedom League in Berkeley, founded by an iconoclast named Jeff Poland, who'd legally changed his name to Jeff Fuck and then had taken the telephone company to court when they wouldn't publish it in the directory, a case he won. The wide open spouse exchanges, foursomes and group sex at the SFL meetings convinced Bob that the sexual revolution was a literal fact, not just a phrase—or a phase. He told me he was overwhelmed by what he called the "uninhibited enthusiasm of the wives. I just had no idea a woman could show the same sex drive as a man. These were middle-class ladies, like from Oakland, not hippies up from Haight-Ashbury." As he would write years later in his Ph.D. thesis, he believed that what he was seeing was "recreational social-sexual sharing"—not the wife swapping he'd been reading about in the press.

Alfred Kinsey was then being cited in the media reports as having declared swinging a convenient way for men to have extramarital sex, so Bob went to the source—the first time he looked into a textbook on sexuality. What he found was that critics of swinging were ignoring Kinsey's finding that most of the husbands wanted to give their wives the opportunity for additional sexual satisfaction. Instead, the critics quoted Kinsey's findings about the other husbands who were essentially bartering their wives. "That's why when I wrote my thesis ten years later on swinging I called it, 'Challenge to Published Reports,'" Bob said. "Sure—some women hated it; some men flipped out that their wives loved it; you saw the occasional bad scene and jealous fights. Couples dropped out and there were a few drinkers, uncouth types, bigots, a few hippies, some unstable personalities. But the majority were just like everyday couples. When I read about swinging in the press, though, there would be the miserable ones, and there would be Kinsey selectively quoted."

He theorized that the observers were purposely ignoring the majority of swingers because they wanted to warn people away from the activity by reporting its worst side, much as homosexuality was then being reported as a perversion. "No one wanted to give gay men permission to have sex with each other and no one wanted to give couples approval to swing," he explained. "In those days there were some homosexuals who attended the parties. We got to talking about what they'd gone through, and what I'd gone through, and they told me something that has always stuck with me: 'Now you know how we feel.'"

In 1968, at one of the SFL parties, Bob met a swinging woman with a charming accent named Geri, from Biloxi, Mississippi. Geri's husband had got her involved in swinging the year before but he'd wanted everything to stay the same in their relationship thereafter—in what she calls his "dominator role in our marriage"—so she was then divorcing him. "Bob certainly had no interest in being my dominator," Geri told me, laughing. In fact, Bob was beginning to scribble theories in notebooks about the reasons men possessively dominated women and about the possibilities of combining what he called "an emotionally monogamous married life" with a sexually-sharing swinging life: in other words, combining American values with American fantasies. That fit right in with what Geri wanted. "I wanted the sexual freedom of that culture, but I wanted the conservative element, love, and romance, and a permanent relationship, from which to enjoy the freedom. Bob's ideas touched all the right chords in me. He was politically and emotionally conservative, he believed in one country, one main partner, and one love, but he was sexually and spiritually radical."

They both reaffiliated themselves with religion, the New Age type, Earth Church of the Pacific. Bob eventually became an ordained minister of this church and was licensed to perform weddings and officiate at funerals. A year later Geri and Bob got married in a full-service wedding—gown, tux, flowers— attended by fellow swingers at the Wayfarer's Chapel, designed by Frank Lloyd Wright, a maverick for whom Bob had infinite respect. As a symbol of their marriage and lifestyle, they chose Frank Sinatra's "I Did it My Way" for their wedding march. They moved to the treeless flats of Orange County, not far from where LSO is located now. When Bob won his appeal against the Air Force—a precedent-setting case for swingers as well as for gays and lesbians—he went to work at Douglas Aircraft, but it wasn't the same. "I wanted to be my own man," Bob said. "Just as important, Geri and I wanted to help people who were just getting into swinging."

———

It was the morning of the Bob-and-Carol-and-Ted-and-Alice era. In the seventies a poll would show that almost 5 percent of Americans had shared spouses at least once. Swing clubs were opening all over the country. In the Los Angeles area alone there were eighteen clubs, one a sophisticated resort called Sandstone Ranch, high in Topanga Canyon, which attracted leading leftwing intellectuals, feminists, and artists. Other clubs were essentially bath houses for indiscriminate orgies. Still others were steel-and-cement discos where sex took place to deafening music. None fit McGinley's vision of a homey club where middle-class folks could feel at ease. "The clubs weren't run right," he remembered. "A screw house wasn't my perception of what everyday people wanted." On the other hand, he felt, Sandstone was intimidating. "It was encounter-group oriented. You were supposed to go through some big psychological change there, have a catharsis, find the serious truth of life." Bob and Geri didn't believe people had to be put through the psychic ringer in order to experience sexual freedom. "You just had to be given permission and the social context to be who you were naturally. We had a vision: a fireplace, a swimming pool, a very warm, casual environment where people could be comfortably erotic, rather than weeping hysterically because they'd just seen God or the devil in a gestalt session while their partner was screwing in the next room."

And so he and Geri founded Club WideWorld and eventually purchased the big house that fit both their visions of a "life-style club," rather than a sex parlor or an Esalen Institute-type center where a personality makeover was the goal. WideWorld was set up as a members-only organization. Before couples were allowed to pay the thirty-dollar initiation fee they had to fill out application forms and then go through an hour-long interview that acquainted them with what they would see at the club and test their willingness to see it. Of the 1,470 members who joined WideWorld by the mid-1970s, roughly two-thirds were white-collar professionals, business people, or skilled workers—almost all from the surrounding suburbs—and three-quarters were between twenty-six and forty-five years old, about five years younger than the average age today, which hovers somewhere between thirty and fifty.

Before each party began, Bob stood in front of the fireplace and led warm-up discussions on sexuality, marriage, religion, or whatever the crowd wanted to talk about. Then people sat around chatting, changed into sexy clothes, danced, went swimming nude, climbed into the hot tub, and many eventually began making love, usually in the boudoirs in the back, some in the glass-walled "group room." The erotic rituals remain unchanged to this day. "I'm not going to be a Pollyanna about what went on back then," Bob said. "We had some of the same problems that went on at SFL. Couples dropped out and there were others we'd never let back even if they begged us. But we're talking about hundreds and hundreds of couples. Most of them left happy and came back year after year. They were changed in just this one important area of their life and their relationship. Everything else stayed the same."

The motto Geri and Bob chose for Club WideWorld came from a line McGinley had read in the collected works of Jack London: "The proper function of a man is to live, not to exist." In 1972, the couple took the hyphen from between "life" and "style" and the word that would become synonymous with swinging fifteen years later was born. Bob and Geri founded something called "The Society for Alternative Lifestyles."

"Pretty much everything grew from that," McGinley told me as we risked our lives crossing La Palma in the middle of the block to get back to headquarters. "We had our first convention at a ranch in Riverside in 1973, which we didn't call a convention and had no idea it would turn into what it has now—a million-dollar extravaganza. We just had a crowd of 125 people for two days of lectures and one dance. Then we started dances on Friday nights at hotels, and then we began organizing trips for couples. And all of a sudden that word *organize* became very important to me. The press was getting more and more derogatory. There were a lot of police raids around the country. I thought, It's time for me to get accredited and its time to make this official, not just an isolated club or a local society for alternatives."

In 1974, McGinley went back to school and began the five-year haul to get a Ph.D. in counseling psychology, and in 1975 he and Geri formed the Lifestyles Organization.

———————

While McGinley would not create the playcouple philosophy until 1993, he began looking at ways to mainstream the lifestyle the day he founded LSO. He knew it would mean organizing what everyone thought of as unorganizable chaos: swing clubs and swinging holidays. Until McGinley started bringing businesslike order to the swing world in the mid-seventies there were few if any resorts that accepted crowds of openly swinging couples or major hotels that would accept thousands of playcouples for a "million-dollar extravaganza."

But it was organizing the clubs themselves that was most important to McGinley. "Swingers are really independent people, but they're not treated as independent by the media and the law," he told me. "If Joe Redneck in Mississippi opens a club and discriminates, or allows nonconsensual activity, we all get tarred with the same brush. The two things I have always been opposed to are racism and unethical behavior. But how do you persuade a club owner to follow professional guidelines? Who can a club member complain to? Who can you go to for advice if your club's raided? Who responds to the press? Who prints up a book with all the clubs and what they offer? I felt that if we believed what we were doing was respectable, and I did, then we should have a regulatory body to keep it respectable."

By the end of the seventies, McGinley had succeeded in persuading big hotels in Southern California like the Town and Country and the Pacifica to host his increasingly profitable

Lifestyles conventions and these weekend gatherings began to draw over a thousand people. Soon club owners from around the country came to realize it was in their economic interest to show up. In the meantime, McGinley had used his academic contacts to enlist seminar leaders who were pretty impressive. There was Dr. Edgar Butler, the chairperson of the sociology department at the University of California at Riverside, a non-swinger who was studying the lifestyle. He would eventually publish a college textbook called *Traditional Marriage and Emerging Alternatives*, which contained a large section on swinging. Butler, who in the 1990s would win a National Human Rights Award for his writings on racism in jury selection, was so offended by the way swinging couples were being maligned in the media that he volunteered to become co-director of Lifestyles conventions and the senior member of the board of advisors of the Lifestyles Organization, a position he still holds, and which McGinley announces proudly in every TV inter-view. McGinley also succeeded in recruiting as a lecturer the distinguished science writer Edward Brecher, a close friend of William Masters and Virginia Johnson and the author of *The Sex Researchers*, a book which also contained a chapter on swinging, and which argued that swingers were "inherently normal." At least a dozen academics gave talks on sexuality at every convention, and once the club owners saw this roster of speakers, and heard McGinley deliver his own seminars on such topics as "Contemporary Human Sexual Behavior," many began to view the LSO president as a spokesperson who could help ameliorate the media's stereotype of a swing-club leader as something between a pimp and a pornographer.

Everything came together for McGinley in the summer of 1979, at the Convention held at the Pacifica in Culver City, California. He gathered two dozen club leaders from Canada and the United States in one room and persuaded them to form a trade organization that would address all the problems he listed for me, plus set standards of ethics and establish a professional management plan for prospective owners. The North American Swing Club Association would operate independent of any club, including McGinley's own. That winter NASCA came up with a logo—an apple with a bite out of it—and a motto, "For those who want more than just one bite." The extra bite was the one McGinley believed suburban North Americans fantasized taking.

McGinley had hoped the club owners would all be happy with the idea of an overseeing body, but there was some fervid opposition to it from southerners at the 1980 Convention in San Francisco, where they argued that NASCA represented the imposition of McGinley's ideals on their free spirits, and that it would provide the FBI with a master sheet of owners. He countered that something had to be done or they would all wind up being raided by morality squads who took the negative coverage in the press as good evidence that swingers were violating community standards. In the end, a few of the owners refused to join, and McGinley wound up managing NASCA as the swing world's watchdog and publicity person, a role he was happy to fill. "Here's why it's a success," he said. "It's *important* for a club to be a member. It means something to be listed in the book or on the Web page. We publish *Etiquette In Swinging*, that's our position paper on the proper way for people to behave at clubs. We have an Equal Opportunity Lifestyles Organization—no discrimination on the basis of race or religion. And if an owner breaks the standards and I get a complaint, I'm there to say, 'Look, you advertised here such and such and you're not delivering.' It's for the good of the lifestyle, so that people can be secure in a nonracist, ethical club environment. I'm really dedicated to NASCA; I poured tons of time into it for five years just getting it set up."

That happened to be the period during which his second marriage fell apart. At age fifty, Geri still wanted the sexual freedom of the culture, but she'd never changed her desire to swing within a permanent marriage of "love and romance." Putting his energies into NASCA, McGinley had neglected two things: preparations for his own club's parties, the handling of which Geri took over; and Geri herself, which Geri was too strong-willed to handle well. For the first time in a decade and a half, Geri felt she was open to having an affair.

"I suppose everybody would find it strange," Geri would tell me at her desk in LSO headquarters one evening, where she still works as the vice-president and co-owner of the company. "What happened is what happens to every couple that breaks up. I felt I was not being acknowledged by Bob any-more—ignored while I ran the financial side, took care of half of what was going on at the conventions, which by then were really growing and which I had a large part in planning. And we began to fight over the tensions of running a business and a marriage at the same time. I met someone at the club and would look forward to being with this fellow. It was exactly the same as happens in a normal breakup, except this was in the open. The idealistic goals of our lives—giving people a chance to increase their eroticism by this means if they wanted to—that never changed. But we always said that just because you're in the lifestyle doesn't mean your marriage lasts forever. It's just a part of the big picture. Nothing is really different."

"If you guys were running a used-car lot together, you don't think it would have been different?" I asked. "At the club you always had the opportunity to sleep with other people."

"If Bob and I were running a used-car lot together, we would probably have had secret affairs," she said. "Marriages break down, inside the lifestyle and outside the lifestyle."

As Geri acknowledged though, why their breakup would seem "strange" to those in the straight world was that these two leaders of the comarital swing movement ran the swing-ing business uninterruptedly as apparently happy partners throughout their 1985 separation and divorce, and continued through the following years to present to the world a model of affectionate, if platonic, cooperation. On the weekends, Geri and Bob oversee LSO's hotel dances and the parties at Wide-World, although Geri has since moved on from her relationship with the man she met at WideWorld to a permanent relationship with a swinging cop who is with the LAPD.

Without breathing a word to his clients, Bob was actually crushed by the failure of his second marriage and wandered around for months in a depressive daze, hurt and full of self-recrimination. At the time, the business was being run out of a dinky, crowded office on a back street. McGinley's director of operations, Bob Hartman, a swinging patron of WideWorld who'd come on board the year before, was using his travel agent's license to expand McGinley's newest addition to the company, Lifestyles Tours and Travel. Hartman had helped get LTT rolling a few months before by booking the airline tickets for couples attending the convention. Then he added a tour called the Houseboat Getaway, during which 120 swingers floated about on Lake Meade for four days in twelve house-boats chained together. Today Hartman is a tall, silent presence in the office, as inscrutable and soft-spoken as McGinley is emotional and vocal. When he does talk, he usually has something pithy to say, with one eyebrow raised as if to punctuate his words. "There wasn't too much room in that office to get away from yourself," he told me. "Robert needed a cruise to nowhere to get away and *with* himself." However, Hartmann did not have the Houseboat Getaway in mind since the floating swing club could get pretty hectic. Instead, he took the initiative and booked his shattered boss on a free bonus trip for travel agents from Los Angeles called the "Cruise to Nowhere." It turned out to be a most fortuitous holiday for McGinley.

The tour was for straight agents, nine out of ten of whom were females. McGinley had eyes for none of them, until a lean,

attractive Japanese-American woman named Jan Moriuchi
Queen walked in and sat at his table. She was going through
her own divorce from an Air Force pilot—although, despite
what had gone on all around her and her husband near the
Strategic Air Command base, she had never been involved in
the lifestyle. "I was immediately attracted to Jan," McGinley
said. "It was not returned on her part. I questioned her in
Japanese. No answer, because she doesn't speak Japanese.
Anyway, we got up to dance and started telling each other our
stories. When we got home I started dating her—just a
straight dating relationship, and she kept saying, 'This won't
work.' She's a very conservative woman and she wasn't very
comfortable at the time with the whole concept of the lifestyle,
particularly swinging. Not that I even brought the subject up
as an option for us."

While Jan could not accept swinging for herself, as a fifteen-
year-veteran travel agent she could see the potential of couples
going on civilized holidays to glamorous destinations where
resort owners might be convinced that discreet swinging would
be acceptable. The more she thought about it, the more she
realized the enormous business possibilities of making swinging part of the allure of a tour package. And so, a nonswinger
to this day, she accepted McGinley's offer to take over Lifestyles Tours and Travel in 1987, a responsibility Bob Hartman
was glad to give her since he had his hands full dealing with
the growth of the company in other areas.

With Jan in full-time charge of LTT (and in a full-time
relationship with McGinley), the business took off. Swinging
became the subtly unspoken subtext of the tours rather than
the main event as it was on the Houseboat Getaway. Jan brought
glamour to the travel side of the operation, throwing a gold
silk sheet over the old image of debauchery. Code-word phrases
such as "for open-minded, adventurous couples" and "adults-
only holiday" were used in ads for Lifestyles' holiday spots.

The word swinging was never used at all, in the same way it would not be used in the playcouple philosophy. Indeed, the Lifestyles holiday gave birth to the concept of the playcouple. Playcouples *played*, and you did not have to swing to be one yourself. As McGinley would phrase it in his codified philosophy: "Playcouples believe that romance is one of life's greatest adventures just as love is one of life's greatest joys."

It was an amazingly effective tack. The travel end of the business skyrocketed. When Jan had first started, there had been only the biannual Houseboat Getaway, and only herself as an agent. Within a few years there were four agents working full time, then overtime. Rather than booking couples on tours arranged by others, LTT ran its tours the way Lifestyles put on its conventions. It booked, transported, and accompanied couples to its destination resorts on all-inclusive packages, and it often took over entire resorts with hundreds of couples, even in the off-season—to the point where many four-star spots started becoming dependent on its business. In Jamaica, LTT destinations included such electric blue ocean paradises as Hedonism II, Bracco, and Club Lido; in Mexico, LTT booked couples to the Caribbean Reef Club, the Eden Resort, Pepi's Retreat, and the Qualton; in the South Pacific they patronized a private island called the Paradise Club and Fiji's Treasure Island. Like Club Med, LTT rented tall-masted vessels and sent dozens of couples on its windjammer cruises throughout the Caribbean, and organized twice-yearly tours of Europe, with stopovers in the big clubs in France, the Netherlands, and Germany. By 1996, LTT was running twenty tours, pulling in $1 million, and booking thousands of couples. In 1998, bookings were up by 25 percent and Air Jamaica and the Jamaican Tourist Board signed on as paying sponsors of the Lifestyles convention.

"We've actually invented and proved profitable a whole new concept in the travel business," McGinley told me in his office. "Playcouple travel *is* the playcouple lifestyle. We're not talking swinging anymore. We're talking people who accept open eroticism and sensuality. At every swing-club party you find a certain percentage of couples who aren't swingers." That included McGinley and the nonswinging Jan: they were a playcouple and Bob hadn't swung for years. "I never argued for a minute that every couple should adopt the lifestyle," he said, tapping the edge of his Ping-Pong table-sized desk piled high with page proofs for the latest booklets on NASCA and the convention. "It was always the *possibility* I fought for, the freedom of thought and expression—so that if it was for you, and you wanted the experience in your relationship, it was a dignified option, a *mainstream* option. My message is: you can be responsibly married and free to responsibly enjoy your dreams with your partner, if that's what you want; and here's where you could do that and be safe. Just look how we've grown. Just look how we *can* grow. Doesn't that tell you something?"

As he made his case, I reflected that McGinley now had a local base of several thousand regulars who patronized his year-round activities at which many, like David Alexander, just wanted to dance. I knew that every Saturday night Club WideWorld drew couples from Santa Barbara to Long Beach. McGinley ran big, Friday night theme dances at hotels like the Holiday Inn and Day's Inn, plus two giant bashes at Halloween and Mardi Gras that attracted about five hundred lifestylers, most of whom stayed over at the hotels he'd booked. He had an international PlayCouples Club, with thirty-two thousand member-couples who received all his mailings as well as a pin to advertise that they were in the lifestyle, and which was growing by about two thousand couples a year. And McGinley had the most sophisticated Web site in the swing world, with eight separate home pages for all the various arms of his corporation—each page providing links to thousands of browsing opportunities, including PlayCouples On-Line,

Lifestyles-America Mall (a shopping center for erotic businesses), Lifestyles Tours and Travel, and NASCA International. He was even planning to open a Lifestyles clothing boutique on the floor above his office.

"You put all this together," he said, spreading his arms, "and that's what I mean when I say we're mainstreaming the lifestyle. What we're about now, and have been about since we branched out from the club and started this whole concept in big events and travel, is that a playcouple just accepts that they're a sensual and erotic couple—and accepts that acting openly erotic can help them feel that way, too, whether they swing or not."

That, McGinley suspected, would sound dangerous to some, considering its mass appeal to the suburban middle class. "I don't know which Cronin-type is going to pop up out of the woodwork, or what my next pebble's going to be," he said. "But I know the future of this lifestyle is going to be damned close to what you experienced in Mexico last month, and what you'll experience at this convention next month. And nothing's going to stop it. We're organized."

CHAPTER THREE

The Unmentionable

Hast thou eaten of the tree, whereof I commanded thee that thou shouldest not eat?

GENESIS 3:11

Humanity has been playing a little game and its cardinal rule is: *Do it if you have to, but make sure you feel bad about it and make sure you don't tell anyone.*

LIFESTYLES ORGANIZATION EROTIC ARTS
EXHIBITION BROCHURE

My experience in Mexico in June of 1996 marked the beginning of my year in the lifestyle, or what a writing colleague called my "year of living flagrantly." I joined thirty married pairs on a long weekend to the Lifestyles Organization's "newest, all-inclusive, adults only travel destination!"—the Eden Resort in the Lower Baja. The Eden sat by itself on the blue-green Sea of Cortes, five miles south of the colonial town of Loreto. It was a Club Med-style, twenty-five-acre development of pools, palms, and pink adobe buildings, surrounded by desert and walled on the west by the towering Sierra de la Giganta mountains. Over ninety tourists were on Aero California's DC-9 flying above the emerald square on that scorching off-season weekend, and, as the plane landed, the outnumbered straights still had no idea they'd just spent two hours sitting beside spouse sharers and open eroticists.

That, of course, was the playcouple point. Not until all the gringos had plodded patiently through the customs hut in the killing heat and then taken the airport mini-buses to register in the Eden's lobby did the crowd separate into identifiable groups. The straight couples on their vacation packages were given blue wristbands and assigned to rooms that fronted the part of the beach where bathing suits were required. The Lifestyles Tours and Travel tourists were fitted with pink bands, and headed off in a different direction.

In age the LTT tourists ranged from early thirties to late fifties and in physique they spanned the spectrum from the aerobically fit to the droopy—though there were none you would call portly. They wore golf shirts and halter tops, tennis shoes and sandals, and chatted with unexpected reserve in their drawled Western vowels and nasalized Eastern diphthongs as they followed tour leaders General Joyce and her husband Richard to the Optional Clothing Club—the nude beach—where McGinley had reserved a three-storey block of rooms for their exclusive use. Almost all were white-collar professionals, including a nuclear-power-plant manager and a third-grade teacher; a school principal and a counselor; an advertising executive and a physician. The group was, according to Joyce, "exactly typical of who take our tours these days."

It was Joyce's job to ease these staid souls into the holiday frame of mind and so, at the hot tub patio in front of their adobe quarters, she festively announced that the orientation would begin in half an hour beside the thatch-roofed beach bar, ten steps away. "*Don't* miss it, guys! We've got a surprise for you!"

The surprise was sixty "oral sex drinks"—a thick white-rum-and-punch concoction with a banana stuck in it and a pink straw barely rising above the tip. To draw the drink, you had to mouth the banana sculpted in the shape of a penis. "Well, I've been sexually active since eighteen and eatingly active since conception," said one woman, laughing, to Joyce by the bar. "Might as well put them together."

A handsome man in sporty whites, Pascal Pellegrino, the resort's Italian general manager, moved to the edge of the cabana to face the crowd. Before I'd left Vancouver McGinley had told me that he'd become good friends with Pascal on an LTT tour to the Eden. "He's totally accepting of the lifestyle, to the point where he wants our tours every month—every *week* if we could get the customers."

"Welcome to the Eden and we wish you happy days and most romantic nights—surrender to the experience," Pascal greeted his guests. "Here you can lose or find yourself," Pascal went on. "Whether you want to relax or stimulate your senses is up to you. But, as the sun sets," he pointed west with an elegantly ringed hand, "the evening air is filled with romance and excitement."

"Sure like his turns of phrase," said a big-boned Oklahoman named Carla.

The school principal, a New Yorker named Chuck, toasted Carla with an approximate line from Montaigne: "The beautiful souls are they that are open and ready for all things."

Carla curtsied, then clinked his glass.

Pascal passed his orientation over to the activities director, Ricco, who ran through the hours of operation of the facilities and how to arrange for horseback riding, golf, and whale watching—then concluded with a request. "We ask something of you, *por favor*," Ricco said, smiling. "We know you will appreciate that for the sake of our other guests you are not permitted to engage in any romantic activities of a public nature that might cause discomfort to those who do not wish to observe those activities. Thank-you—and enjoy your stay in Eden!"

"Shoot," Carla said. "And I come all this way so I could discomfort little old ladies in the hot tub."

I noticed a pair of couples who seemed to be showing affectionate signs of linking up. They headed down to the water, undressed and waded in, not exactly arm in arm, but close enough to distinguish them from nonswinging couples at a regular nude beach. They swam around the area protected by the breakers for a half-hour, sometimes gliding up against each other in laughter, and then they came into shore and sat in the shallows, holding their knees against their chests with their arms. From the water's edge I heard the four of them talking about how wonderful it was to be away from home and work and in the bath-warm sea in the middle of a spectacular desert. They pointed to the mountain peaks, now glowing bright orange beyond the tall, dark date palms, and marveled at the quiet. There was nothing but raw coastline for miles in either direction, a wilderness of rock and saguaro cactus. I took off my shorts and walked into the sea up to my thighs. Even in the fading light the water was so clear I could see the yellow minnows nibbling at my body.

"Nice night," I said to the four.

We exchanged the usual intros—name, home, occupation —with handshakes all around. One couple consisted of a petite court stenographer by the name of Phyllis and her mustachioed husband, Jay, an executive-type with rebelliously long hair, both in their mid-thirties. The other couple were a bit older but were actually physically more glamorous—a muscular gym teacher named Neal and his honey-blond wife, Corrie, who was a parole officer.

After I'd explained why I was on the tour, Jay asked if I was going to be describing any graphic swinging sex in my book.

"Actually, I don't know how I'll handle that part," I replied. "Right now I'm just basically asking why everybody here is into the erotosexual lifestyle."

"Well, it's not everybody *with* everybody," Neal said. "It's the law of thirds. One third you like, one third you can take or leave, and one third you don't like at all."

"You want to know what I always find, the bottom line, the root of it all?" Phyllis said. "It's that everybody wants that family connection. They want that feeling of being desired, wanted—and not just in a sexual way—socially and otherwise."

"I think it's because we all kind of revert back to our school days for a bit," explained her husband, Jay. "You can socially interact, be wild and crazy, but yet you can still feel accepted, that it's cool if you're wild and crazy."

"Then, of course, we all go home and live our responsible

anal lives," Neal told me. He drifted over to Jay's wife, Phyllis, then turned in the water and moved back against her body. Phyllis slipped her arms around Neal's waist and ran her palms up through his chest hair.

"Well, you know, from a woman's point of view," said Neal's wife, Corrie, "my personal opinion is that this is the best thing to come to without fear of being raped, mugged, or misunderstood." Corrie moved forward along the sandy bottom to sit beside her husband Neal. She stroked his hand, which was stroking Phyllis's knee.

"And feel sensual," said Phyllis, tracing circles on Neal's chest hair. "Feel fun, because most women—I should speak for myself—but I think we all are very inhibited."

"Just as men are," commented Neal, leaning his head back to Phyllis.

"But men have a—I don't know," Phyllis said. "Either they've been trained better than women to supersede their inhibitions and they're not so intimidated by the idea of someone's thoughts or looks or whatever. The internal stuff. Whereas here, it's great; you can be in denial of your upbringing for a little."

Jay, Phyllis's husband, moved behind Corrie and ran his hands up over her tanned back. Corrie lifted her wet blond hair off her shoulders and inclined her neck forward. "That's nice," she said, responding to Jay's firm neck massage.

There it was, I thought. Phyllis and Jay, Neal and Corrie, had now become Phyllis and Jay and Neal and Corrie. The law of thirds had dealt four-of-a-kind. We all waved to a few other naked couples wading into the water.

"In the lifestyle I've also enjoyed the conversations with women," Phyllis told me. You could see in her face that she was trying to remember all the pertinent points she appreciated about swinging. "We're sitting here talking like this—*like* this; where else do you get to talk about what we're talking about?

I never get to talk about sexuality except with Jay and our friends. Sexuality is way more important than sex. It's mental. It's heart. I've appreciated this kind of honesty of sharing with people, struggles with sexuality as well as triumphs with sexuality."

"Which isn't to say there are times you would never do this," Corrie said to me. "When you first fall in love you wouldn't. Also when you've got very little ones this isn't what you're after. Or when you're dealing with something like illness. It really is a *recreational* lifestyle. Don't say it's *serious business*."

"I wouldn't argue with that," Phyllis agreed. "You should tell people it's got to be balanced. It's got to be fun or it's no fun."

"Boy," said Jay, lifting his foot around Corrie and shoving water my way, "I don't know how you'll ever explain this to normal society."

"Hey, we *are* normal society!" a fast-food distributor by the name of Mark called from where he'd been listening in with his wife, Julia. "*They're* all weird." He meant that the real world was weird.

"Weird in secret," Neal said, twisting around and putting his arm around Phyllis's slight shoulder.

Mark drifted over with Julia in his arms. "No, seriously," he said, "I think like everything, you got the bell-shaped curve —the majority of people would never do it. But then there are those who are freer thinkers, freer spirits, and who are really very secure in their relationships, which is absolutely vital."

Mark was about forty-five and he thought he looked a little like Burt Reynolds, which you couldn't deny once he'd mentioned it. He sat back in the shallows of the beach with Julia, his wife of twenty-five years on his lap, her full breasts clear of the water and her arms around his neck. "There is no question that you gotta be secure. When Julia and I first started this thing, I said, 'Do you really wanna have another guy?'"

"And I said, 'As long as you're watching, Mark, and enjoying, I'm fine,'" Julia said.

Everybody broke up at that remark.

"You've *got* to watch, Mark, or she ain't fine."

"You probably got holes drilled in all your closets."

"I gotta admit," Mark said, "watching the ecstasy in her face the first couple of times, it was *great*. I loved it. I felt this closeness, a lot more love surging up in me—And I'm thinking to myself, 'This is crazy.' I really enjoyed it."

"Now it's gotten to the point," Julia said to me, "where they have to be really good friends, we really have to like them, and even then it's more we bring a woman in. Because as much as I enjoy men, I like women, to tell you the truth. Which is something I never considered before we got into this lifestyle. I love Mark, but I like women. And if a fellow I'm attracted to happens to come along with the woman, then that's really a wonderful experience for me—but it takes time. We're not indiscriminate like some."

"The top priority for both of us is her," Mark said. "We have one good friend who sometimes stays over, and when she gets excited she comes down to our bedroom. The next thing I know, she and Julia are out by the Jacuzzi, on one of the chaise lounges. Or else she'll come down and say, 'Okay, Mark, I'm taking your wife now.' I say, 'Okay.' She says, 'Leave the bedroom, but watch.' Is that a turn on! Can you imagine! And you're watching! That to me is the epitome of marital bliss."

Phyllis turned her head from where it was resting against Neal's back and looked at me thoughtfully. "What did you call this again?" she asked.

"The erotosexual lifestyle."

"Yeah, I like that—I like that name."

I still have an info sheet I received from LSO just before I went to my first Lifestyles convention in 1993. "Enter the 'Playcouples' of the nineties!" publicity director Steve Mason told prospective attendees like me. "Imagine, couples who like to meet, dance and party with other couples from around the world and who, quite frankly, get off on being openly erotic in semi-public settings. What better way to renew passion, to enhance romance?"

Those words—"openly erotic in semi-public settings"—and that sentiment—renewing a relationship by behaving in that way—are at the heart of the lifestyle. To the outside world it must seem mind-boggling that the playcouples at the Eden could be so nakedly at ease explaining and exhibiting to each other the details of what they considered "the epitome of marital bliss." In the real world the conduct of extramarital sex is marked by secrecy and denial, but that is not the way playcouples behave when they feel safe. Married pairs like those at the Eden have been leaping the fence into the forbidden zone for so long, and finding that zone so regularly crowded with respectable people each time they've leapt, that among themselves they hardly even think of swinging as forbidden. Playcouples love open sexual play; they love talking about how much they love it; and they love sharing the specifics of the ways they personally experience it. That's what makes them "different"—and it partly explains why they elicit such indignation, hostility, and fear in people to whom the rules of concealment serve as protections against both intrusion and exposure.

Since the "sexual revolution" of the 1960s we have assumed our culture to be totally open about sexuality, suffused with sex. But the efforts of pollsters tell a different story: suffused with sex we are; open to revealing our sexual secrets we are not. Sex is still one of the only subjects we demur or dissemble about. The academics behind the National Health and Social Life Survey devoted a fair portion of their 1995 book *Sex in America* to explaining why it took them seven years to design and complete what in other cases would have been a standard three-month canvass. To be sure, the U.S. Senate (that paradigm

of sexual openness) passed a law by a two-thirds majority barring public financing of the study, a telling poll in itself. But
even after the authors had secured private backing they had
to agonize over the wording of questions so as not to "make
the interview sexy or provocative or offensive"; they inserted
"checks and cross-checks" that would catch people up on lying;
then they handpicked interviewers from among the most
skilled and tactful professionals in the country—who had to
repeatedly reassure those polled "that the information they
provided would be obtained in privacy, held in confidence, and
not associated with them personally."

"Our study was completed only after a long and difficult
struggle that shows, if nothing else, why it has been so enormously difficult for any social scientists to get any reliable data
on sexual practices," the authors wrote.

So entrenched is our tradition of sexual secrecy and lying
about sex that the evidence for the practice of open eroticism has
been ignored by many scientists when assessing the repertoire
of "normal" sexual options for humans—just as homosexuality
was once ignored. Prominent evolutionary anthropologists
have made assumptions about the behavior of people today
and, projecting it into the past, have implied that what swingers
are up to has been unnatural for humans for at least the last
thirty-five thousand years—even though they don't really know
how people had sex before writing was invented.

For instance, in *Anatomy of Love: A Natural History of
Mating, Marriage, and Why We Stray*, Helen Fisher claimed
that Cro-Magnon couples "must have coupled in the dark or
out of view. Nowhere in the world do people regularly have
coitus in public." And in the journal *American Anthropologist*,
Ernestine Friedl gleaned from the ethnographic evidence that
"hidden coitus may safely be declared a near universal." The
logic offered for the universality of the public-sex taboo is that
it must have arisen either to hide adultery or to exclude those

who could be aroused to interrupt sex and, in a competitive struggle, steal the body most desired for passing on genes. But when Fisher and Friedl decided that hidden coitus was universal, they may not have considered that the NHSL Survey showed that more men and women think group sex is appealing than think same gender sex is appealing. They certainly did not acknowledge the behavior of swingers, surprising in Fisher's case because just ten miles from where she teaches at Rutgers University are two big swing clubs, Beginnings and Entre Nous. If she had made the drive she would have seen dozens of her neighbors regularly having coitus in public every weekend. And if she had spoken with her colleague at Rutgers, Dr. Norman Scherzer—who sometimes lectures on the swinger phenomenon both at Rutgers and as an adjunct professor in human sexuality at New York University—she would have discovered that today in North America at least three million taxpayers in the thirty- to sixty-year-old age bracket are frequenting places where the opportunity to partake in open sexuality is the main drawing card. What is significant, Scherzer says, is that swingers are practicing their behavior in a subculture where there is very little competition for sexual mates, no desire to procreate, and no attempt to be secretive about sex. They are engaging in open eroticism as part of their marriage —and if you examine their behavior both historically and cross-culturally, Scherzer says, you will find that they are actually not doing anything new at all.

———————

There are two components to the overt sexual culture of the lifestyle. One is a couple's engagement in sex with groups of other people—generally referred to as orgiastic sex. The other is spouse exchange, which historically has been more discreet.

Let's look first at orgiastic sex, the behavior that never "regularly" takes place.

Organized, open sex is not unique to our era, our culture, or our hemisphere. It has occurred regularly for at least four thousand years, or since the time the Caananites held yearly sex festivals to honor the goddess Asherah and the god Baal in Abraham's day. Unrestrained group sex and public intercourse with priestesses were frequent practices in the towns we know as Sodom and Gomorrah—until they were stamped out in a series of "righteous" wars led by the "avenging angels" of the same God who had thrown the biblical forebears of these citizens out of Eden. A little farther east, according to Herodotus, the highborn wives of Babylon worshipped the goddess Mylitta by going to her temple and having sex openly at least once in their lives.

As far as the West goes, the catalogue of public sex is almost continuous right down to today. The Greeks held several national sex fests, called Aphrodisia, Dionysia, and Lenea, the latter two subsidized by the state. First there was fasting, then there was feasting, then the population dressed as nymphs, bacchantes, and satyrs, marched through town and into the country, and, by late night, were having intercourse in sight of each other. They even had a special lesbian Dionysia practiced by Attic women, according to the ancient Greek travel writer Pausanias. The wild-haired worshippers dressed in goatskins, linked up with crowds of Delphian ladies, and climbed to the top of Mount Parnassus where they held ritual dancing and orgies. In the reign of Augustus Caesar, thousands of Romans who were members of the cult of Bacchus held orgies no fewer than five times a month. One raid of this ancient swing club by the Roman guard led to the arrest of seven thousand socialites.

After Rome fell, pagan Europe—which had been practicing orgiastic rites when Rome rose—continued on its merry way with festivals such as Beltane and the Feast of Fools, which eventually became our Mardi Gras and Fasching. In the late Renaissance a mystical cult of European cabalists held regular séances enlivened by orgies. And when the West's explorers sailed the seas and began "discovering" aboriginal cultures untouched by their social norms, they found so many instances of public sex that for years the prime focus of the missionaries was imposing the position named after them.

Intriguingly, two of the matriarchal cultures they stumbled onto reversed Western norms regarding the secret consummation of sex and the public consumption of food. In these societies, the abundant availability of sex and the scarcity of food seems to have played a role in the reversal. On Vakuta Island in the Trobriands and on Tahiti, people ate in secret, guarding their meals in the face of fresh memories of famine. Not wanting to excite envy and conflict among diners, the Vakutans and Tahitians evolved norms that branded public eating shameful. Yet in both South Sea societies, citizens publicly copulated on special occasions. Women possessed status and property comparable to males and were relatively free to express their sexual desires, thus increasing the otherwise dear supply of sex that reigns in patriarchal societies where women have always been rigidly controlled to assure paternity. In addition, the myths of these islanders were erotopositive, and it is probably no historical and economic coincidence that pro-women pop stars such as Sarah McLachlan and painters such as Lilian Broca are now promoting an alternative "original" woman to the biblically demure Eve. She is Lilith, the apocryphal "first wife" of Adam, who is alleged to have been edited out of the Bible by the ancient patriarchs because of her openly expressed sexual desires. After leaving Adam, Lilith fulfilled herself on the shores of the Red Sea by having group sex with hundreds of male demons.

Today, a yearly trip to Brazil will reveal that the citizens never quite buckled under to the imposition of one man, one

woman, one-at-a-time sex: for over a week during Mardi Gras
Brazilians lift proscriptions against sex in public and group
sex and combine their aboriginal, African, and European pagan
heritages in a rite of consensual nonmonogamy they've idio-
matically named *sacanagem*. It's a loaded word understood by
every citizen of the country, and when wives and husbands use
it they mean they are going to publicly "seek pleasure" with
other partners.

"Many peoples of the world, prior to European coloniza-
tion and its attendant Christian missions, seem to have openly
celebrated their sexuality, at least on occasion," the British
archaeologist Timothy Taylor observed in *The Prehistory of
Sex*. "Days of sexual license, where adults had sex with as many
partners as they wished quite publicly, seem to have occurred
among North American Indian groups like the Huron. Jesuit
missionaries were eager to crack down on such activity, so
that by the time trained anthropologists arrived to study these
communities in detail, from the nineteenth century onward,
they found a very different culture from what the Jesuits had
encountered." Alluding to swingers, Taylor asserted that
modern anthropologists like Friedl were "wrong to think that
coitus is entirely hidden even in modern Western society.
Although it is not an everyday public act, it is regularly performed in small private groups."

———

Most swingers, of course, tell you they are not orgiasts. They
may have sex with others in front of their own partners, but
"it's not everybody with everybody," as Neal pointed out to me.
Partner-sharing is far more common in swing culture than
pile-on orgies and requires no historical digging to demonstrate as regular. The practice of spouse exchange is institutionalized in many cultures, partly because in some societies it

has made good economic and political sense, partly because it has spiced up the sex lives of the participants. Its most famous practitioners are the Inuit, whose lifestyle at the time they ubiquitously practiced spouse exchange bore an intriguing resemblance to the modern suburbanite's. The Inuit family tends to be nuclear, without the broad affiliations of a clan. Until the advent of the snowmobile, hunting for meat in the Arctic required them to be isolated from others, and when they did encounter their fellows, they often shared spouses as a way of increasing cooperation and lessening competition. Swingers, too, live in nuclear families, and they find their lifestyle an effective means of abating the isolation of suburban living. Couples in the lifestyle will tell you that in many ways their clubs are networking centers, since the range of members' professions they are likely to meet extends into all fields. At a club like New Faces New Friends in Vancouver or WideWorld in Orange County, it is not extraordinary to see people exchanging business cards at the end of an evening and longtime acquaintances often offer each other advice and services as an extension of the sexual exchanges that take place on the weekends.

In a much less casual vein, some lifestyle spouse-sharers become so close they do resemble a clan. Here they approximate the customs of aboriginal societies that in the past practiced extra-mateship liaison as a way of solidifying a tribe or, as we have seen with World War II pilots, as a sort of insurance policy against the death of a spouse. The Banya Remarra of Rwanda shared spouses among "blood brothers"—relatives near or distant within the clan. The Siriono of the Bolivian Amazon had a clan culture of partner exchange that resembled that of the Remarra, while allowing almost complete sexual freedom as well: husbands and wives maintained the primary pair-bond but had as many as ten lovers within the clan, knitting a sexual web of solidarity.

The Toda tribe of India, however, extended the sexual freedom of marital partners to include just about anyone who struck their fancy, without requiring any clan obligation. "A [Toda] woman may have one or more recognized lovers as well as several husbands," wrote anthropologist Clellan Ford and psychologist Frank Beach in 1951. "There is no censure of adultery. In fact, the Toda language includes no word for adultery. As far as these people are concerned, immorality attaches to the man who begrudges his wife to another."

Ford and Beach discerned that 39 percent of the 139 cultures they studied throughout the world practiced approved adultery. While some of these societies forbade sexual liaisons as a general rule, "on certain special occasions the prohibitions are lifted for a short time and everyone is expected to have sexual intercourse with someone other than their spouse."

Married lifestylers, then, combine all four varieties of spouse exchange: sometimes they reciprocate sexual liaisons with favors, like the Inuit; sometimes they become extraordinarily close with a few couples, approximating a clan; sometimes, like the Toda, they have casual sex; and sometimes they practice celebratory group sex, as when they partake in Mardi Gras or Halloween parties. They are typically North American in this regard, taking a little bit here and there to form a new twist on an old and varied practice.

Aside from a very small minority known as the "polyfidelitists," however, lifestylers do not practice group marriage or communal living. As McGinley's former employee Frank Lomas once told me: "Swingers like to share bedrooms, but not bathrooms—at least for more than a weekend." Here, too, they are typically North American, and if you recall the origins of modern swinging you can see how the behavior has been consistent for over half a century. Fighter pilots were fiercely independent souls who would probably die for you, even live for you—but they would not live *with* you.

In 1979, when the sociologist Edgar Butler tried to determine how many people were regularly engaging in swinging rites, he found widely differing estimates offered by sociologists and anthropologists, ranging from a low of one million people to a high of sixteen million. One pair of sociologists predicted in 1972 "that eventually 15 to 25 percent of all married couples will adopt swinging," based on its growth curve in North America. According to McGinley, however, it seems likely that at no time has the figure been above where it stands today, at about three million participants—based on the number of clubs, the roster of club memberships, attendance at parties, and samples of private parties in selected cities—although he points out that the number in 1998 is up by about one million from the late eighties. Around the world there are probably another million or so active swingers, with offshore clubs most numerous in Germany, France, England, the Netherlands, and Belgium, and with other clubs scattered from India to Ecuador to Australia.

The point here is that swingers are not doing something historically irregular, just currently unusual. As Edward Brecher wrote in his chapter on swingers in *The Sex Researchers*: "Everyone is not like you, your loved ones, and your friends and neighbors—and even your loved ones, friends, and neighbors may not be as much like you as you commonly suppose."

———————

By my second day at the Eden I'd noticed a couple who were hanging back from most of the goings-on at the clothing-optional beach and at the resort's disco: they went kayaking on their own in the morning and rented horses or played golf in the afternoon. Joe and Doris were a couple of handsome, 40-year-old businesspeople, and, as they quietly explained to me over breakfast on the open terrace by the pool, they were not swingers. Before they came on this trip they had had no idea that the word "lifestyle" meant swinging—they had thought it was just the name of the tour agency.

"We wanted to come to the Eden's nude beach," Doris told me, "but when we called the Aero California office they said the flight was full—that we should phone Lifestyles Tours because they had a whole bunch of seats reserved."

I was skeptical, but it could have happened that way. Lifestyles agents do not specifically describe their tours as swinger vacations because nonswinging playcouples often take them. The phrases "adults-only tour" and "for open-minded couples," plus some fleshy photos of nude bathers in the brochures, were generally thought to signal the right message. A Lifestyles tour was actually cheaper than going on your own and the atmosphere was spicy if you chose to hang around with the people you flew in with.

"So—what do you think of them?" I asked.

"We don't judge people," Joe replied. "But I will say this. There's a big difference between being open about your sexuality and being maybe too fond of it. That's what I'm reading so far." He creased his cheek and wavered his hand to indicate that he thought swinging might be a bit dicey. "I'm not sure when it comes to kinkiness. It depends what's in the head—motivation, compulsion, that sort of stuff."

"Last night, two rooms down from us—" Doris rolled her eyes to the spinning fans, then looked back through palm fronds in the direction of their block of rooms, where most of the lifestylers were still in dreamland, eight-thirty being the crack of dawn on a swing vacation. "I could only imagine what was going on in there," she whispered. "They were sure hollering."

"The women were," I said.

"Yeah! God, did you hear it? Wasn't that something? It was like opera."

"Personally, I think people can fool themselves on all kinds of levels," Joe said. "This could be one of them. Not that I'm not curious how they handle all the issues though. Like there's just basics I don't know how they overcome. Jealousy's a big one. Also, I didn't even know this stuff was going on. But I was talking to the manager, Pascal, he says there's a zillion people doing it—the whole place is gonna be taken over in the fall by swingers. So, why is that now? It's like it's come from out of nowhere."

"Actually," Doris said, "I'm noticing these women are all very extroverted—and they're all in professions."

"Yeah, but that teacher gal—the nuclear guy's wife—you know what she was telling me? She dresses up—they go out and just pick up a guy in his twenties. She likes 'em young. Then she goes and teaches little kids Monday morning. The whole morality issue—how can they reconcile it?"

CHAPTER FOUR

Beyond Good and Evil

Our virtues/lie in the interpretation of the time.

WILLIAM SHAKESPEARE, *Coriolanus* IV,vii

"Sometimes the nude must go naked and the naked must go nude," Chuck declared, sitting among a dozen lifestylers under one of the palm umbrellas that lined the clothing-optional beach.

"Don't confuse me now!" Carla called back to him from the shore's edge. "I'm trying to get this right here. I don't get asked this every day."

She drew her legs up from the sand and placed her elbows on her knees and the heels of her hands against her temples. A few feet from where I sat beside her a flock of pelicans rose and fell in the waves of the Sea of Cortes, keeping their beady eyes on Carla, who'd been moodily tossing them crusts of her sandwich. She was a man-sized Westerner, as much a presence on the sand as she probably was in the corporate office where she ordered around personnel. She wore two-inch dangling earrings, a thin necklace, a thinner waist chain that caught the sun just above her bellybutton, two ankle bracelets, and bright red polish on all twenty nails. When she'd shown up that morning on the beach Joe and Doris had opened their eyes wide at the way she adorned and sexualized her naked but definitely not nude body.

"I suppose, when it comes right down to it," Carla finally told me, "an immoral act's gotta be something you do that's gonna benefit you which you *know* is gonna hurt someone else. That's my definition of an immoral act. Seeing as I'm being quoted."

She turned around from the water and mussed up her short,

wet hair. "Ed!" she said to her husband, seated on a lounge chair behind us. "I get that right from your point of view?"

"It ain't quite 'If it feels good do it,'" said Ed, a craggy-featured construction boss. "But then you never did do unto others what you didn't want others to do unto you. Why I'm a fortunate man."

"Correct," Carla replied. Then she swiveled around and yanked on my ear. "Moral's what other people put in here. Being kind's what we're born with here." She pressed her forefinger against my chest, then repeated the gesture on her own reddening breast. "Uh, oh. Gimme back my suntan oil, Bill!" she yelled to an ad executive she'd slept with last night.

Wearing only a blue yachting cap, skinny Bill stood up from where he was massaging oil onto his wife's bottom beside the umbrella and ambled obediently over to Carla. "There's another question you should write about when you look at morals," he said, lathering up his hands with Paba 21 and smoothing them over Carla's shoulders and breasts. "When you look at morals, you have to look inside the person telling you what's moral. Nine out of ten times what moralists say is not what they're thinking of doing." He squatted and kneaded the lotion down over Carla's belly and onto her thighs. "Look around here. Eyes are the window to the soul. Everyone is saying exactly what they're thinking, doing what they're saying."

"Ask me, that's why the moral majority's pissed off all the time," Ed reasoned, moving from his lounge and sitting beside Carla. He too lathered up his hands and began to massage his wife's lower back. "They *want* to do it but they ain't allowed— even to say so."

"Oh, they're doin' it, they're doin' it," Carla laughed. "Most moralists are not only mean—they're unscrupulous."

I shifted my eyes to Chuck, the New York school principal, who lay on a plastic lounge chair sipping a Cuba Libre beside his wife of twenty years, a counselor named Leah. Both were bemusedly contemplating Carla—their favorite among the threescore lifestylers scattered around the disks of shade provided by the thatch umbrellas posted along the shore. Chuck and Leah had recently accompanied our tour leader, Joyce, on the most orgiastic Lifestyles holiday—the Houseboat Getaway—but they were soft swingers. As they'd told me last night at the disco, they liked to watch other couples make love and often made love while watching, but they didn't exchange partners. Like the six other couples around them who had coalesced into an intimate clique since landing in Loreto a couple of days before, they were trim and good-looking. Leah had a curly, thick mane of red hair and narrow, refined eyes that squinted at the world with pleasant intelligence. Chuck, at first glance, seemed like a ferociously intimidating schoolmaster— tall and black-bearded, with dark eyes that focused on you intently when you talked—although more often than not he was searching his mind for the maximum riddling direction he could yank a conversation.

"Oh, is it *my* turn now?" he asked when he noticed my gaze on him. "God made man and man made religion! See that cloud over there?" He hitched his head at a big cumulus, kicked up probably by the hurricane passing south near Acapulco and towering like a Himalayan peak over the arid Island of Carmen. "See that under it?" He meant the white mist trailing from the cloud's middle as it passed over the island. "Is that an immoral act? Quick!"

Everyone in our circle of naked couples looked to see what he was talking about, including Joe and Doris who, while not far enough away from the group to be out of earshot, kept at a safe distance. I watched Carla narrowing her eyes at the cloud and island, trying to bring them into focus without her glasses. "What in hell you talking about, Chuck?"

"Desire and gratification!" said Chuck, grandly sweeping his arm across the water. "'Generate me!' says the land. 'Here

I come!' says the cloud. And that's without the benefit of religious morality, societal morality—"

"But what about that indiscriminate aspect of sex without morality?" Joe piped up from the southwest point of the compass. Everybody turned and held up hands to block the sun to look at him. "Can't it just be a lot of strangers groping in the clubs you were talking about?"

"Oh, I agree, that's exactly what it *can* be," said Leah. "I don't know about them being immoral, but they certainly just fuck and don't even know each other's name. They don't even talk. It's just 'Hello,' touch-touch, fuck; 'Hello,' touch-touch, fuck. That's the main reason we don't switch partners."

"That's the main reason you go to clubs!" cracked Ed.

Leah leaned forward and slapped his shoulder.

"For a fringe element it can be like that," Mark, the fast-food distributor, informed Joe. "Arms and legs waving out of a pile—that's the stereotype. The vast majority aren't orgiasts."

"Just the vast minority," his wife Julia laughed. "No, we pretty much stay to ourselves in that kind of environment," she reassured Joe. "The club we go to, the main thing is just display—people dressing up. It's really the erotic value we're after—for each other—that's really what it is."

"I don't understand what your moral problem is anyway," said Greer, Bill's wife, a golden-tanned executive in her late thirties who was getting fed up with my constant call for commentary. Over dinner the previous night she'd told me she was a strict moralist in all ways but one and thought the drug dealers in her neighborhood should be executed. Like many of the lifestyle tourists on the beach, Greer voted Republican. "The people who are involved in this are consenting, responsible adults," she said. "Nobody is being forced or coerced into anything. It doesn't have to be defended on moral grounds. Defending myself is the last thing I feel like doing on vacation."

"We have a lot of fun at our club because we *know* everybody," Carla remarked to me, as Bill worked the oil around her ankles and between her toes. "I come from two abusive marriages which were really immoral. Don't *tickle* me!" She put her arm around Bill's waist and pulled him back. "I can tell you there isn't a thing Ed's gonna make me do I don't feel comfortable with." She put her other arm around Ed. "You want to write a book, write it straight. Don't worry about the moral criticism. Just tell 'em we wear saucers in our lips. They'll think it's holy business."

From the direction of what the swingers called "the prude beach," General Joyce presently leaped through a border of feather shrubs in a splash of white sand and came running toward us waving her bathing-suit top above her head. "I got the scoop on the togas, guys!" she yelled. "I got the scoop on the togas!"

She pulled up breathless beneath our umbrella, the center one on the beach. "Ricco's working on it right now!" she shouted left. "At four o'clock I'm gonna pick up the togas!" she shouted right. "*Everybody*—meet at the pool to get your toga at four!"

As there'd been some question of whether the seamstresses in Loreto could supply the togas for the disco party tonight, there were cheers up and down the beach.

"How big are the pieces of material?" Leah asked.

"Well now," Joyce said coyly, "I don't know. But they are see-through, you know. Muslin."

"Can we wear 'em to dinner?" Bill asked.

"Hey, no sheet, no eat," Greer said. "Come on, Joyce—talk to Pascal, the restaurant's Italian."

"That's right, and we're *pre*-Italian," argued Chuck.

"I just got through giving this guy a definition of immorality and you want me to impose myself on those who don't want to see me in a restaurant?" Carla asked. She leaned forward, picked up the last crust of her sandwich from the sand, and roundhoused it into the water, causing a near riot among the pelicans.

"See them birds," Ed said. "You show up in a toga at Caruso's, you're looking at the staff's reaction."

Carla stood up, brushed the sand from her broad cheeks, and yanked hard at Ed and Bill. "Know what reaction I want from you two? You're gonna help me wash this grease off."

————————

As I watched Carla walk arm in arm with her men into the water, her hands on their bottoms, their hands on hers, I thought of why there was not one swinger on the beach who was out of the closet, despite their claim to being free and honest spirits. "Open to life, the joys of sensuality and deeply felt relationships," Bob McGinley had once described his clients to me. But I'd learned how greatly they feared a society that considered them as living at the bottom of a moral pit. They knew that when mainstream media discussed swingers it was usually not as "a recognizable part of the rich mosaic of human sexuality," as the evolutionary biologist Robin Baker wrote, but to call them grotesque, obese, and deranged. In its 1993 article on the Lifestyles convention, "Strange Bedfellows," *GQ* led off by describing a friendly male participant as "resembling nothing so much as a flirtatious iguana." Swingers at the '94 convention persuaded the *Details* columnist Anka that she was "in front of the hippo cage at the San Diego Zoo." And the British edition of *Marie Claire* spiced its own report of a convention by calling lifestyle women "slightly mad, like Stepford Wives." The swingers at the Eden knew that their marital morals, if ever confessed, would make them into laughing stocks or worse.

From the very first time I started sounding out the reaction to a book on the lifestyle it became apparent to me that trying to discuss swingers without condemning them the way I had in 1989 made most editors and journalists suspect I was working on a profoundly immoral project. Not only was co-marital sex viewed as a perversion leading to death and hell, but swingers wore no saucers in their lips that made them ethnically exotic and forgivable to liberals. Nor were there any "rogue genes" journalists and their bosses could point to that could earn swingers recognition as "naturally" occurring minorities. Unlike gays and lesbians, playcouples cannot be considered sexually self-segregating; hence their moral threat to tens of millions of heterosexuals who are susceptible to being seduced into their ways; hence the conflicted attention shown them by the press, which at all times reflects societal norms. Religious or not, most people raised in the traditions of our Judeo-Christian-Muslim culture believe they have a good idea of what would happen to society if all their neighbors suddenly began behaving like the naked playcouples pictured in *Marie Claire*.

The fears for the future of civilization that swingers arouse are so ancient, and the metaphors used to describe them so consistent over time, that our modern judgments on their practices shed light on the origin of moral preaching itself. Why, for instance, do the authorities get so angry at swingers that they barge into their private clubs, charge them with being "found-ins in a common bawdy house," and then force them out into the street in front of leering cameras—denigrating them as a lesson to all who transgress? A 1998 raid on Club L'Orage in Montreal publicly humiliated forty-two white-collar people, including a physician, an airline pilot, an ophthamologist, and a hairstylist. The police actually phoned the press beforehand so they could photograph the raid. Back in 1992, a team of thirty-five officers wearing riot gear surrounded Club Eros in Mississauga, Ontario, then poured through the doors and arrested 149 people. Six months later the police phoned the press to ensure coverage of a judge's decision—which turned out to be an acquittal. As this book goes to press the Club L'Orage case is still before the courts—but why is it there to begin with? Why, by sexually indulging themselves, do swingers become liable to the baleful exorcism of rulers, backed up by priests and scribes, who declare their pleasures a violation of a universal moral order founded on the laws of nature?

———

Most of those who are certain that morals and sex are synonymous rarely pause to consider that both the *Oxford* and *Webster*'s definitions of "moral" mention sex almost as an afterthought. The Latin root *moralis* merely means "manner, custom, or habit," and, true to its origin, "moral," (in *Webster*'s), is "concerned with establishing principles of right and wrong in behavior" and is "characterized by excellence in what pertains to practice or conduct." The standards of right and wrong in sexual behavior are astonishingly variable among societies, and the sexual customs of societies are all moral *within* societies— sanctioned by their own gods even though considered immoral and of the devil by other gods.

This is a disquieting thought for those who believe there is only one kind of sexual morality governed by "the laws of God." But some religions worship gods and goddesses who flaunt their licentiousness before congregations and some of these have been around longer than the gods of the West. The five-thousand-year-old deities Vishnu, Lakshmi, Parvati, and Shiva are depicted in Hindu shrines across India cavorting amid daisy chains of copulation and fellatio. The pantheon of Greek gods, which lasted a thousand years and still crops up in literature to this day, was filled with promiscuous tricksters such as Priapus, Dionysius, Silenus, and Aphrodite (who ordained that men hold their testicles while taking an oath, giving us our word testify). Not so lucky in his competition with the West's gods was Topileta, of the openly sexual Vakutans, who once guided moral worshippers to unending sex after death on a heavenly island called Tuma. And then there was the fertility goddess Asherah in Canaan who welcomed orgies in her temples and whose destruction by the Hebrews marked the establishment of a new morality that would come to dominate the lives of 2.3 billion Muslims, Christians, and Jews. More than a hundred nations are now peppered with thousands of multimillion-dollar shrines where if an artwork depicting sexual couples is shown at all it is of Adam and Eve fleeing malediction, or the souls of Sodom and Gomorrah falling to hell and being torn apart by wild animals (whose sex lives they supposedly mirrored).

Indeed, given the age-old image we have in our minds of sexually immoral humans behaving "like animals"—implying that the worse one is at controlling a pleasurable urge the more animal one is and the less human—it is understandable that we don't blink when we read of a swinger described as an iguana or a hippo. The truth is—cloven-hoofed gods of the Greeks notwithstanding—we are unwittingly being unfair to animals, most of which have sex less in any given year than an average human. In fact, almost all species of mammals and birds that live in social groups are rigidly bound by their own codes of sexual behavior, and if we look closely at that behavior we notice something telling about morality: it serves the interests of the beasts who enforce it. Morals are without exception dictated by the dominant figures in a group, who ruthlessly attempt to constrain the sexual expression of others. Animal morality may not be based on a righteous code handed down from a holy gazelle or a lion god, but it is enforced by the kings and queens of the herd, flock, or pride who act like gods—and it is tied strictly to reproduction for the most part.

There are, however, two animals that do not adhere to this reproduction-oriented morality. They engage year-round in sex acts that in the vast majority of cases do not result in off-spring. One species is our closest relative, the bonobo chimpanzee. Whether females are in estrus or not, male and female bonobos enjoy sex several times a day with an ever-changing array of partners in their close-knit group, reproducing only once every five years. The other species is modern humans. About three-quarters of men and women in the United States have sex anywhere from a few times a month to four or more times a week. They do so in sessions lasting from fifteen minutes to over an hour, with about one-third of women and more than half of men having five or more partners after the age of eighteen—and whose total copulations produce an average of only two offspring per female per lifetime. This seems consistent with what the archaeologist Timothy Taylor discovered in his comparison of the sexual behavior of prehistoric peoples to bonobos. "Sexual pleasure has been taken yet further by humans—and so has sex as an aspect of power," he wrote in *The Prehistory of Sex*. "Effective plant-based contraception was available to our prehistoric ancestors, freeing sex from any necessary reproductive shackles." For Taylor there seemed to be a clear "evolutionary development of sensual and sexual pleasure."

Given the thousands of species of animals that have sexual intercourse only during the widely spaced intervals when they are likely to reproduce, and the mere two species that have intercourse week in and week out without reproducing—one human, the other humanlike—an argument can be made that sex done purely for pleasure with a variety of partners is actually *more* human than it is animal, while sex done strictly for reproduction is actually *less* human than it is animal. After studying "the varied, almost imaginative, eroticism" of the group-sex-loving bonobo for a decade, the zoologist Frans De Waal concluded: "The possibility that these aspects have characterized our lineage from very early on has serious implications, given how often moralizing relies on claims about the naturalness or unnaturalness of behavior: what is natural is generally equated with what is good and acceptable. The truth is that if bonobo behavior provides any hints, very few human sexual practices can be dismissed as 'unnatural.'"

In terms of a moral assessment of the behavior of lifestylers this natural versus unnatural debate does indeed have "serious implications." For the morality that we employ to judge them is founded upon ancient rules dictated by the supposedly divinely inspired chiefs of a sparsely populated tribe, once surrounded by enemies and desperate to procreate in a manner that assured paternity. According to the *moralis* prescribed by the rulers of that Hebrew tribe, masturbation, birth control, homosexuality, abortion, group-sex fertility rites, prostitution, spouse exchange, sex during menstruation, and all other forms of nonprocreative sex-pleasure the human body is capable of were banned as "immoral," and they still retain that taint. How did the leaders of the Hebrews convince their followers not to have a nonreproductive orgasm when and where and how they felt like it—when all around them other tribes were doing so in a manner "natural" to humans? The ancient rulers and priests, in league with their well-rewarded scribes, convinced their people that their sexuality was not their own but was controlled by God and His agents on earth. The mechanisms of sexual control were fear, as in "fear of God," and guilt, as in guilt for the "original sin" of sex—the ultimate taboo humans were condemned to break again and again, keeping them perpetually fearful and guilty and in need of priests, rulers, and literary proselytizers who all claimed to be closer to God than they were.

At the turn of the second millennium A.D. the wealthy and powerful officials of the Jewish, Christian, and Muslim faiths, their allies in the state, and their moral mirrors in the mainstream media have two things in common besides their roughly consistent brands of sexual morality. One is "the sexual hypocrisy" evidenced by the exponents of morality, which is "of particular interest" to evolutionary biologists such as Robin Baker "because...the most successful exponents are those who try, through force or criticism, to prevent other people from behaving in a particular way while secretly behaving in precisely that way themselves....Rule-makers and enforcers are in fact the people who most indulge in behavior they seek to prevent in others." The other pattern of conduct they share is that they regularly help us to assuage our sexual guilt by asking for our money. Religious leaders pressure us for donations; their allies in the state, who swear themselves into office holding not their testicles but a holy book, solicit campaign contributions and levy taxes; and most moral advocates in the media harvest ample rewards in wages and royalties paid out by a chastised public.

Instead of continuing to accept on faith what the agents of God and their scribes tell us is immoral, or even what our own good sense tells us is moral, we can reappraise all our ancient proscriptions by posing a single question at every juncture in our analysis of the history of sexual morality. It is a question employed by evolutionary theorists who like to sharpen the discussion surrounding moral rules pronounced by politicians, preachers and reporters.

"*Cui bono?*" is the question. "Who benefits" from the preaching of these moral rules?

———

Moral preaching began in earnest in the West in 2000 B.C., when God appeared to the wandering Abraham and commanded him to take his wife, Sarah, and his nephew, Lot, to Canaan. "I will make of you a great nation, and I will bless you," God told the seventy-five-year-old patriarch. "I will give this land to your offspring." The land was already occupied, of course, but since the Canaanites resembled today's pleasure-loving swingers and homosexuals, they "were very wicked sinners against the Lord," and were therefore less worthy of the territory than the new arrivals from Babylon. Thus, the man who laid the cornerstone of sexual morality upon which Moses built his law and Jesus laid his capstone was also the man who gave the West its first lesson that morality could be used as a justification and inspiration for invasion and conquest.

In return for Canaan, however, God required a sacrifice from Abraham and the followers he was then recruiting: the agonizing cutting off of a part of the penis in circumcision, which at the outset of life put the imprimatur of God and His priests on the pleasure source of males, who in the patriarchal society of the Hebrews ruled their wives' sexuality as well as their own. It was to be the founding ritual of our Western religious heritage and the origin of all the moral rules that teach us our sexuality is not our own (and that to behave like the Canaanites is to risk dying like dogs). Still practiced by Muslims and Jews, the sacrifice has been superseded in ritual by Christian faiths, but the original message remains the same: your sexuality is the property of a moral power you must obey, or pay the consequences. "Thus shall My covenant be marked in your flesh as an everlasting pact," God decreed to the new chieftain-cum-head priest, a double portfolio not infrequently held by rulers throughout history, right down to our time of mullahs.

The moral Abraham dutifully circumcised himself and his son Ishmael, the antecedent of all Muslims, then ordered the circumcision of "all his retainers, his homeborn slaves, and those that had been bought from outsiders." No one knows how many "retainers" he had at this time, although the Bible tells us (without moral judgment) that a famine in Canaan had forced Abraham to move to Egypt and prostitute Sarah in the Pharaoh's palace for a few years, making Abraham "very rich in cattle, silver, and gold" as well as slaves. "And because of her, it went well with Abram."

What happened next in this morality tale was catastrophic for the sinners of the capital cities of Canaan—and serves as a warning to all the rest of us, equivalent in historical terror to Adam and Eve's expulsion from Eden. "The outrage of Sodom and Gomorrah is so great and their sin so grave!" God told Abraham regarding the swingers and gays. Then He sent down two destroying angels who announced to nephew Lot in Sodom, "We are about to destroy this place, because the outcry against them before the Lord has become so great." Lot and his wife and daughters fled for their lives and "the Lord rained upon Sodom and Gomorrah sulfurous fire from the Lord out of heaven" (which the King James Version of the Bible famously refers to as fire and brimstone, the antisexual sparks of preachers ever since). "He annihilated those cities and the entire Plain, and all the inhabitants of the cities and the vegetation of the ground." (God did this, we are told, not Abraham's warriors.) Now much of the land of Canaan belonged to the sexually righteous leader and his people.

As with Abraham's prostitution of Sarah and his adulterous fling with Hagar that resulted in the birth of Ishmael, the Bible then reinforces the message that there are two kinds of sexual morality: one for the rulers, who get off scot-free for their sexual crimes, and one for the ruled, who wind up slaughtered if they transgress. No sooner were Sodom and Gomorrah annihilated for their sins, taking Lot's wife with them as a result of her curious backward glance (wives who like to watch, beware) than Lot, over the course of the next two nights, committed incest with both his daughters—supposedly at their coercion. "There is not a man on earth to consort with us in the way of all the world," they pined. "Come, let us make our father drink wine and let us lie with him." So we are told. Who benefited?

Four hundred years later, on a mission from God to reclaim Canaan for the Hebrews returning from bondage in Egypt, the warrior Joshua again used the "accursed" sex lives of the Canaanites as justification for razing every other town between the Jordan and the Mediterranean. In this time-honored fashion one sexual pogrom followed another over the next thirty-five hundred years. Sexual immorality was used as righteous justification by the mass murderers of the Inquisition, who pocketed the possessions of their victims; by the judges of "concupiscent" women at the Salem witch trials, who profited in a similar manner; by the American settlers when they slaughtered some groups of openly sexual "savages," then seized their land; and it was behind the whole range of nineteenth- and twentieth-century sexual-degeneracy theories and "vice" laws that led to the imprisonment of thousands and the empowerment of judges, police, and preachers. It was certainly the motivating logic behind the oft-repeated call for God to do to America what he had done to the violators of nature in Sodom and Gommorah.

The problem for swingers is that enlightened media oracles still take these medieval imprecations seriously. Consider the judgments made in an article in the April 1997 *Vanity Fair*, titled "Polanski's Inferno," written by Jill Robinson, daughter of the former MGM boss Dore Schary. Reflecting back to a night twenty-eight years before, when Charles Manson's minions broke into a Bel Air ranch house and taunted, beat, hanged, stabbed, and shot a pregnant Sharon Tate and her three houseguests, Robinson deduced that Manson was a moral avenger. Why? Tate and her absent husband, Roman Polanski, were, like many others in that summer of '69, swingers. "The murders seemed the consequence of everything all of us had done," Robinson wrote guiltily, confessing that she too had sped wildly down the fast lane during the years she identified as "the Golden Age of Sex," the "period between the invention of the Pill and AIDS." "We had gone too far, done all the things our parents had warned against—and more. But Polanski, it was believed, had gone farther than anyone. 'It's not like it came from out of the blue,'" Robinson quoted Polanski's former neighbor Bob Rafelson as surmising. "Something he had done had tempted the Fates."

The mysterious "Fates" were never named, their workings never explained, probably because most readers rooted in the moral myths related above would have understood Robinson's mystical logic that powerful gods and their avenging angels punish orgiasts by massacring them. Perhaps that was why Robinson reminded us that "Manson...loomed large" over a sexually liberated America that "had got heavy, dark and complicated.... 'I am what you have made me,'" Robinson quoted a Manson hex. "'In my mind's eye my thoughts light fires in your cities.'"

Now, Polanski himself is not to be defended as a sexually liberated hero. Eight years after the slaughter, he seduced a thirteen-year-old and fled to Europe. But we should examine why Robinson could imply that, long before Polanski's crime, Sharon Tate and the others died in this insane way because of *their* noncriminal sexual sins. The essayist Lawrence Osborn has labeled the belief in this murderous karma "sexual pessimism...the equation of sexual love outside the prerequisites of reproduction with death," and the sexologist John Money has coined the term "sexosophy" to describe the negative philosophy of sex reinforcing our dread of the Fates. "Sexosophy is to sexology as alchemy is to chemistry, or astrology is to astronomy," he wrote in a volume he appropriately titled *The Destroying Angel*. "With the certainty of doctrinal truth revealed" sexosophy uses occult logic or pseudo-science to prove eroticism *causes* "depravity and degeneracy [which] in turn are accused of being the cause of the afflictions of both the individual person and the society."

In "Polanski's Inferno," the very modern Robinson was a metaphysical practitioner of both sexual pessimism and sexosophy, since the nonsuperstitious fact of the Tate-La Bianca killings is that Charles Manson's motives had nothing whatever to do with the sexual lifestyle of his victims. According to the court testimony of his cohorts, Manson planned his mad butchery so that it would seem the work of black terrorists, which he hoped would ignite a race war that would lead to his emergence as king. He had 35 other millionaires of no particular sexual immorality on his hit list when he was arrested. But Robinson mentioned not a word of this courtroom evidence; instead she told us: "Polanski himself, working in London at the time of the tragedy, became a citizen suspected of lasciviousness, excess, even witchcraft." What realistic connection those suspicions had to do with the mass murder of innocent people across the ocean we are never told.

Who is benefiting from this non sequitur posing as moral logic?

Vanity Fair's conclusion was that Manson's victims paid the price of their pleasure—yet, paradoxically, Robinson's moral message rubbed shoulders in the same issue with a titillating sexual carrot—a bunch of carrots, actually. "HOLLYWOOD 1997, THE GLAMOR, the stars, the scandals," read the tabloidesque coverlines, with a foldout triptych featuring ten languorous starlets whose erogenous zones were minimally covered to maximally stimulate the sexual imagination. "Starring MADONNA, Nicole Kidman...and dozens more." Abutting a nude Giorgio Armani ad, just a short flip from portraits of the avowedly orgiastic Madonna in crotch-peeking fishnets and Kidman in furry heels and a see-through teddy on a bed, Robinson concluded that everyone had learned their sexual lesson from the bloodbath in the Bel Air sin house, and now things were safe again in a more moral Hollywood. "I noticed how much the city is returning to the family feel that the studios had tried to maintain before blacklisting, before the 60s," she wrote. "The conversations are about children and bringing them up the way we lucky Hollywood kids were brought up. Implicit is the sense that at some time things had slipped and are now being put right."

Implicit, rather, is the sense that things are as they have always been in Hollywood, and in *Vanity Fair* as well, where producers and editors almost always imbed an absolving message of moral condemnation within their profitable sale of forbidden sex. That tactic is the way of the West, where, since Abraham, religious and political leaders have regulated sexual expression by warning against the wrath of invisible Fates, frequently visiting that wrath on offenders as they have enjoyed the forbidden pleasures themselves. "I call it the moral hypocrisy of the commanders," Friedrich Nietzsche observed in *Beyond Good and Evil*, at the height of the Victorian era's hypersensitive repression of sex. "They know no way of defending themselves against their bad conscience other than to pose as executors of more ancient and higher commands."

Every step in the elaborate codification of moral rules in the West illuminates the superstitious vulnerability of humans to threats of divine punishment for their excessive enjoyments, which has allowed the savvy to profit from that vulnerability. Nietzsche discerned a cynical conspiracy between religious and political rulers who, by declaring sexual pleasure a sin, and themselves as protective intermediaries between sinners and avenging angels, established their divine power over the guilt-burdened multitudes. Recently rediscovered by evolutionary psychologists, the iconoclastic Nietzsche was one of the first to have conducted a "revaluation" of the sexual moral history of the West, from the Dionysian orgies of the Greeks, which he believed emancipated individuals from the power of rulers, to the antisexualism of his own day, which he believed enslaved them to rulers. "I know no higher symbolism than this Greek symbolism of the Dionysian festivals," he wrote in *Twilight of the Idols*. "Here the most profound instinct of life, that directed towards the future of life, the eternity of life, is experienced religiously—and the way to life, procreation, as the *holy* way. It was Christianity, with its *ressentiment* against life at the bottom of its heart, which first made something unclean of sexuality: it threw *filth* on the origin, the presupposition of our life."

In a secular era when we no longer burn or jail pagans and when sexual orientation is supposedly a human right, it might seem that the moral revisionism, revivalism, and profitable hypocrisy of *Vanity Fair* are harmless vices in their own right. But a mainstream writer donning a black hood and concluding that the lascivious deserved to be murdered for their sexual enjoyments sounds too much like an ancient call to arms to swingers, who are not comfortable with the idea that some Oswaldesque "loner" might take a Christian hint.

What happened during the sexual revolution of the swinging sixties that made Jill Robinson grateful that it was "now being put right"? Nietzsche might have explained that for the first time since the Greeks the multitudes had assumed the Dionysian privileges that historically had been reserved for the rulers. And since ungoverned sexuality was *never* meant to be the privilege of the likes of Ed and Carla from Oklahoma, it is not surprising to see a mouthpiece for the very wealthy, *Vanity Fair*, declaring that immoral lust leads to mass murder by punishing messengers like Charles Manson—while at the same time exciting the very lust that needs the saving grace of the rulers.

"Boy, if I knew we'd be talking about Nietzsche I would have studied for this vacation," Leah said to me on the nude beach. I'd just offered her and Chuck my surfside analysis of the moral structure of Western civilization. "I can just picture this conversation on the Houseboat Getaway," she laughed to her husband. "They certainly experience the profound instincts of life."

"Truthfully—Nietzsche died a nut," Chuck said to me. "He was the only virgin who ever contracted syphilis. Immaculate Infection."

To my left, the others in the lifestyle clique under the umbrella were now swapping stories about the delight they felt whenever they went to clubs and encountered a mix of "normal, everyday" people—the same delight they'd been experiencing here at the Eden. Swingers are genuinely thrilled by the reassurance they offer to each other. All the swingers at the Eden were sexual outsiders who in their professional lives behaved like insiders. Whenever insiders who are outsiders get together, they marvel at the experience of no longer having to lead dual lives.

"I hate to use the term, but it's almost like a cosmic experience!" said an ad executive named Linda, expressing her enthusiasm to the others. At thirty-four, Linda was one of the youngest women on the tour. She and her husband, Elliot, were sprawled at right angles to each other by the log pole supporting the circle of thatch that shaded them. "When you have conversations like this you walk away with such a feeling of refreshing openness," Linda went on, repeating the sentiments of Phyllis the other evening. "You really want to talk to other people about it but you'd be crazy if you did. I mean, I can't talk to my friends about this. I wouldn't dare! Then you have to go back into normal society and you have to watch what you say all the time. You can't talk about what a great time you had at the Eden with your husband."

"Right, then you have to get back with a certain group of friends and colleagues and stand on yourself with both feet," offered Ed, who just a few minutes before had left Carla alone with Bill in the sea and had swum to shore. She was now embracing Bill far out past the pelicans, with her head thrown back in what seemed like sustained laughter. I looked around at the couples. One or two briefly glanced in Carla's direction and then looked back at Ed. They were all focused on the heart-to-heart. All but Joe and Doris: their eyes were still glued thirty yards offshore at the shoulders above the waterline.

"And it becomes very annoying at times," Ed said, with his back to the water. "Because if Carla ever sat in a group'a friends and said she liked sex for fun—not one'a them's not gonna think, uh, oh, home-wreckin' tart. Take them seven months'a talking to understand you're normal and they're weird. Seven months'a talking or one good party!"

The group broke into loud laughter and a few claps.

"I just think it's unfortunate," said Greer, the law-and-order Republican. "Very unfortunate."

"About three months ago when Elliot and I went to the club we're members of," Linda said, reaching back and stroking her husband's head resting on her bottom, his eyes fast shut, "we met some people and had a wonderful experience with them, and we both found, hey, we'd like to spend time with them. So it's almost developed into a steady relationship now. And he runs a trucking business, and Elliot's got the plant—"

"So it's a perfect fit!" Greer chirped.

"Perfect. Whereas we have good friends, they've been married twenty-five years, she's never had another man in her life, and they have a very passionate relationship—but it's nice to be able to add the spice to your relationship just by the atmosphere, whether you have sex with somebody else or not. But when she approached him about it—wow!—like putting a pin in a balloon. Kaboom! Threatened! Totally threatened!"

"The male ego is very delicate," Ed pronounced, "like a fine piece of china. All you gotta do is tap it and it shatters." He flicked his forefinger at air and spread his hands at the pieces falling between his legs.

"I'm not sure I see anything delicate about that guy's reaction," Joe said, taking the floor with a pertinent point. "Wouldn't he figure that if his wife wants to go to a swing club then maybe she wants to have sex with another man? Or else she wants to have an affair?"

"I think that a lot of people take that mind-set," Ed said. "That's the way they're brought up, though. Doesn't *have* to be like that."

"After four days observing the congress of many couples on Lifestyles' houseboats, I am *convinced* it does not have to be like that," Chuck said, winking at me, his drink resting on a long scar beneath his chest hair. As I'd found out the night before, he'd had surgery about a year ago to replace some coronary vessels, and the veins from his leg now threading his heart were expected to last, at most, five years. There was no possibility of another operation. "'In all these things connected with love, everybody should act according to his own inclination,'" he intoned from the *Kama Sutra*.

"You know, when we travel," Leah said to me, "it's like riding with one of those headsets you rent at a museum. We pass a mountain, he's got a quote from Whitman. A woodpile, Robert Frost—"

"A porno shop, *Hustler*," Chuck said.

"Hey, I just thought of another point for your book," a husky fellow named Harvey from Washington State said. "You look at the native Americans, and you go way back and it was a great honor to share your wife. If you go anywhere in the South Pacific, New Guinea, all through Samoa, and all the islands down there it's been part of the culture forever. North American Indians, it was part of the culture up until the 1800s."

"Oh yeah," Elliot said, his eyes still closed. "There was a

movie I saw about Indians, where they welcomed a guy to the tribe by letting him sleep with the chief's wife. Have a cup of coffee and my wife."

"Well, we look at it as strange but they don't," said Harvey. "It's a way to say 'We welcome you.'"

"But isn't that in their culture?" Joe asked, sounding as if he thought he was the only rational man in the vicinity. "If you tried that over on the other beach with the wrong guy, wouldn't there be a scene—a fight?" He looked at me, eyeing my camera around my neck and my notepad on my lap. "I mean this guy's a *reporter*."

"I think he means what would you do if the *National Enquirer* showed up?" I asked, separating myself from the tattle-tale press.

"Scariest thought ever on my mind," said Elliot, opening his eyes at the sky. "Deny, deny, deny."

"Actually, there was a club raided last year," Mark said. "They published some names in the papers, I hear. What a mess that was."

A silence fell over the group. After thirty years of activism gays might have progressed from "pervert" to "deviate" to "diverse," but swingers were still stuck somewhere between the two former terms. Who would want to come out and be referred to publicly as "Deviates in Love"—never mind "sweaty, smelly and uncivilized"? In fact, Greer had complained that very morning to Joyce that I took too many pictures and asked too many questions, although there was not much Joyce could do about me since both Robert McGinley and Jan Queen had encouraged my accompanying Lifestyles events right through to the end of the convention two months hence.

"Do you guys have kids?" Joe asked everyone in general.

"Yes and we keep this completely from them," Linda said. "I don't want them ever to know. They're too young."

"What did you do last week you don't want your kids to know?" Ed asked Joe. "What did you do this morning?"

"It's relative to the chances of getting caught I guess I'm talking about," Joe said.

"No, it's not. It's relative to what society tells you don't get caught at."

"Anybody ready to go eat lunch before they close up?" Greer asked, having had enough of the discussion.

"If I can get our other halves back," Ed replied, craning around at the water. "*They're gonna close for lunch!*" he shouted. "Like they could give a damn," he laughed.

"Our feeling is that our kids would just be overwhelmed by the whole situation," Leah said to me, becoming animated. "We draw a strict line." She emphatically chopped the lounge with the side of her hand at the same time as she drew a towel over her lap. "I mean there are kids that are really screwed up by knowing what their parents are doing. They can't comprehend that. Kids don't need to know that mom and dad have fantasies; they can hardly accept that mom and dad have sex. I know with our parents, you can't picture it, you don't want to. A kid's world is where it's at, they know that mom and dad create them, but the potentials of sexuality are just not a part of their consciousness yet. I had a real hard time when our kids came home and they'd been to a porno, I told them that's not really what sex is. Because kids take it and they distort it; to me, the first part of sex is what you have with someone when you're intimate and you love your partner. And that's the healthy part of sex that I want my kids to know before they're exposed to anything else—that they would know what normal sex is, by my standards. This kind of alternative evolves in a very long-term relationship. It's not what you should start out with."

"I totally agree with that," Linda said, and all the other mothers nodded assent. "It's just a natural barrier that should be there. But in its proper context, when you're ready for it, old enough, in a committed relationship, the lifestyle is very effective in reviving what was there all the time, but which probably would have died without it."

"But," Doris spoke up for the first time, "this is all very— what's the word—paradoxical. To me, anyway. You must be all so guilty all the time, leading a secret life. You know what I'm saying? If what you do is moral—and I'm not saying it's not—then why do you have to keep it from your children?"

"Because we are still parents," Julia said. "We're not out of it. If my kids grow up and after so many years they decide on their own to do this with their partners, then it'll be all right. It's moral when no one gets hurt, like Carla said. It's moral for consenting adults. Kids can't consent. That's why we say 'below the age of consent.'"

"No one should use sex and hurt someone," Elliot said.

Carla came out of the water arm in arm with Bill. "You all look like you been cogitatin' the infinite," she declared, looking around at the somber crowd. She gave Ed a kiss on the lips and a stroke up the thigh.

"Chewin' on the infinite," Ed nodded. "Chewin' on it."

"To everything there is a season," Chuck sang, playing his scar like a flute. "And a time to every purpose under heaven. There's your liberal-existentialist's definition of morality." He raised his drink to me. "No man can find out the work that God maketh from beginning to the end," he said, enunciating a rarer line from Ecclesiastes.

CHAPTER FIVE

Ethical Hedonism

I see a different law in my members warring against the law of my mind and bringing me into captivity under the law of sin which is in my members. O wretched man that I am!

—ST. PAUL *Romans*, 7:23–24

Why is it that whatever we touch we turn into a problem? We have made God a problem, we have made love a problem, we have made...living a problem, and we have made sex a problem. Why? Why is everything we do a problem, a horror? Why are we suffering? Why has sex become a problem?

J. KRISHNAMURTI, *The First and Last Freedom*

At most Lifestyles Erotic Arts shows you will find reproductions of two venerable works that elegantly illustrate the open sharing of love between couples—the kind you see on an average toga night on a swingers' holiday. One is Western, Nicolas Poussin's sixteenth-century painting *Bacchanalian Revel Before a Term of Pan*; the other is Eastern, the bas-relief frieze of bending and twisting couples on the Tantric Temple of Kajuraho in India. In both orgies, all the participants are deities who seem exuberantly happy to be in the middle of their erotic spectacle. Their passion is light, voluntary, and feminine as opposed to satanically driven, vicious, and probably deadly. In other words, they are portraits of social gatherings in which everybody has agreed to have guiltless sex. The galactic wheels of carnal engagements are immoral in our time, but by virtue of their consensuality they are curiously ethical, since they obey Hillel's maxim, the source of all ethical codes, paraphrased to me by Ed and Carla: "Do not do unto others what you do not want others to do unto you."

That was the ethical ideal of all the veteran lifestylers I visited under the beach umbrellas in the bright Baja daylight, and it is probably why, like the deities in the art works, they could be sexual with one another without being riven by guilt. They simply did not accept that they had passed through Alice's mirror into a wicked, swinger's version of Wonderland. To their minds ethical rules, which urged individuals to live in a way that did not harm others, made sense, whereas moral principles of right sex and wrong sex did not. It seemed eminently logical to them that people could indulge in a sexually immoral lifestyle and still lead decent, ethical lives, whereas people who were fully entitled to be described as sexually moral might break ethical codes daily.

In putting their beliefs into promiscuous practice they were, without doubt, challenging society's bedrock orthodoxy that sexual morality and ethical behavior are inextricably linked. The logic of the ages tells us that if people were ever freed from moral censure to cultivate hedonism they would become slaves to their bottommost desires both inside and outside the bedroom and be rendered incapable of thoughtful, ethical behavior. Thus, with the partial exception of Tantra (which has its own idiosyncratic orthodoxy), each of the world's major religions, their mystical traditions, and even some humanist schools of thought, have for the betterment of humanity arranged the pursuits of life along a vertical scale, with those that encourage lust at the hellish bottom and those that encourage chaste love at the heavenly top. From the seven spinal chakras of the Hindus to the seven rungs of Jacob's ladder in the Bible, and from the seven links of the Elizabethans' great chain of being to the seven tiers of the psychologist Abraham Maslow's "hierarchy of needs," the directional arrows are all the same: saturnalian pursuits drive one downward to the lowest sphere of genital instinct, selfishness, and evil; spiritual pursuits lift one upward to the godly crown of superconsciousness, selfless service, and goodness.

This hierarchical scale, which to this day is accepted as a valid metaphor for a standing person's centers of awareness, accounts in part for why swingers push so many apocalyptic buttons in the media. The metaphor was certainly at work in *Marie Claire*'s coverage of the 1991 Lifestyles Convention. Surveying two thousand couples who bore a "glazed look of generalized lust" that made them "revolting" and "repellent," the writer, Louisa Young, concluded that they formed an

undifferentiated mass of soulless debauchers who had jetti-
soned all ethical responsibilities in their blind pursuit of "recreational sex." "After all, these people haven't even got as far as
realizing that there is a connection between the body and the
rest of a person—heart, mind, intellect—so how can you
expect more from them?" Young asked rhetorically at the end
of her article, reflecting the vertical scale of awareness that had
informed her upbringing.

Of course, there is no denying that redneck louts and beach
babies have always been present in swing culture in about the
same proportion as in straight society and that they have given
writers the opportunity to pound tables with the same bigoted
pejoratives once used to demonize all gays. On the other hand,
there just doesn't seem to be enough room in the tiny medium
of an article to weigh evidence that, relatively speaking, there
are as many high-minded heterosexual couples in the swinging
lifestyle as there are cultured homosexuals in the gay and lesbian lifestyles. For example, the concluding event of the 1991
convention, completely ignored by Louisa Young, was a round-
table discussion of the lifestyle co-hosted by Dr. Edgar Butler.
It drew hundreds of mostly white-collar conventioneers,
including physicians, psychiatrists, and social workers, all of
whom believed they lived at the other end of the value scale
from those whom Young had assessed as having nonstop group
sex with "no thinking or feeling (beyond 'Mmmm, feels good')
involved." Indeed, in the years since then the ratio of the mentally vigorous to the vacuous in the lifestyle has shifted ever-
steadily upward. In 1996 the keynote speaker at the Lifestyles
convention was an Auschwitz survivor and psychologist, Dr.
Edith Eger, who lectured to a thousand swinging couples on
"the dance of life," which, as a girl, she had perceived as taking place even in the midst of hell—a decidedly nonerotic topic
for a sex convention. Based on the survey form they'd filled
out at the registration desk, three-quarters of these folks were

college graduates. And at the next year's convention people just like them would crowd into seven seminars and workshops that addressed the question of how swingers who believed in God—even a fundamentalist Christian God—could integrate their faith, their sexuality, and their sense of themselves as ethical people.

For a journalist to honestly report on such seminars he or she would have to open up a Pandora's box of questions cutting to the core of our conventional notions that unbridled eroticism cannot coexist with civilized codes of conduct and noble discourse. He or she would have to weigh the code middle-class swingers claimed they lived by, which went by the brain-twisting name of "ethical hedonism," and which was defined by Dr. Susan Block, the most popular seminar leader at Lifestyles conventions, as "an erotic etiquette to guide you (and me) toward fully and dramatically expressing our sexual, animal nature, while maintaining the peace as civilized, considerate ladies and gentlemen." It was, as Chuck had casually mentioned, a "pre-Italian" etiquette deriving from the 2,400-year-old formulations of one Aristippus, a Libyan Greek who founded the hedonist school of Cyrene, where he taught that if wisdom consisted of making the most of the present in sexual pleasure and avoidance of pain, it followed that pleasure's pursuit must be attended by thought for the future, since pleasure's consequences should never be painful. That was one of the finer points of Cyrenaic philosophy, and it is why scholars have generally acknowledged Aristippus's teachings as a bona fide system of ethics that in its ideals promotes pleasurable solutions to the painful problems born of sexual competition and jealousy. "The Greeks realized what hardly anybody else appeared to observe during most of the ensuing two thousand years, that a passing lust for A is not incompatible with a more permanent love for B," wrote the British historian Burgo Partridge back in 1960. "Moreover, the Greeks realized what the Victorians did not, that the restraints imposed on married women, whether desirable and justifiable or not, were imposing a strain, and one which it would be well to alleviate from time to time." Aristippus, perhaps the first of the West's swing-club owners, therefore worked to alleviate Grecian marital strain by gathering together couples at Cyrene for regular, open bacchanals, which he had observed could be gentle affairs if exercised according to the usual rules that governed all other interactions.

Today, in the neohedonist swinging lifestyle, Aristippus is a pagan hero, and Susan Block—a doctor of philosophy, sex therapist, and host of HBO's *Radio Sex TV*—is his most outspoken promoter. According to Block's application of ethical hedonism to marriage, couples may "enjoy the intimate camaraderie with other couples that the swinging or 'playcouple' lifestyle fosters" provided they do so from the base of a "very loving and trusting" relationship, use condoms, and do not practice any coercive behavior. Refuting those who called hedonists mindless and Godless, Block reconfigured some age-old irreconcilables by claiming the lifestyle did not necessarily take one away from spirituality or from leading the kind of unselfish, "good" life that benefited oneself and humanity. "We have so much potential to be sexy, peaceful, gracious bonobo ladies and gentlemen," she wrote in her book, *The Ten Commandments of Pleasure*, published just one month before the Lifestyles tour I was on had taken off for the Baja, and two copies of which were being passed around on the beach. "The mystical experience and the erotic experience are the most intense in human life: both connect desire with awe, anguish, fear, pleasure, pain, and extreme logic-defying *passion*. Religious mystics love God with a passion that can be feverishly romantic, and who do most lovers call out to in the throes of erotic passion? God, baby, God, baby, God...! *There is nothing unsacred about sex*."

The extremely colorful Block had even applied evolutionary logic to Cyrenaic thought, coining the term "primemates" to describe the happy halves of a hedonist marriage and establishing the Bonobo Foundation "to educate individuals in The Bonobo Way, that is, how these chimps use sex to create and maintain peace in their societies." Bonobo-like marriage partners had "very strong values," Block maintained. "I'm not talking about 'family values,' at least not the narrow, paternalistic, 1950s-style family values that politicians swoon over. I'm talking about personal values. The value of pleasure, and not violence. The value of love, and not war. The value of lust, and not greed. The value of knowledge, and not ignorance."

I once sat with the skinny, blond, middle-aged Block in her hotel room while she got ready for her TV show, which was taped at a Lifestyles convention the day after she delivered her "Bonobo Way" seminar to several hundred hedonists. "This Everest of smugness from a radio station interviewed me yesterday," she said, making up her face before the mirror in a shapeless T-shirt that came to her knees and would soon be replaced by the lingerie she wore for the show. "He said, 'A lot of people are looking back to the morals of the fifties and here you guys are doing this stuff.' So I said to him, 'In the fifties there were a lot of people cheating.' I mean, *morals*? Morals are what people break if they can get away with it. Ethics are what they *don't* break if they can get away with it. These people are trying to work it out as a team. Whatever their sex drives are, whatever their needs are—at least they're trying not to cheat on each other." She turned to me with a liner brush at her eyes. "It's not a perfect solution at all, but life doesn't have any perfect solutions. They're *so* straight, God bless 'em! I think they're great—ethical hedonists—most of them!"

On the beach where I sat at the Eden Resort, all the couples were quite convinced that they had combined ethical living with hedonism. They were *proud* of their lives, which in some cases went beyond Hillel's restraining maxim and followed Christ's more positive prescription, "*Do* unto others what you would have others do unto you." Chuck, for instance, could have headed a safe, suburban school if he'd wanted to but had chosen instead to work in an inner-city battleground. Leah, a one-time concert violinist, could have held a genteel job as a music teacher but had gone on to get a postgraduate degree and now worked with students from poor households who had severe problems. Carla headed a troop of Brownies two evenings a week. Ed was an officer in the Rotarians. And Joyce raced home from work at Lifestyles headquarters several evenings a week, ate a dinner prepared by her husband, Richard, and then raced around to various civic centers to organize events for children.

"I have three rules," Joyce explained to me under the beach umbrella while everyone slipped on bathing suits before heading back to the pool to collect their togas. She waved a hand north and south to include the people she was now guiding through their weekend, then began bending back fingers to enumerate the ethical ideals of swingers. "Number one, you act considerate of your spouse, because he or she comes first in the lifestyle. Without your spouse, there *is* no lifestyle. If your partner doesn't want it, then it's not going to happen—end of discussion. Number two, you act decent at all times—you don't touch *anyone* that doesn't want to be touched. And the last one is, you act polite—you obey a woman's wishes when it comes to condoms, and you immediately stop doing *anything* as soon as you're told to stop."

Rule for rule, these precepts, which in Susan Block's words allowed for "the pursuit and cultivation of pleasure within strict limits of consensuality for the peaceful benefit of the individual, the couple, the family, and society," were repeated every weekend by swing-club overseers throughout the uniform subculture of the lifestyle. Japanese couples belonging to the Liberated Lifestylist League followed the same rules as those at the New Adventures club in Ecuador, the Couples Club in Australia, the thirty-acre Club Maihof in Germany, and the ten-acre New Faces New Friends club in British Columbia. Jam-packed every weekend were party houses from Scotland to the Philippines—yet an inappropriate grab in any of them, no matter how crowded, got a partygoer thrown off the premises. The club owners might be business-minded entrepreneurs catering to the fantasies of swingers by encouraging couples to dress for the brothel and openly exchange spouses in mirrored rooms, but they knew that no lifestyle club could stay in business for long if it did not promptly evict rowdies who violated the principles of ethical behavior. It was an absolute prerequisite for diminishing the volatility of extra-partner sex. The lifestyle was not, at least in its ideals, a lawless world—just a subculture that could, admittedly, appear very unattractive to an outsider on the occasions when uncouth types were in the majority.

"Swinging never made a bad marriage good but it can make a good marriage better," averred Joyce's curly-headed husband, Richard, who had walked over from a neighboring umbrella as part of his constant patrolling to earn his free holiday. "It's not for everyone, but if you look at who's in it, everyone's represented. These aren't stupid jerks who take drugs to have a good time. They're socially great people. You know what the biggest shock is to people who go to our club for the first time?"

"Nothing shocking about the folks in there?" I asked.

"Exactly. You should write that."

I was being agreeable, of course, but in order to be objective about noncriminals who've been historically hated on strictly moral grounds, you have to offer them dignity and sympathy—favors not usually granted to revolting heterosexual hedonists.

I noticed Chuck and Leah, Ed and Carla, and Elliot and Linda veering off from the other pool-bound lifestylers and I broke from Rich and Joyce, plowing through the sand and catching up with the six at the brick path before the bar cabana at the top of the beach.

"Principal is as high as I want to go, it's where I can do the most good," Chuck was telling Linda as they entered the cabana. Beyond us was the hot tub where a school of lifestyle women were drifting against each other, shiny as porpoises. Two of them waved and then mooned us. "At the level I'm at you have a practical proximity to the kids and to the people that work under you, and you can take the *bullshit* policies that are coming down at you and work them into your effective curriculum goals. We've got a tough school in a heavy gang area. But we've got a very good learning environment."

"So are you known as the principal that makes a gangsta school work?" Linda asked him.

"Never been tempted to enter that bubble," Chuck replied. "I've been asked to go on speaking tours but I told them, 'Look, what I do, the *way* I do it, is not transferable.' The goal is pretty universal, but I could tell ya that in one sentence: get 'em to understand that every single thing they do has consequences. *Everything* proceeds from that."

I looked at the four women in the hot tub rubbing their breasts together for a couple of husbands who were videotaping them, then at Chuck, then at Joe and Doris, who were walking up the brick path on their way to catch a taxi to the mission church in Loreto.

"There's no conflict here at all, hombre," Chuck said, following my gaze. "This is harmless entertainment. The consequence is pleasure."

"It's just real hedonist enjoyment with the right people," Leah said, and by turning her back on the hot tub she seemed to be excluding the four women who were now tightly encircling the two cameramen. "The people that we're attracted to require a certain level of intimacy prior to having sex."

"You know what?" the garrulous Linda announced. "I think it's really important when you talk about this practice that you describe the results for a lot of people, not just the crude stuff."

"What's wrong with the crude stuff?" Chuck protested. "Nymphs and satyrs are *supposed* to be crude."

"This is where I disagree with society's conception of what I am doing—internally," Linda said as we took our beers from the cabana and headed down the path to the straight part of the hotel. "Because it's created such a strong intimacy between Elliot and me. It's really increased our communication skills. What it does is eroticize a relationship. It's an aphrodisiac. Your whole body, all your nerve endings are so sensitized by the experience. It's the afterglow. We make such amazing love afterwards."

"Seventh heaven sex, kind'a deal?" Carla asked. "Can't say it's ever happened to us. Fifth heaven, maybe. Fourth for sure."

"How many heavens we had this weekend?" Ed asked.

Carla sipped her beer thoughtfully, then looked over at Ed. "I'm goin' blank all of a sudden. Guess it's like a dream ya gotta write down soon as it happens."

"I meditate when I have the time," Linda interrupted the banter, and I suddenly remembered her reference to swinging being like an ineffable "cosmic experience." "I've had very, *very* blissful feelings—like my brain's on the top of a flagpole and my body's at the bottom? I'm filled with such ecstasy. With Elliot, what I'm talking about, it's *physical* ecstasy. But it's the same ecstasy."

"You get that?" Chuck said to me. "It's important to a Californian. Maybe Canadians wouldn't understand."

Linda gave him a shove down the path, under the varnished archway that separated the nude beach from the prude beach.

"So were you the one who first suggested it?" Leah asked.

"Actually, Elliot saw an ad for a dance and I said okay," Linda related. "At that point we loved each other as much as we ever did—but we didn't make love. We had no passionate times anymore. I always thought you loved a man and you had passionate sex on an ocean of romance, blah, blah, blah. Well, ten years of marriage, the kids, a job, and no more oceans. But what the lifestyle definitely did for me," she went on, "it taught me to separate sex from love, to have an experience with a man and then to come back with it to us again. Right, Elliot? That first time, we just got so *passionate* about each other, it was *amazing*."

"It was like I was watching a movie star in a love scene," Elliot said. "I can't believe how *beautiful* she gets. So *hot!* I went out and spent two hundred dollars on sexy underwear for her for the next time."

I knew that this sort of erotic collaboration—the first of Joyce's rules for a couple's ethical involvement in the lifestyle—was incomprehensible to the straight world. Hardly anyone I'd ever talked to could accept that two everyday heterosexuals could *both* want to stay in this forbidden world beyond a single experimental evening. The repeat expression of wifely bisexuality—and male voyeurism of same—was a little easier for people to understand as a motivating factor for a couple to remain swingers. "Generalized" male lust and grudging female concurrence, or the abusive hauling of women to clubs, were the easiest to comprehend. Unethical as it was, *normal* people had adulterous affairs.

"It's really increased my appreciation of Carla," Ed said in agreement with Elliot as we turned the palmy corner and came parallel with the dancercise pool where lines of couples wearing blue ID wristbands were doing split jumps and calisthenics. Noticing our pink Lifestyles wristbands, a couple of them beckoned with cheerful innuendo for us to join them. The

Eden and a dozen other lifestyle-friendly resorts were on the points plans of many staid North American businesses and all around the world that season the poker-straight middle classes were getting a first-hand peek at a subculture they'd never expected was still alive and well—and which (judging by the lack of complaints) they seemed to find less offensive than the reporters who had noticed swinging was still kicking.

"See, the way I was brought up, I would never even fantasize over another man," Linda was saying as we crossed onto the main pool deck where Joyce was tearing open the boxes of togas. "It was always buried. I was really naive. I just thought it was wrong, immoral, a betrayal. I was clueless that it was natural if the two were separate sometimes."

"You mean lust separate from romance?" Carla asked. "Animal attraction?"

"Yeah, like for the general manager," Linda laughed, gesturing to Pascal who, wearing his tennis whites, waved to us heartily as he entered the administration building.

"There's something about that guy, ain't there?" Carla mused. "Pascal. I think he's very intriguing."

"Those were Linda's *exact* words!" Elliot laughed. "See, I'm just learning the girl code for 'I wanna do that guy.'"

"I can actually think that about a man now and my head doesn't have to go through the woman thing, 'Do I really want a full relationship?'" Linda said. "Like my friend's having an affair she got into over pure lust, and she's worried, my God, am I gonna lose my husband? But here, everybody understands it's not that way. It's so tremendous. And I must say that there's never a time that I go down to our club with an expectation of something happening. If it happens and it's spontaneous, that's fine. But spontaneous is a big deal for me. Because I love Elliot. It's just for us."

"What would happen if you found yourself crossing the line between sex and love?" I asked.

"For myself I don't even have to answer that question," Linda said. "If I even *thought* it, that would be the end of it."

————————

Lest I get hate mail from neophyte couples attending a back-woods bacchanal hoping to find thirty intellectuals sitting around in togas debating the simple and profound truths of Cyrenaic thought, it must be stated that the wealthier and better educated the crowd the more prevalent will be those swingers dealing from the top of the Tarot deck. Conventions are big draws for these articulate sorts, as are expensive Life-styles tours, although on your average Saturday night at, say, Select Friends in Alaska or the Dixie Group in South Carolina, you will more often than not have to bring up a high-minded topic on your own. All I can affirm is that whenever I've been around to ask the right questions about God or morals or ethics, most swingers have not been averse to addressing issues you would never expect them to take seriously.

And so, as the uniformly college-educated couples gathered round Joyce and took their yard of muslin, I completed a conversational poll of the Lifestyles tour I'd been working on and determined that, as in the general population, not only did most of them take God or a Supreme Being seriously, but they believed in Him. There were a few, like Chuck, who were determinists or agnostics, but the fact that more than a handful actually *prayed* to Jesus Christ or meditated on Buddha-consciousness and admitted it was consistent with most groups of couples I'd met at conventions and clubs. Everyone I'd ever talked to in the straight world always found this one of the strangest bits of information about swingers, as if, smart or stupid, they must be in deep denial about opposing the moral laws enjoined by God that it was their duty to obey. Combining God with an orgy seemed as impossible as combining ethics with hedonism.

"This, if it's done right between couples, is not aspiritual," a Catholic nurse by the name of Evie told me, trying to figure out how to wrap her toga creatively. "It just expands the accepted definition, I guess."

Beside her, Carla said, "You call this *material?*" She held it up to the light, lowered it, held it up again. "I'm lookin' through a fishing net!"

"If you're not into it you can't interpret it as pleasant or a turn-on," Evie said. "It's hard to understand from the outside. Most people think it's a terrible thing, and so they say that women are doing it against their will."

"That's exactly what they think about it," said Evie's husband Lance. "All the guys taking their wives out—it's all abuse."

"It really confronts all your issues in life," Evie explained. "You have to throw off so much to be in this environment. I'm looking for my pure energy, I guess. If I get through all these hang-ups and all these walls, then I can truly love people. That's what I'm looking for. You get that ecstatic energy with other people, and that's something!"

"That's the pagan philosophy," said Harvey, the anthropology buff. "You get so far into your sexuality so that all the personality stuff falls away, and what you're left with is the bare humanity."

"A poor soul is he who does not love or lust under summer's sun!" Chuck called—offering a paraphrase, I later learned, from his favorite piece of music, *Carmina Burana*, whose libretto sometimes just informed his thoughts or sometimes was quoted verbatim.

"Maybe ecstasy's what all people in this movement recognize they're struggling for, and that this is the way to get there," Lance said.

"Well, that's a pagan belief," repeated Harvey. "Ecstasy means to get outside yourself. It's a Greek word. That's the main pagan belief. I've been all over the world and that was the belief before the missionaries arrived."

"Whether it be through sexuality or spirituality or some form of our emotional being," Lance said, "what I'm after is to tear away the shell and get at the inner being. I really believe that."

"To admit who you are, to tear away all those layers, then you can really kind of laugh and love yourself when you've been hating yourself," Evie said. "You're not presupposing so much, and you're not so fickle of other people's personalities, you can just have your core being and flow with it without judgment. We went to Lance's birth mother's funeral about six months ago. I hadn't been in a church in a long time, and it was kind of sad for me, because I was remembering how it was *all* judgment, *no* forgiveness. And I was just thinking how bad religions are if you're different—you have to go outside the church to reach out. I seek it, or God, or whatever on the outside. I don't have to be in a church to be spiritual. I can be here and be spiritual. Churches are all about orthodoxies and I just can't stay hidden in that box, hiding myself from God."

"Here's something else for your book," the ever-helpful Harvey said to me. "I spend a lot of time on the Internet and there's Christian groups in the lifestyle promoting the pagan roots. Liberated Christians."

"Actually, I've looked them up," I said.

They were a Phoenix-based organization whose evangelical preachers presented one of the more popular seminars at the annual Lifestyles convention—its theme: "Swinging: Not a Biblical Conflict." God-loving playcouples weren't "guilt-ridden and shameful slugs of the sexual underground," the Christian Libbers preached on the Internet, and we shouldn't be shocked "that the innocent-looking wife next door likes to drag two or three men onto a bed at a time and be smothered with their attentions without guilt." On their Web site, visited by thousands of spiritually inclined swingers a month, Dave Hutchison, an exile from the Billy Graham Crusade, and Bill Paris, a certified theologian, attacked the belief that lust was sinful, based as it was on a "Bible that has been misquoted and mistranslated to falsely suppress sexuality." In their view, adulterous lust in the Old Testament was declared an evil not because of immoral sexuality, but because of unethical "covetousness, the desire to deprive another of his property...the essence of adultery." Since lifestyle couples were supposedly not covetous of their extramarital partners, they were not sinful but ethical. "The loving women-centered sensuality and satisfaction of natural desire for sexual variety has absolutely nothing to do with 'lust' as most assume it to mean. Lust is the selfish desire to take something from another."

It was a question, again, of ethics, not morals—of motives and ends. Instead of staying morally loyal while unethically cheating, swingers stayed ethically loyal while immorally exchanging spouses, having group sex, or watching others do both. The world might view secret adulterers as angels compared to orgiasts, since adultery was sometimes redeemed by love and thus closer to God than a four-in-a-bed scenario, but swingers viewed themselves as actually having taken a step *up* from this moral code. They claimed that the ethical lust they cultivated with others was a plaything of their loving marriage and that they were not doing anyone harm by enjoying affectionate encounters with like-minded couples. They *did* have love on their minds, they said—for each other—and so they did not feel separate from God and His goodness.

Yet you would be hard-pressed to find a paragon of ethical and spiritual goodness in any culture's pantheon of saints who would reflect this reasoning. When Mahatma Gandhi titled his autobiography *The Story of My Experiments With Truth*, the big truth was not pacifism or independence for his homeland, but *brahmacharya*, "literally conduct that leads one to God. Its technical meaning is self-restraint, particularly mastery over the sexual organ." By mastering sexual desire, one became master of oneself. "Purify one's mind," was the first lesson of Buddha. "Flee fornication," was Saint Paul's advice. "Hell has three gates: lust, anger, and greed," the *Bhagavadgita* warned us, lust being immoral, anger and greed unethical, and all three interlocked at the low level of a hedonistic existence. "No man," Christ said atop the Mount, "can serve two masters." And so on across all religious barriers and national borders, even unto that moral pit America, where triple-X-rated movies are still "wicked" and "dirty" and all the more profitably promoted as such by purveyors of porn.

This fundamental theological and cultural tenet—that hedonism is separate from "good" behavior and from God; that chastity is completely unified with both; and that matrimonial sex is somewhere between—is so ancient that we need to look beyond its cynical exploitation by kings, priests, scribes, and pornographers and ask: where, in truth, did it come from? Why did sexual pleasure, persistent across millions of years of evolution and the perfection of nature's and presumably God's reproductive laws, come to be considered the basest of human pursuits, involving one in a web of selfishness and evil? And why has the struggle against hedonistic enjoyment always been waged with appeals to our "higher," spiritual nature, with threats of irredeemable harm for those who ignored the appeals?

When the righteous American general in the film *Dr. Strangelove* raged against women because they corrupted men and stole their "vital juices," he gave a clue to at least one of several possible answers, which, in this case, could derive from what John Money has called "an ancient bit of proverbial sexosophy." The notion that one's goodness or evil fluctuates up and down on a divine scale according to one's orgasmic self-restraint or hedonistic expulsions may in part have originated in the mistaken belief of our male ancestors that they were losing something precious when they lost semen.

This singular misapprehension probably dates back at least ten thousand years to about the time of the domestication of herd animals at the dawn of civilization. Farmers would have noticed that the castrated animals in their herds grew up tamer, weaker, and smaller than the breeding males who were allowed to keep their testicles. Warriors, too, would have learned the same lesson: after they had castrated the male children of their conquered enemies to keep them from reproducing, they would have watched them mature into passive, stunted, beardless men. Since the castrated boys and animals produced no semen, the implication would have been clear: semen must be a fuel required for growth and development, and its loss had negative consequences. It was one of the great sexosophical discoveries of civilization, rediscovered again and again throughout the world.

But it was completely false. "The error in the folklore," Money assessed in *The Destroying Angel*, "…stems from the centuries when absolutely nothing was known about hormones." It was not known, for instance, that when a male is gelded, his body loses testosterone—the hormone testicles secrete into the bloodstream—without which males appear weak and unmanly. "The ancients knew that without testicles an animal is sterile and also unable to ejaculate semen. But they did not know that almost all the fluid of the semen is produced in the prostate gland and that only the sperm are made in the testicles. Thus, it was easy to arrive at the wrong conclusion that, because castration causes loss of semen, semen itself must be the vital fluid that should be conserved in order to be virile, strong, and healthy."

If they had known about testosterone, and that it was not ejaculated with semen, we might have wound up with a slightly different version of sexual morality. But by the time writing was developed in 3000 B.C., the sexosophy was already part of the fabric of society, and it was codified for the first time by the chaste Brahman priests of the Indus Valley, patriarchs of the world's oldest living religion, Hinduism. Semen was declared *sukra dhatu*, "sacred white metal." It was believed that by some mysterious process semen—the essence of the divine "life force" known in Sanskrit as *kundalini*—was converted into spiritual energy if retained, and would rise up the spine through the various "spiritual centers," the chakras, lifting one's mortal consciousness from the urge to expel semen to a superconscious godhead completely removed from sexuality. The spine became viewed as a sort of evolutionary thermometer, with the seven chakras its mystical scale markings and the transmuted semen, in the form of *kundalini*, its quicksilver.

The belief in this vertical "ladder to God" is pervasive across cultures. Indeed, the baroque sexual mythology of the Hindus (which arose a thousand years before the codification of the Eden myth) is so obviously an antecedent of many of the other traditions equating sexual self-control with Godly behavior, that the imagery is worthy of some scrutiny.

According to the Hindus, in most unevolved humans, that is, in those souls who had not evolved much over thousands of incarnations on earth, the hot fuel of *kundalini* sat coiled like a snake at the two lowest chakras—survival and sex. There they whispered seductive entreaties for expulsion, much like the Satanic serpent in Eden did as it lay coiled about the tree of knowledge of good and evil, which yogis to this day interpret as a metaphor for the spine, with the fruit representing orgasm. The expression of *kundalini* through the sex chakra, while reproducing life, tied one's consciousness to the body and its "gross" perceptions and needs. By retaining one's sexual energy, meditating on God, and practicing yogic breath techniques that helped remove the buildup of evil karma, one sped up the reincarnational process and one's *kundalini* began to rise through the various centers, expressing itself in ways commensurate with the higher states of more evolved beings.

When, for instance, the *kundalini* passed the third "power" center and reached the fourth center, opposite the heart, human love began to be expressed selflessly. When it reached the fifth center opposite the throat, Platonic ideals and the uniformities underlying all differences were perceived—taking one even further from earthbound emotions and desires. The divine vision center, the sixth chakra or "spiritual eye," sat in the middle of the forehead: here the arrival of *kundalini* caused one to behold God as St. Paul reportedly beheld Jesus—which caused him ever after to denounce sex as a grievous sin that kept him from union with this infinite being. Had he held onto his semen, according to the lore, he would have found all separateness finally transcended when the *kundalini* reached the seventh, *sansara*, center, situated on the crown of the head within the "thousand-petaled lotus of light"—the center of cosmic consciousness, the "self" of self-realization. At that moment the *sansara* blossomed open and one experienced a flood of bliss thousands of times more powerful than the expression of *kundalini* in sexual orgasm. That is why the yogic goal of life was crucially dependent on the mastery of sex. Sex short-circuited the rise of *kundalini* and wasted the latent potential for eternal orgasm. By expelling semen in orgasm, one lost the spiritual fuel, leaving one stranded in earthly delusion and evil.

Thus, the true purpose of sex was revealed: it was not reproduction but God-realization. Sex, in the words of Elisabeth Haich, a modern proselytizer of this sexosophy, was "the only fuel absolutely indispensable for this purpose." Since God-realization was the most important goal of life, the retention of semen became an obsession of the Brahman rulers. It was vile when emitted, holy when retained. And so they developed their mystical beliefs into a science, the world's oldest sexosophical practice, *kundalini yoga*—literally, "joining together with the life force"—which occupied one's every hour with breath techniques, meditation, a "noninflammatory" diet, and a host of other ascetic practices to keep one's mind off that fruity repository for semen offered by Eve.

There is an argument to be made that upon that mythological belief in the conservation and transmutation of sexual energy into spiritual energy rests almost all the religious, sexual, and moral laws man must follow if he is to live an ethical and spiritual life. Whatever encourages the excessive expulsion of semen is at the bottom of the scale; whatever encourages its retention is at the top. The belief may have arisen from sincere faith, but it was a faith that fit in nicely with the agenda of priests and kings who, as we have seen, are always anxious to keep the lustful masses guilt-ridden and beholden to their powers as intermediaries between a God who condemns those who indulge in sexual pleasure and loves those who strive for chastity. It led eventually to all the crackpot sexual-degeneracy-disease theories of the Victorian era, one of which claimed that sexual excess led to spermatorrhea—the uncontrollable "leaking" of vital essence. It led also to those equally crackpot notions purveyed to this day in the rafts of yogic texts in every New Age bookstore that explain the precious energies required by the body to produce semen. Such as the theory that the body "purifies" semen from "vital spirits in the blood." Or that semen is made from "neurine" taken from the blood. Or that when semen is expelled it drains away brain fluids down the spinal cord—an old hammer used to keep nineteenth-century boys from masturbating.

Although you will find lots of testimonials in passionately written books with names like *Arousing the Goddess*, *Sexual Energy and Yoga*, and *Kundalini: The Evolutionary Energy in Man*, there is not a shred of scientific evidence that the retention of semen accomplishes anything except egotistic pride in accomplishment. It does not increase a male athlete's performance in sporting events or raise scores on IQ tests or increase concentration in any way that has ever been measured by external observation, the foundation of all scientific hypotheses. As for women, although most texts on *kundalini* and yoga "emphasize that everything said in this book about sexuality and the development of consciousness applies as much to the female as it does to the male," as Elisabeth Haich has stated, I have not been able to discover a single volume that postulates the female equivalent of "sacred white metal" that is lost during sex. (Rare women do expel a clear fluid during "female ejaculation," but no *kundalini* text—sacred or popular—has ever pointed to the need to *retain* this fluid; on the contrary, as we shall see below, that expulsion is *cultivated* by aspiring Tantrics.) Even if we are dealing only with a "psychic" loss that sidetracks the mind and ensnares one mentally in illusion, there is still no observable evidence that *kundalini* exists beyond the realm of metaphor, much less that it rises through the equally unobservable seven chakras, purifying the body and uplifting the consciousness as it goes. Lastly, while meditation demonstrably calms people and vastly increases their alpha brain waves and immediate powers of concentration, there is no evidence that the techniques advocated by *kundalini* yogis and yoginis cleanse the soul of "bad karma" or speed up one's psychospiritual "reincarnational" development. We are dealing simply with a matter of faith.

And yet there is a swinging twist to this story of faith. *Kundalini* yoga has seen an amazing resurgence in the West. Some people follow the original tenets of the tyrannically ascetic Brahmans but others follow the rebel branch known as Tantra. Tantra emerged four thousand years ago to promote the same "conservationist" truth as the Brahmans—for men, that is. At the same time it radically affirmed that sexuality did not have to be denied in order to obtain enlightenment. If semen retention was the goal of *kundalini* yoga, the Tantric masters decided, then they could offer another route to that goal. Their erotospiritual alternative accommodated human lust by actually encouraging the night-long pleasures of God-conscious lovemaking—including the sort of outrageous group sex pornographically pictured on Tantric temples all over India—but with one fabulous benefit: no loss of semen. The key was for males to delay their eight-second orgasm indefinitely so as to: 1) cater to the female's endless capacity for orgasm even unto a G-spot-stimulated waterfall; and 2) save the precious fluids in their own bodies.

Needless to say, the lifestyle movement has seized upon the Tantric version of *kundalini* yoga to validate its philosophy that such a thing as high-minded, spiritual hedonism is possible. Susan Block considers herself a "bonobo Tantric" and every Lifestyles convention has a few Tantra seminars in which couples who belong to groups such as the Liberated Christians, the polyamorists, Loving More, and the Temple of the Goddess switch partners and have "sacred sexual" encounters with other ethical hedonists. In the words of Dr. Deborah M. Anapol, a clinical psychologist who has offered "Tantra and Sexual Pleasuring" workshops at Lifestyles conventions, and who is a cofounder of the polyamorist *Loving More* magazine as well as the author of *Love Without Limits* (and who, by the way, is on-record as being opposed to the "recreational sex" of fastlane swingers): "Any tool for increasing your flow of life force—variously called *chi*, *prana*, or *kundalini*—and opening your energy centers or chakras will help prepare you for multi-partner sex." She recommends "yoga" and "meditation" as "very effective" means toward these ends. The goal is "to access heightened energy states and expanded consciousness through specific sexual practices." Thus, couples having group sex should make italicized love *"to the god or goddess within your partners*. This focus lifts us out of our usual overidentification with the ego or personal self, and makes it easier to see ourselves and our partners as different manifestations of a single universal male or female." On the physical plane, Anapol asserts, "Tantra can provide effective techniques for the man who wants to satisfy more than one woman. By learning to *separate orgasm from ejaculation*, any man is able to match women's innate capacity for multiple and continuous orgasm." Anapol recommends that to properly experience a group-sex encounter—one in which "each partner experiences union with the cosmos and consequently with each other"—one must learn "to direct the flow of sexual energy." She concludes by saying Tantric techniques "are useful skills for solo and coupled sex, but they are critical for an optimal group sexual experience."

Strange as all of this sounds, the point is that lifestylers generally do not feel they have joined a culture in which all ethical values have been reversed. Far from feeling they are perverting the teachings of the masters, many believe they are correctly interpreting the truth of God that in both the West and the East has been misinterpreted, or mistranslated, or just hijacked for economic reasons. They have woven freely expressed sexuality "back" into the moral fabric of their religions, redefined the "erroneous" tenet of monogamy upon which the institution of marriage has been based for ages, and reconfigured the approved method for the worship of God to include the lifestyle's forbidden hedonistic pleasures. Some have actually fully worked through the texts of their faiths to find evidence that multipartner sex within marriage is spiritually permissible for those who can handle it. Others who believe in Jesus Christ as the literal Son of God are just counting on forgiveness for what they see as a far less egregious transgression than has been proselytized. For many of them the ancient directional arrows that have always pointed

upward to spirituality and downward to sex are actually connected in a circle—and God is equally present at all points on
that circle.

———————

"You're asking how do we reconcile it?" Rita said to me in the
quiet restaurant where we'd sat down for a snack. She was
forty-five, with the complexion and flaxen hair of a Swedish
model, the waist of a woman in her twenties, and the unrecon-
structed breasts of an erotic statue. Yet she was curiously prim:
she wore no makeup except for a wash of pink blush on her
lips and on previous evenings, had dressed in a knee-length
skirt, silk, sleeveless blouse, and flat leather sandals. Not for
her the bra-and-garter get-ups that were standard fare at
swinger dances. Perhaps that was because she and her husband, Palmer, were members of the Mormon church.

"I'm wondering how people can act in a way that their
spiritual belief system tells them is not the way to act," I said,
since I knew that at home Rita and Palmer were engaged in
long-term affairs with two couples in their club and that they
sought out casual encounters all the time.

"I think they believe they can make up for it later," Rita
said. "Forgiven later. I know I'm like that."

"The traditional message of the church is that people can
be forgiven if they go to church and repent—if they do pen-
ance, all sins are forgiven," Palmer said. He had the emphatic
syntax of a physician-specialist who was used to heading a
hospital wing and giving talks to lecture-rooms full of his colleagues. He too was attractive, with a square jaw, a full head of
hair, and gold-framed glasses that enlarged his sky-blue eyes.

"But isn't this *the* ultimate forbidden behavior for a
Mormon?" I asked Rita and Palmer. It sounded as if they had
struggled to reconcile the contradictions in their prayers, as

have many religious people with unconventional sex lives, but the evening before I had seen the Mormon pair entering their room with two couples. That gathering, I was sure, would have been considered demonic beyond forgiveness to the members of their congregation.

"On the surface it's forbidden," Palmer said, "but yet for centuries most of society has been doing it anyway. As a matter of fact, you go back to the early days of the church, they were polygamous. Some of the church founders had two or three wives—obviously when they got together they had two or three wives at the same time, they got to have their own little swinging party. In Latter-Day Saints they stopped polygamy only because the federal government said if you don't stop, we will destroy you."

"And I don't believe it's as forbidden a sin as with a victim," Rita said. "I mean you have people here of age, and they're all agreeing to do this. In our society adultery is sort of part of the institution of marriage—so that when you get married you also join the club of adultery, just like swingers belong to swing clubs. The thing about this that contrasts with adultery is that it's the couple that makes the mutual decision. They believe that this is more acceptable than adultery; I can still love and care for my partner and I wouldn't go behind my partner's back. So as far as Christian morality goes, I would still like to think I can do this and still be the kind of person that I am: I offer help to the people around me, I give to charities, I volunteer all the time. But we live in a society that says I am an evil person because of this one area, when in my heart I know that I am really not. I know I'm still involved in the church and with the people there I like to be involved with, and can be the way I like to be and all of the other things that make up the virtues of being a Christian person. Will He really punish me for this time here? Probably in reality there's a little doubt in my mind. But are all of these people that have this aberrant lifestyle, will they *all* be punished too, even though they have hearts that are really good, yet they have this one thing that makes them take liberties with their faith?"

"You know that this is purely hedonistic," I said.

"I guess by definition it is," replied Rita.

"So then you have to deal with the following: if there's a God, then it's our duty on earth to know Him—God is the goal," I said. "Does that mean that involving yourself totally in the flesh takes you in the wrong direction from God?"

"Well, I think it does in the sense that it is a material involvement," Rita said, "but whether it pulls you in that direction more is the same as should be asked of many material things. It depends on how you handle it in the context of your other life responsibilities. Anybody really involved in this shouldn't let everything else go, should make sure their family is well taken care of, and that they are a unit and there's love, that you make wages and everybody has money and all the necessities of life. They're sort of all part of the same thing; the family situation can be just as threatened by people who read the Bible all together but who really aren't living together as a family unit."

"Ultimately, maybe there's no hard answer," I said. "We'll have to wait for the moment of death."

"Well, I think you've put your finger on it," Palmer said. "A lot of this has to do with the way people think they'll be judged by God. People think that when you die, you're gonna go to judgment, you're gonna be judged on what you did good, and what you did bad, what you didn't do that you should have done, and what you did do that you shouldn't have. They think, that's it: God's gonna add up the good things you did and the bad things, and it's gonna come to a grand total, and see where you fit in the grand scheme of things. But I don't think that's all it."

"Yeah!" Rita agreed enthusiastically, taking Palmer's hand.

"I truly believe that the rules that the Lord has down for us," Palmer went on, covering his wife's hand with his own, "about being honest, and virtuous, and courageous and kind, meek and humble—they're all designed to help you find the way to be like—well, you're supposed to be like God. Jesus Christ said 'Be like my Father.' All these rules are set down to find how to be like God, how to be Godly. But I think on the Judgment Day, you're not going to be judged on all the things you've done sexually, you're going be judged on how close you are to God, how good have you become, what kind of a person are you. There are going to be some people who've done a lot of good things, who have put their money here in this and that, but they never really got themselves as close as they should to becoming God."

"People feel they can buy their way to goodness, for instance," Rita said. "I know in our church that's a big component of showing that you're a good person."

"That's my point, you're going be judged on who you are," Palmer said. "You can't take your money and bribe God. All you're going to be is you at the end of the day. What are you? Are you a loving, kind person who would love to serve anybody and help anybody in need; would you go that extra mile to help anybody that was in need, would you be like your Father, or would you just whip out your checkbook and say, 'I can help you with your need but I can't really stick around'?"

"So why did sex get thrown into that mix?" I asked. "Why are you an evil person if you're involved in this lifestyle, or something like it? I think it's extraordinary, from the point of view of other Mormons, that you two could possibly be in this. I still can't get over that you still consider yourselves Mormons."

"Well, our church would not approve," Rita laughed. "Someday we'll have a coming-out party. Our church is opposed to teaching about birth control or anything about your own sexuality, unless it's within marriage. But there is that foundation of polygamy, so in a way they've gone back on their original teachings."

"I'll tell you my perspective," Palmer said. "You use the word *why*. I've always been interested in why since I've been quite young. I always was resistant to the rules unless I knew why they were there; I wanted a good reason. The only exception was the church. Legal rules, I knew if I broke them I'd go to jail. School rules, if I broke them and I got away with breaking them, I'd just do what I wanted to. The only rules I never questioned were the church's. I believed in God, and I still do as much as I did then.

"But at one point in time I began to talk to myself and say, 'The more serious rules in our society, religious rules and cultural rules that have been around for a long time, why are they that way?' I think of God, I don't think He's somebody that just makes up rules and says you follow them for no reason, I think He's got a reason for what he does. He's the most reasonable person out there. By following the rules, there's some specific, expected results both for individuals, families, and societies in general. And I think those rules are there for those results.

"For example, most people today eat ham or pork, no problem. But it was forbidden in the early church, because Moses said you don't do it. The Jews didn't and they still don't. But in reality, why was that? Now we know why it was forbidden. Because they didn't know what to do with trichinosis. You eat pork that hasn't been adequately cooked and you get trichinosis and your body gets this disease, you get really sick. And so the only way to avoid that was to say, 'You don't eat it.'

"And so I think in all these sexual cases the rules have been designed to make sure that society moves forward, children are raised in a proper environment, and families continue to have relationships. The elders knew the only way to have children brought up in a proper environment was to have a father and mother who were together and bonded and committed to raising them. You do that by having a marital situation where you have a child born into that marriage. But where you have willy-nilly sex before marriage, then you really don't get a bonding relationship of man and woman. Many times you get children out of wedlock, which in the past presented a problem. So I think the rules against fornication arose to ensure that children had a good chance of being raised in a situation where they had a happy, healthy, stable environment.

"And the other thing is, they didn't have any methods of birth control, except withdrawal, and that's not very reliable. How could you maintain a society if you're swapping wives and you're not sure who's getting pregnant with who? You really couldn't have that kind of thing and maintain the security of the family and the future of the people.

"But that brings us to the other thing, which is the emotional problems. Jealousy is one of the biggest problems in this lifestyle. There's no way you can be a jealous person and be in this lifestyle. Rita and I, for example, jealousy at the beginning was a real issue. We've worked through it to the point where we don't experience it, or if we do we sit down and talk about it. In reality, so many people in our society have a significant jealous aspect that they could not go around swapping, even if one day they said, 'Sure, let's go do it.' The next day they'd feel so jealous, it would destroy their marriage. Fidelity was established by God to maintain the integrity of the marriage and to sustain it, because God knew the emotions of the men and women He created.

"If you put all those things together, how is God gonna say, 'You can go have sexual intercourse outside your immediate marriage as long as you're using condoms all the time, as long as you ensure the paternity of your children, as long as you ensure that everybody's emotional needs are taken care of, and as long as you ensure that there's no hurtful results, and that it will enhance your marriage.' Well, that requires too much maturity. It's easier just to say, 'Don't!' My own opinion, not as a Mormon or a physician but just as a civilian who's seen couples come and go in this lifestyle, is that God was right when He said 'Don't.'"

"There's a lot of people who benefit from the lifestyle," Rita said. "It increases their self-image, it spices their marriage. But it would be counterproductive to the majority of people. That's my view."

"We agree on that," Palmer said. "Those that want to go against the prohibitions and get out there on the edge, they'll do it anyway. For everybody else, there should be these brakes that make them think long and hard before taking the chance."

Outside the Diamond Eden's colonial lobby entrance stood a twenty-foot-tall, three-pronged saguaro, the middle finger of which had exploded into rampant fruit sometime during the day. Several flowerlike pods, red as a mandrill's backside, now oozed a kind of Varathane oil that dripped the currantlike seeds over the thick, ripe petals. Long, sticky strings hung partway to the flagstone driveway. The obscene sight was not wasted on a couple of dozen swingers who, walking from the cool of the lobby into the massive night heat of the outdoors, paused on the hot stones in their gauzy togas and marveled at the plant.

"Ain't it from outer taste, though?"

"*Too* crude!"

"The impossible dream to me."

"Maybe that thing should charge us just for looking at it."

"I'd sue the damn thing for false advertising!"

"Noble Venus!" Chuck toasted the vaginate flowers with a beer bottle.

"Hey, how much you allowed to drink with your condition, Chuck?" Carla asked maternally, since Chuck had put away a bottle of wine at dinner.

"Only time I drink is when I exercise my pantheistic enjoyments on these kinds of nights," he replied as we crossed the driveway on the way to the thumping beat emanating from the disco. "My chances of living are the same as you guys'—you might get hit by a garbage truck in three to five years."

"Sounds like you got it worked out real good," Ed said, putting his arm around Chuck.

"Extraordinarily simple and sensual," Chuck replied. He put his bottle down on the stone, turned and embraced Carla. "Summer, love, wine, sex!" he called out with his head against her cheek. "Pagan joy in *divine ecstasy!*"

"Why Chuck!" Carla said. "You're takin' my breath!"

He grasped the Oklahoman's hand and kissed it. "'Your beautiful face makes me weep a thousand times,'" he shouted, kneeling, looking up into her eyes then pressing his face against her belly.

"Oh, Chuck," Carla said, "you gonna make me cry. Damned if you ain't." She lowered herself in a billow of diaphanous cotton to the flagstones, took Chuck in her arms, and kissed him passionately.

"Conga line! Conga line!" Leah called, embracing Carla from behind.

Bill and Ed ran up to the feather brush plants lining the driveway, ripped up handfuls of stems, and came back twisting them into wreaths with which they crowned their wives and then themselves, handing out the rest. "Conga line! Conga line!" Bill shouted.

"Behold the pleasant!" Chuck called, getting to the head of the line, with Carla hugging him tightly from behind. "'I am eager for the pleasures of the flesh more than salvation!'"

As if connected by snapping wires the couples began an

exhibitionist, bouncy march up the alley. The optometrists and lawyers and teachers and housewives on their straight vacation packages turned from the lineup at the disco to behold the hedonists rocking and snaking in their direction.

"You're requested not to disrobe until you're inside." Harvey yelled.

"Now you're putting me at a disadvantage," Ed replied. "My ass looks better'n my face."

"Now, now," Leah said, "you're only old when you start being proud of the shape you're in."

"That's alright," Carla called back over her shoulder. "He likes to concentrate less on his brains and more on his butt anyways!"

"Ba-ta-ba-ta-boom-BOOM! Ba-ta-ba-ta-boom-BOOM!" they chanted as they congaed into the crowd, most of whom caught their lawless spirit and pushed past the doorman, heedless of his calls to check their wristbands.

It was absolutely freezing in the disco, at least after the sweaty dance across the atrium in heat that couldn't have been below 95 degrees. The weightless togas of the swingers were knotted in a dozen different ways, none of which provided warmth or minimal cover when the glacial air bathed their nakedness. The women with great physiques, like Carla, Greer, Leah, and Linda, had fashioned their cotton as G-strings then twirled it in a rope about their waists, from there letting it rise as a loose blouse knotted around their necks. Others wore the fabric as standard Greek skirts over Fashion Fantasy underwear—straps pulling French nylon tops taut about the thighs, and panty triangles floating in and out of focus beneath the white film. The men, advertising tight or fallen buttocks, Herculean pectorals or breasts as big as a woman's, sported their muslin as jockstraps and cross-blankets, gladiator kilts or diapers belted round by blue silk. Bellies were mostly flat, but some were big and hairy, which you noticed more when they were partly dressed than when they were completely naked. Many of the swingers were barefoot, with the women, some of them, wearing Fatima jangles on their ankles and insteps, rings on their toes. Others wore four-inch, dangerously spiked heels.

Joyce ran to the D.J. who promptly announced: "The Eden welcomes the Lifestyle!"

At her urging, to warm her group up, he slipped on their theme song of the season, Prince's "Erotic City." Immediately the lifestylers hit the dance floor as one and commenced the Electric Slide.

Watching sixty outlaw swingers power into the Slide is a little like watching sixty Hell's Angels start up their bikes and roar onto the highway. It's their dance, their stage, their expression. It's no more than a step-turn-clap Texas line dance, but they performed it like a school of fish moved by a single mind. From scores of cities and as many professions, with IQs that spanned the spectrum from adequate to genius, with passable grace or professional rhythm, they fell into line— one culture, one body, hands twirling, eyes on the walls, eyes on the floor, sometimes with hyperbolic nonchalance. The most intimate grinds and grasps were executed with a sort of hypnotic efficiency. From Club Eros in Toronto to the Wild Wyoming in Caspar, they knew it that summer. Proud as Masai warriors, they did it. It was the dance of the lifestyle for 1996.

Even Joe and Doris were out there on the black stone floor under the green and red spinning floodlights, picking up the step, trying to stay in line, watching their feet and hands. It was too cold not to be doing something. Meanwhile, the fully clothed straight guests, encountering the sixty swingers en masse for the first time, in action and in sync, sipped their drinks at their tables surrounding the floor, smiling ear to ear. Doris seemed to fit right in. It seemed part of the chaste routine of dance for her to accept the male body parts pressed against her bottom at each turn. But Joe looked downright embarrassed when the sheerly covered bosoms, pointy nipples, and pillow flesh brushed solidly against his bare back. He looked as if he were smelling these strange bodies and not liking it. It wasn't the smell of sport, definitely not the smell of Doris. As the bodies heated, the cold air did in fact become filled with an oversweet vapor you could feel on your nostril hairs. He seemed grateful when the dance was over.

I fell back into a leatherette booth with them. "Well, do you think you guys could ever become involved?" I asked—or rather shouted.

"Even if I were single and horny as a goat I could never be attracted to a woman who'll take any man whatsoever," Joe said. "Never."

"I only think a few of them are like that, Joe," Doris said. "I quite like Leah, and Carla, and certainly Chuck. They're very entertaining. I could see, if someone were to ask me now, 'So whaddya think of these lowlife swingers?'—I could see saying, 'Well, ya know, I went on this crazy holiday, and there were some people there I could probably be friends with—just friends.' Because the way they pour their hearts out, it's really touching in a way. Don't you think, Joe?"

"I would never be able to relax; I'd know *exactly* what was on their minds," Joe said. "Like I know for a fact Julia's bisexual—*look* at her." She was out on the floor with two of the gals from the hot tub, plus the Catholic nurse, Evie. They were posing in blunt body statements, with hand gestures that stroked and teased. "Which is great, fine, this is her outlet," Joe said. "But she's got her eye on you, I saw." He looked over at Doris, appraising her toga with a gawking figure-eight movement of his head. "And I'm thinking, Oh great!"

"You want to hear something interesting?" Doris said. "The guys aren't allowed to be bi at all. They call it 'bearing,' like if one guy makes a mistake and touches another guy in bed. Like they say, 'Hey, don't bear me.'" She snorted beer through her nose. "Excuse me—Bill told me that gem."

I asked them if any of this was having an affect on their lovemaking.

"Oh, come on," Doris said, giving me a shove. "Everyone's a voyeur. We're having a good time."

"At some level any person would find this entertaining, sure," Joe said. "But I could really see worrying about them if they were friends. Like some of them are pretty high up in society. Suppose they did get exposed? They're all talking how they make business contacts in clubs and how they can really trust people after they have sex. I don't think I'd want to do business with a swinger guy. You could wind up getting sucked into a scandal. No pun intended."

"I guess that's why they say they're *in* the lifestyle—they think of it as being in a community," Doris said, looking at our tourmates out there becoming progressively more obvious in their embraces, several at a time entwined and cooperating. I raised my camera and took a picture of Carla sprawled on the dance floor with Bill on top of her. Leah was pulling at Bill's hair, Linda was pulling at Leah's toga, Ed was dancing the lindy with a barely clad Julia, and Greer was leading Chuck by the hand to join Bill and Carla on the floor. "It really is another world," Doris said. "I can't get over it. It's not like they're misfits in any other way. Except for this, they're just everyday people."

"That's a big except," Joe said.

As the disco heated up in physical temperature, toga tops came undone beyond caring. By one in the morning the older straight guests had gravitated over to the swinger side of the bar, talking shop and talking sex. Most of the younger ones, however, stayed where they were, rolling their eyes. A physical and psychic divide between baby boomers and twentysome-things formed, which became more pronounced when the

swingers began their musical-chair party games on the dance
floor: "Pass the Stick Stuck Between Your Legs"; "Pass the
Orange Held Between Your Neck and Chin." Two in the
morning found them playing a favorite swing-club game,
"Find the Fruit on the Person on the Table With Your Mouth
While You're Blindfolded." Good sports, just before heading
off to sleep Doris found a papaya slice on Joe's chest and Joe
found a mango on her tummy.

By three in the morning the disco was quiet and empty
save for the booth where I was sitting beside Chuck and Leah.
Leah's bare legs were thrown casually over Elliot's lap, while
Elliot was leaning over and kneading her shins below the knee.
Linda was embracing her husband from behind, biting at his
ear, while Ed was working at her wings with twisting thumbs
and kisses. Down the line, Chuck was smooching with Carla,
and Bill was sitting yoga-style on the floor, accepting the tick-
ling of Carla's painted toes. Like all the others, Bill's wife,
Greer, had found some friends and, I supposed, gone back to
the rooms or the hot tub.

"Young men and women are rightly coupled!" Chuck said
to me, turning from Carla and giving me a manly hug. "Hail,
light of the world, Hail, rose of the world—noble Venus!"

"You got that whole libretto memorized, Chuck?" I asked.

"'The soul of man is urged toward love,'" he intoned,
clunking his head down on my shoulder. "'All joys are governed by the gods.'"

"Chuck," I said.

He raised his head. "Huh?"

"You're *bearing* me!"

Nonplussed by my tone, the whole crew looked over at
us—then tittered in satyric approval at how quickly I was
catching on to their world.

"Where I'm headed," I said, "anybody that bears me dies!"

CHAPTER SIX

New Horizons

Partner swapping is not particularly common in Western society, but it occurs often enough to form a recognizable part of the rich mosaic of human sexuality—a part, moreover, that promotes sperm warfare.

ROBIN BAKER, *Sperm Wars: The Science of Sex*

New Horizons is a place: to openly communicate with others and experience a caring atmosphere; to realize a new appreciation of your mate and a maturing of your relationship; to add to pleasurable memories as you lounge around the fireplace, talk and laugh in the hot tub, or become involved in a fantasy group scene.

FOR PLAY MAGAZINE

The woman who volunteered to take my medical advisor, my wife, and me on the orientation tour of New Horizons was a former military officer who now had a degree in health science. Every weekend she drove across Washington State to this thirteen-acre "Disneyland of swing clubs." Sometimes she showed up with her boyfriend and sometimes she came alone. It was a little over a week after I'd got back from the Baja, which had given me just enough time to attend the Eleventh International AIDS Conference in Vancouver before driving south for this four-day convention that because of its elaborate setting attracted a clientele sometimes referred to by sociologists as "hard-core" swingers. In most of the literature I'd read, hard-core swingers were said to account for about one-quarter of the lifestyle—which argued for about 750,000 of them—and even within the subculture they were judged "fastlane," that is, more promiscuous than the rest and more willing to participate in a group-sex encounter. They were the ones you usually read about in the press, rather than the other three-quarters who behaved similarly to the discreet partner sharers I'd vacationed with at the Eden Resort. Nevertheless, the fastlane swingers came from the same staid ranks of the white-collar middle class as did Chuck and Leah, and it was my belief that if I could explain the behavior of this quarter of the lifestyle biologically, I could explain the central mystery of the overall culture. The sociologist Dr. Brian Gilmartin had posed that mystery in 1978: "To most Americans it is inconceivable that a person could allow his or her own spouse to engage in casual sexual intercourse with another partner in his or her own house. To the swinger, on the other hand, to do so is most often seen as an aphrodisiac." Eager to see the club that was famous for drawing fastlane lifestylers in greater proportion than might be seen elsewhere, I made sure my wife, Dr. Josef Skala, and I arrived early on that cool Thursday afternoon. I'd warned them both, however: "Fast means fast." The convention was called "Northwest Celebration: A Celebration of Intimacy Among Friends."

"The first time I came here a year ago, I said to myself, '*I have found what I have been looking for all my life!*'" the chipper, forty-year-old Jodie told us in the empty banquet room that could hold hundreds. "By the way, I went ahead and put tags out so that you'd get good seats." She pointed with scarlet nails to our first names, which she'd placed on plates. Jodie was such a regular visitor to the club that she often worked closely with the management in attending to guests. "There's another dining room upstairs and unless you claim a table early, you wind up there. You get to see everything better from here," she added, indicating the dance floor, the bandstand, the chandeliers, the hardwood paneling, the glass wall behind us that overlooked an Olympic-size indoor swimming pool, and the tall windows that gave a great view of a gold-green garden bordered by tall cedars with little lamps that marked the start of Hansel-and-Gretel trails. Just to the right of the windows, leaning against one wall, was a six-by-ten-foot stage prop, with white puffy clouds painted on a sky-blue background. Five squares of paper showing red numerals were pasted on the board above waist-high little doors. Written across the top of the board were the words "Blind Fondle Wall."

"There'll be three couples at every table," Jodie said. "We'll probably have about a hundred couples tonight, a hundred and fifty tomorrow, and by Saturday things will be really ripping with maybe two hundred couples. They pretty much come from all over the country and from up where you are in Canada. Everybody just relaxes and eats and dances and then gradually they filter on back to what we call the Annex. The 'Inhibition-Inhibitor Wing,' I call it."

"Are most of the couples married?" my wife of a quarter-century asked, her arms folded against her chest as if she were chilled.

"Oh yeah—I'd say practically all. Some get married here. They like romantic ceremonies."

"Interesting," Dr. Skala said.

"Of course, some of them decide to have two ceremonies: one regular in church and then one here. Well, why don't we walk outside first, then I'll take you over to the main part," Jodie said, leading us across the dance floor and up the wrought-iron stairs into the sunny garden. "I meant to tell you, I was very impressed with your credentials, Dr. Skala."

Skala, Josef P., MD, Ph.D., FRCP(C)—as I'd mentioned over the phone to Connie, the youngish matron of New Horizons—was a senior teaching professor and cancer re-searcher on the faculty of medicine at the University of British Columbia. He was one of those Nobel-prize-contender types who accumulated "credentials" in his spare time. He had spe-cialties in gynecology, obstetrics, physiology, and pediatrics and was the first to grow lymphoblastic leukemia cells outside the human body. He was also a visiting professor of medicine at Charles University in Prague, where he headed up projects in the Czech Republic's pediatric cancer research program. I'd invited him to accompany me to this convention partly because he was the medical advisor to this book and partly because I wanted to show him evidence for what I thought might be the complementary reasons husbands and wives could be enjoying the fastlane lifestyle. He brought a notepad, and, as I would be on the road for the next couple of months, I packed a small library, including Mary Jane Sherfey's *The Nature and*

Evolution of Female Sexuality, which hypothesized that the "extremes of an impelling, aggressive eroticism" exhibited by women at "orgastic parties" was a manifestation of our evolutionary heritage, suppressed for thousands of years. Skala had read the psychiatrist's once heterodox views on female "sexual insatiability" and was intrigued that they were now being given weight by evolutionary biologists who claimed women possessed the drive to fill their vaginas with the "sperm of two (or more) men at the same time" to promote sperm competition, while men were programmed to cope with that drive. A husband suspicious of his wife orgasmed more forcefully and pleasurably and ejaculated three times the number of sperm cells as during routine sex, with his "army" following commands to seek out and destroy the sperm of his rivals. Sherfey's evolutionary explanations for extravagant female promiscuity and the "sperm wars" theory, now all the rage in academia, shook hands in the lifestyle. In fact, they were the only biological explanations I'd ever heard offered for why the kind of orgiastic sex favored by fastlane lifestylers kept cropping up throughout history among everyday segments of remarkably different populations.

"This is all owned by Connie and her dad and the whole family," Jodie said as we came out to the manicured lawn. "They started out small in 1979 and then gradually they kept expanding the buildings and making the grounds into a park. Here's the volleyball court. Hopefully we'll get a chance to play. Most of the people play nude. It's completely private."

Indeed it was. To get to New Horizons you had to find your way through a strip-mall town outside Seattle, then along a tertiary road that snaked up chip and down dale through the rainforest, watching all the time for two anonymous brick pillars that looked like the entrance to a cemetery. A five-hundred-foot gravel driveway ended in front of an ugly metal warehouse. This was where Connie's father, founder and architect of the resort, ran a manufacturing business. Getting out of your car you hadn't a clue that you were within a hundred yards of the largest swing club in North America, second only in the world to the German Club Maihof. There was no sign that told you to cross the Japanese bridge that spanned a running brook, no arrow that told you to follow the narrow dirt path through the thick, cedar forest, no letters on the huge brick wall that you came upon all of a sudden, nor on the heavy, varnished, Spanish oak doors to the mansion. You had to have either read about New Horizons in its listings in swing-club directories or heard about it from one of the tens of thousands of people who had visited it in the last seventeen years. You had to have called, booked a reservation, and then received directions from Connie, who was no garish-looking madame, but an unassuming intellectual with a couple of postgraduate degrees.

"It's amazing a huge club like this sits in a little town and nobody knows about it," I said to Jodie as I looked back through the glaring sunlight at the connected tiers of brown wood buildings that zigzagged across the lawn and into the forest. Manicured rhododendron bushes, tall, pink sprays of orchids, rosebushes, and lobelias almost completely hid the first floor.

"Well," Jodie said. "It depends who you ask. Most weekends they have the nurse out here from the health department giving her talk on safe sex to everybody, so the health department knows. The fire department knows because they inspect the place. The town council knows because it's legally zoned as a private recreation club and they're always checking that it's in compliance with business and alcohol regs. So the right people *know*. And there are a lot of famous people you'd never expect who come here to inspect it unofficially, so to speak."

"Interesting," Skala said.

"This is the yurt where couples who want economy accommodation can stay," Jodie said, leading us into a windowed tent in a clearing beneath the trees, with about twenty sleeping bags in a circle around the walls. "Mostly the young people stay out here. There's a shower in here too, and they tend to shower together. Actually, this area does not allow sex, just out of respect to those who want to sleep—there's plenty of rooms I'll take you where you can have plenty of loud and screaming sex. My opinion is a swing club is a place where a woman can be *totally* satisfied, *if* she loses all her inhibitions. And you can't in here."

"Interesting," Skala said.

"Here's the start of very romantic trails, they go all the way back, and there's mosquito lights so you don't get bit by bugs—but you can be bit by anything else you want. It's very lovely back there."

We crossed the lawn again and returned to the building complex via a cement walkway that led over another Japanese bridge. "There's carp in there, big goldfish—see?" Jodie said. "An-n-n-d, on that platform up above, there's a hot tub—there's several Jacuzzis on the property." She held a door for us and we walked up a flight of stairs into a glass-walled walkway between the main building, with its swimming pool and banquet hall now on our left, and the mysterious club proper down the hallway to our right.

"Just come this way. One more door and—" She pulled open two heavy wooden doors, the kind used to seal saunas. "Ta dah-ah-*AH*!"

"Holy shit!" I said.

"My God!" my wife said.

"*In-ter-esting*!" Skala said.

The Annex, or, as I would hear it referred to by some astronomy-minded swingers, the "Satellite," towered very much like an extraterrestrial craft almost three stories above us and stretched sixty feet from where we stood to the opposite wall, colorfully enlivened by a mystical, airbrushed mural of naked men and women in carnal ecstasy. The sheer breadth, height, and variety of the layout had us looking upward and turning around with our eyes and mouths agape, since, by design, any visitor could take in from the door a lot of what the club had to offer sexually and (just as certainly by design) many of the couples partaking. Yet, open to the rafters though it was, in its ranch-style construction the vast Annex strived for the warmth of a north woods lodge, built post and beam in the shape of a six-sided tower around a sunken brick hearth, with many surrounding walls containing doorless theme rooms, making for at least a dozen fantasy chambers. Some rooms glowed brightly from their mirrored ceilings and walls; others were softly lit and decorated variously like a sultan's tent, a Victorian drawing room, a railway car with facing passenger seats, and a Harlequin Romance room replete with period couches. Rustic stairways connected the levels; banistered gangways crossed the air; and miniplayhouses— cantilevered out over space—gave guests a high vantage point from which to privately peep at the activities taking place below. Presumably there would be an array of postures worthy of a Tantric temple to peep at, since lining the walls were suggestive arrangements of swivel chairs and attached stools of different heights called "Eros Seats," plus waterbeds, red-plush couches, massage tables, and bunk beds with trans-lucent draw-curtains. At two of the corners on the first floor, alleys curved away beneath red lights that seemed to signal entrances to dark fun houses, and above us a wooden prison door stood slightly ajar to a chamber whose motif I could easily guess. All was cozily quiet save for the crackle and hiss of the central fireplace around which there was room for ten couples to sit below floor level on built-in couches and make love in the light of flames leaping into a black flue hung by heavy chains from log posts that also supported a wrap-around walkway. There was a big sign on the varnished log facing us: "No outside clothing. Partners only beyond this point."

"So this entire environment will be, shall we say, 'occupied' with numerous people on this weekend?" Skala asked in his orotund Bohemian lecturer's voice.

"Sure," Jodie said, "plus the Carebears who roam around to make sure women aren't having any problems. They're almost never needed but it makes everyone feel safe and secure. They all have Carebear badges. Ron—you'll meet Ron—he's in charge of the Carebears. He's a Vietnam vet, a terrific guy.

"But, anyway, isn't it another *world* in here?" Jodie asked, twirling around by the fireplace. "There's no limit. How can you *not* want to feel like this? It's not reality, it's just pure fun, a comfy place where you can come with your partner, where you can have your fantasies, and then you can go back to your real life and your inhibitions." She waved her hand at a wall of pigeonhole lockers lining a cedar passage that led into a room of showers, sinks, and toilets. "And *that* is where you put your inhibitions! There's a bidet in there, a good, powerful one that almost lifts you off the seat," she told my wife. "Now, you guys don't *have* to walk around naked—you can wear a towel or a bathing suit or a nightie or kimono—but they want to prevent fully dressed people from coming in and gawking. And speaking of kimonos, here's the Japanese room." She took off her heels, pointed to our shoes for us to do the same, and led the way into a bright red, velvet-walled room whose floor was completely covered in flowered futons. Stylized drawings of couples with satirically enlarged genitalia were hung on the walls and in one corner there was a stack of pamphlets from the community health office: "Straight Talk for Safe Sex" and "As Safe as You Wanna Be."

"This room's kind of simple and intellectual and sophisti-cated," she told us. "What I like about it is that everyone's on one level. Actually, all these open rooms, if you come in and make love don't be surprised if a couple asks if they can join you. So if you don't want to be near another woman, don't want to be near another man, this isn't the place to lie down. For me it's kind of an all-encompassing, enjoyable sort of thing. You stretch out and look up in a mirror and it's like a fantasy-dream watching all these men adore you. But whatever your boundaries are," Jodie said to my wife, "it's to be respected. And if people hear of someone not respecting your boundary, they'll say something to the Carebears and that person will be asked to leave." She turned to me and Skala. "There are top-of-the-line condoms in each room in these wicker baskets and they're always being refilled. And I suggest that that is a very important step you take before engaging in any activities. And then deposit them afterwards in these metal canisters."

She worked the foot pedal up and down with a clank and led us back to our shoes, around the fireplace, and along one of the red-lit corridors that turned sharply and then opened into an amphitheatre with broad, ascending tiers of beds and form-fitting couches that faced a giant, black TV screen. "This is the video room," she said. "They have pornos playing throughout the evening and you might have twenty couples coming and going in here, so to speak. Myself, I prefer to sit over here and watch the people. Who needs a video?"

As we returned to the central area, she pointed to an electric socket beside a set of five Eros Seats and said to my wife, "If you like power toys, there's outlets all over. They have a woman coming in this weekend, Dr. Ruthless, she sells them if you didn't bring yours." She patted a furry massage table by the stairway. "Also, they have a very handsome Jamaican who comes and does Swedish erotic massage for free. Nothing penetrative," she said, leading us upstairs, "but he works the sciatic nerve in the thigh and buttocks and brings you to orgasm after orgasm—which is an *amazing* experience, honey, so there's a real lineup for him. Okay, these are what we call the condos." She pointed to the dollhouses I'd seen from below, plus several other criblike cubicles built into the landing and overlooking the downstairs. "They're really private, and you can crawl in here and be with your partner and look over the action through the windows. A lot of new younger couples wind up in here and have their private fantasies. You can hear all the moans and groans of everybody around you but nobody can see you. There's condom baskets in here, too—see? Also, you find a lot of the husbands come in here on the sly just to watch their wives without them. It's like a man's fly-on-the-wall fantasy—you know, *what is she really like without me?*"

"This way, this way," she sang. "We'll have to move because there'll be a big tour coming through soon." She led us quickly through the "Sultan's Tent" and "Miss Daisy's Academy" and the the "Amtrack Room," reminising all the while about her experiences on the pillows and divans and benches and tables. Then, walking back down from the top floor "Loft," whose two hundred square feet of mattresses was reflected in beveled mirror-walls to produce multiple images, she stopped and turned to my wife.

"Do you like women?"

"As friends," Leslie said.

"You know, I actually didn't think I liked women sexually either, until this one time, I was in there with three young men"—she pointed to the Sultan's Tent as we passed it—"and I was just enjoying the luxurious oral on all those soft pillows with my eyes closed and their hands all over me and whatnot, and all of a sudden I thought, Wow! does that guy ever know what he is doing, who *is* that? So I opened my eyes and there's long, silky hair on my belly from this young woman who was this guy's wife going down on me. So she says, 'It's just pleasure, darling.' So I thought, Okay, close your eyes, relax. And so I did. And I realized, Hey, I'm comfortable with this—why not? So, you see, whether you just visit once or every weekend, there's always another little room of your mind that you might say, 'Well, I might like to go in there.' Speaking of rooms, I'll take you into the Dungeon now."

"The *Dungeon*?" I heard my wife whisper behind me, which caused Skala, following behind, to erupt in laughter.

"What's that?" Jodie asked, turning around. "Oh, I see. No, no, no, it's not what it sounds like at all." She flicked on a flood light and we made our way down a long staircase, creepily creaky. "This is just play stuff." On the landing above the firepit she pulled back the set of bars and we entered a room painted white and bathed in light from a ten-foot window. "See, it's not *really* a dark dungeon—everything they build here is really middle class. Which isn't to say it's *everybody's* thing. I guess it's a matter of taste." Against the window was a line of beds covered in leopard-print fabric at the foot of which were soft, fuzzy stirrups. "You'd be surprised at how ladies go *crazy* in here, though." She took down from the wall a couple of feather ticklers with whip handles, and then a pair of "chains," which were actually strips of fishing net. She threw the chains over the stirrups and backhandedly tickled and whipped the bed, pointing to the mirrored wall and mocking a tongue-lolling look of lost pleasure. "Not my thing at all," she laughed to her reflection, "but there's always a crowd of couples. You figure it out. Beats me!"

She led us out the other end of the Dungeon, past a king-size waterbed, more bunk beds and other mirrored rooms floored with mattresses and hung with love hammocks, and then to the firepit again, where we ran into a dozen middle-aged couples being led through the main door by a pair with teddy-bear badges on their chests that said "Don and Judy." "See!" Jodie laughed. "The early bird gets the worm and the private tour!"

We were introduced in a blur of names and were walking back down the long passageway towards the pool when my wife asked, "Your boyfriend doesn't mind you coming here by yourself?"

"Not at all. He's a very wonderful younger gentleman—you'd love him," Jodie said. "He knows I don't think I'd ever want to be with one man again. I'm single and a totally independent nonconformist, with all my children grown. I don't need or want one man. And he says he finds me very refreshing."

"Because generally the lifestyle is only for couples," I remarked.

"Oh God, I really get into this conversation with some husbands a lot here—some guys just don't seem to get it, only the women," she said confidentially to my wife. "See, the lifestyle refers to a lot of different things," she said to me. "Most of the people here are couples—and that's the lifestyle for them, it's very arousing for them. But I have several girl-friends in the lifestyle who are single professionals like me—I'll introduce you tonight, one's a massage therapist, another's a welfare-fraud investigator—and we just find we're really at home here; it's a very wonderful life for us. Most of us, we lived our whole lives without knowing this was possible, and then we came here, one way or another, and, like I said, it was like this was really what we'd been looking for our whole lives. My circle of couples here is so close, it's like a real tribe. Oh, by the way, here, this is one of the lecture rooms where they give seminars," she said, rolling back sliding-glass doors into an empty room above the pool. "Some people will be bringing sleeping bags and spending the night here too. See, that's the banquet hall on the far side." She pointed down the length of the pool back to where we had started out.

"You are saying that this is a space that you and your friends feel comfortable in every weekend," Skala said, seeming to want to get it right as we walked above the pool to the second-floor dining area.

"Exactly."

"You and your friends came here," Skala said flatly and with clarity, "and you were looking for something, and when you experienced it here you instantly knew you had found it. There was no adjustment period."

"Well, before my marriage I was actually very promiscuous —my whole life I'd been very curious in sex, but it was never fulfilling because it always felt wrong. Just a minute. *Hi, Stan! Yoo-hoo! Ready or not, here I come!*" she called down from the dining room banister to a young D.J. setting up equipment below. He waved back and blew her a kiss. "I met him last week, isn't he cute? Anyway, this is fulfilling because it doesn't feel wrong. It's just a very natural way for me to be, it feels right. So, yes, I found a place that has always been a part of me, no one introduced something new to me here because it's a part of me. This is the only place I've ever found where I can be that part. "

"I see," Skala said.

The three of us stood leaning against the banister while Jodie ran to the stairs in her heels, clickity-clacked down the flight, and dashed across the dance floor below us to Stan. She embraced him, kissed him passionately, and, getting to her knees, pulled his shorts and underwear right down to his ankles. Skala looked at me and I looked at Skala.

"Interesting," my wife said.

———

"The strength of the drive determines the force required to suppress it," Mary Jane Sherfey wrote regarding female sexuality, and a big swing club is the place to go to see many women like Jodie offering uninhibited evidence of why that suppression might have been so forceful throughout history. It is also, paradoxically, the place to see male jealousy—the irrepressible emotion behind that murderously repressive force—turned on its head, with husbands enjoying rushes of lust for their promiscuous wives, then overwhelmed by volcanic orgasms they cannot explain but which they want to repeat. Here couples lie with their mouths glued in love while they have sex with others. Here there are romantic games of seduction but almost no competition among men for women. Here a wife's jealousy is sparked less by her husband having sex with another than by the possibility that he is feeling love for his new partner. Yet wifely jealousy is minimized because, as Brian Gilmartin says, "Swingers believe that couples with good, strong marriages are highly unlikely to 'fall in love' with someone with whom they are not married." In fact, at clubs like New Horizons, a bond is usually formed among potential female rivals: wives are often casually bisexual with one another, expressing a pleasure that is so sanctioned in the subculture that it bears the name "confirming." Although they may have just met that night, "most swingers value the emotion of friendship with the couples with whom they share their recreational pursuit." And when these friendly recreational pursuits are finally over, another party begins: "After having spent hours in an orgiastic social setting," couples return home "even more erotically charged toward their spouse than when they left" and have the best sex of all—with each other. "Swingers *expect* swinging to have this aphrodisiac function for conjugal coitus, and so it does." Finally, on Monday morning they all go back to work as teachers or pharmacists, therapists or editors—and begin planning for the next event, all the while aware of the central meaning of their erotic rites: "The idea is to protect and defend the marital unions of everyone involved, yet still enable everyone to enjoy playful, recreational sex."

It's another world that doesn't seem to make sense on any cultural, evolutionary, or biological level, although the underlying logic of the lifestyle on all these levels is written so tinily in code and acted out in such a visually overwhelming fashion that until recently we just haven't had the proper instruments and perspective to read its message.

In fact, until the mid-1990s, the message of the lifestyle phenomenon was so indecipherable, its milieus and activities so foreign to the experiences of most people, that most often it was written off as a perverse aberration that should never have been interpreted in the sixties as "sexual freedom." Swinging wives, we were told, could not really be "choosing" to have promiscuous sex with friends, because even nonhuman primates were discriminating in their choice of sex partners. Therefore wives were either being forced into the lifestyle by husbands anxious to swap them for other partners, or they were victims of some psychological malady that compelled them to act in this unnaturally hedonistic manner. "Swinging is fundamentally a male device for obtaining extramarital sex," one of the world's leading evolutionary anthropologists, Donald Symons, concluded in the sociobiologist's "handbook" on sex, *The Evolution of Human Sexuality*, published in 1981. "Presently available evidence," Symons wrote, "supports the view that human males typically experience an autonomous desire for a variety of sex partners and human females are far less likely to do so."

From Darwin's day until quite recently, the belief that there is a profound evolutionary difference between the male and female desire for sexual variety has been the starting point for the analysis of the traditional double standard. It has also been used as a fundamental argument against the possibility that women could be getting any satisfaction from the lifestyle. According to theoreticians, human females evolved to be very choosy about mates for a crucially important reason: they invest far more heavily in offspring than do males. Females produce only one ovum per month to the male's profligate billions of sperm in the same period. A single copulation can result in a long pregnancy and the delivery of a helpless infant who must be breast-fed and protected for years until the child can fend for itself. But while the life of a female is virtually monopolized by the consequence of sex, a male is free to desert her and go off with his infinite supply of sperm and have sex with other females. Over millions of years, therefore, those females who successfully raised children must have delayed mating until they were able to assess a male's potential as a provider and protector during the child's infancy. Then, during courtship and after birth, the female would have assured the male through fidelity that the child could be only his. According to this scenario, female sexual pleasure and the female sex drive must have evolved to be limited and under the female's careful control: if her urges were as powerful and indiscriminate as the male's they would have jeopardized the survival of her offspring, to say nothing of her own survival if she were to have sex with partners other than her mate. "Men everywhere prefer their wives to be sexually faithful," Symons wrote, and men throughout history have been homicidally unkind to women if presented with another man's child to care for. At the end of the day, those women who mated promiscuously for pleasure must have lost out in the evolutionary battle to produce the greatest number of surviving offspring—which is the bottom line of evolution.

Symons said this accounted for why women had almost always been on the receiving end of men's sexual desires, not the initiators; why their genitalia developed to be merely an atrophied version of the male's; and why women were far less driven to achieve orgasmic pleasure than men—whose genetic interests were served well by sowing their seed far and wide in their insatiable quest for variety. "There is no compelling evidence," Symons contended, "that natural selection favored females that were capable of orgasm, either in the evolution of mammals or specifically in the human lineage." Symons even offered explanations for why female orgasm served no biological function, and "might actually be dysfunctional."

Symons, whom the sociobiologist Edward O. Wilson declared had come close to providing "the ultimate meaning of sexuality," summed up the logic behind the female's limited desire for pleasure with steamroller inexorability: "If orgasm were so rewarding an experience that it became an autonomous need, it might conceivably undermine a woman's efficient management of sexuality. Throughout evolutionary history, perhaps nothing was more critical to a female's reproductive success than the circumstances surrounding copulation and conception. A woman's reproductive success is jeopardized by anything that interferes with her ability: to conceive no children that cannot be raised; to induce males to aid her and her children; to maximize the return on sexual favors she bestows; and to minimize the risk of violence or withdrawal of support by her husband and kinsmen. This view of female sexuality is a major theme of this [Symons'] book; it is the biological reality that underlies W. H. Auden's observation that 'men are playboys, women realists.'"

Not surprisingly, Symons scorned Mary Jane Sherfey's theory that the female's "insatiable" capacity for orgasm had been successfully reproduced because it served an evolutionarily important function: to make her promiscuously search out fertility and variety. While the admitted capacity of some women to experience ten, twenty, or fifty orgasms in a single hour seemed to contradict Symons's own evolutionary logic that a sexual trait would not persist over thousands of generations unless it aided reproduction, in fact, Symons had a ready explanation. Multiple female orgasm could very well be a "functionless artifact" of female human anatomy, standing in relation to the vitally functional male orgasm as the male's inutile nipples stood in relation to the female's lactating ones: "The ability of females to experience multiple orgasms may be an incidental effect of their inability to ejaculate," Symons, with a straight face, told men and women alike—a deduction that, these days, prominent female anthropologists such as Sarah Blaffer Hrdy and Meredith Small view with some impatience. "To my knowledge, Sherfey's argument has not been taken seriously by evolutionary biologists," Symons wrote, about a dozen years before his own theories would begin to be questioned by the evolutionary biologists Robin Baker and Mark Bellis. Baker and Bellis were the first to document how men's sperm were programmed to kill one another in the female reproductive tract, a battle the female actively promoted. In his book *Sperm Wars: The Science of Sex*, Baker hypothesized that "the traditional double standard may even betray an innate male understanding that if given the cultural freedom to do so, females would behave as licentiously as males." This contrasted with Symons's contention that "the sexually insatiable woman is to be found primarily, if not exclusively, in the ideology of feminism, the hopes of boys, and the fears of men." "Happily promiscuous, nonpossessive, Rousseauian chimpanzees turned out not to exist," he claimed, again a few years before scientists began to report that bonobo chimps were happily promiscuous and nonpossessive of partners in their very sensual social structure. "I am not convinced by the available evidence that such human beings exist either."

Symons's view of human sexuality is sometimes referred to as "the standard model." Back in 1993, when I stopped thinking of swingers in terms of the standard model, I began to search for the evolutionary and biological inside story of their professed delights—the underlying logic to a lifestyle that seemed to defy logic. Here were thousands upon thousands of middle-aged wives behaving in a way once thought nymphomaniacal; here were middle-aged husbands who had discovered that the promiscuity of their wives mysteriously turned their own orgasms into explosive events, involving what seemed to them like more seminal spurts than they usually experienced in "routine sex." Weighing the usual explanations for "why couples swing" in the many cases where women admitted to no abusive coercion, I arrived at my own hypothesis for the persistence and growth of the lifestyle. Swinging couples of a certain age who were no longer threatened by the prospect of losing their mate, or, in the case of the men, having to raise a child not their own, had freed themselves to "play" at what humans and most other animals on the planet had very likely been programmed to achieve through multiple mating: the competition of the sperm of several males in the female reproductive tract. "Advanced preparation for this warfare is so strongly programmed into both the male and the female," Robin Baker maintained, "that it continues blindly throughout life, even when the chances of such warfare seem minuscule to the conscious mind.... Why? Because, disturbing as this observation may be, past evolutionary imperatives have dictated that a female who promotes [sperm] competition may better the chances of her offspring having good genes."

As Skala and I reviewed some of this literature after our tour with Jodie, it seemed to us that the evidence of evolution argued for, not against, the complements of pleasure and domesticity pursued by men and women at all levels in the lifestyle. "The swingers believe that human beings (both male and female) are intrinsically monogamous from a psycho-emotional and residential standpoint, but polygamous from a *sexual* standpoint," Brian Gilmartin had argued in his National Science Foundation study, and Skala and I could see how many adulterers of both genders might secretly agree with that. While I'd learned that the behavior of swingers at a club like New Horizons could be culturally shocking, requiring some forbearance to behold, and was certainly not the preference of the couples I had just spent time with in the Baja, there were telling social and biological explanations for what fastlane lifestylers were up to in their mirrored rooms. Responsible couples—leaders in society—do fill hundreds of swing clubs every single weekend around the world, and their pursuits have a basis in the evolutionary forces that have in part shaped all of us. Hidden within the unconscious processes that serve reproduction—processes that have evolved over millions of years to ensure the best male's genes are received by the female—are our lifelong sexual yearnings for variety. In a Liberalia involving married swingers these yearnings are employed openly as aphrodisiacs, instead of secretly in the model followed by many couples. In fact swingers are intuitively aware of what evolution seems to have designed for them in the way of matrimony *and* promiscuity, and display a grandiose appetite for incorporating their urges into an acknowledged part of their emotionally monogamous pairbond. Their "openly unfaithful" behavior, Baker noted, "promotes sperm warfare."

———————

"Every new couple we meet, we always say, 'It's the sex that puts you here, but it's the people who keep you here,'" an auburn-haired woman named Edith said to Leslie at our table in the banquet room that night. It was about eleven o'clock, we were dawdling over dessert, and a slow country tune was playing too loudly from the speakers. The dance floor was no longer populated enough to absorb the echo, since three-quarters of the couples had gone back to the Annex—a stroll we were just now getting ready to take ourselves.

"Haven't you ever gotten yourself into a situation where

what you're feeling with one of those people becomes love?"
Leslie asked.

"No, not really. I don't need that emotional commitment
—I've got Sol." In contrast to the playful underwear costumes
which had been on parade about us all night, Sol and Edith
were unspectacularly covered in baggy white cotton. Perhaps
that was because the two of them ran a health-food store and
eschewed artificial fabrics. Certainly nothing about their
organic appearance would have given you a clue that they were
longtime members of New Horizons. They were in their early
forties, with two teen boys now at home with Sol's mother.

"We're not having sex with someone because we're looking for emotional commitment," Sol said. "We're looking for
the open communication; then you have the ability to shed the
mask that you put on for everyone else. We've found we can't
really do that anywhere but here, or with friends we meet here
and get together with."

"See?" Jodie said to Skala. "Wasn't I telling you that this
afternoon?"

"Yes, precisely," Skala said. "Interesting."

"You should understand," a real-estate agent named Larry
said to me, "once you draw down the wall of secrecy through
sex, there are no more secrets. Once you see all your friends
like that, all together—once they see you—everyone's made
themselves so vulnerable you're not going to laugh at them
over all the stupid things people laugh at each other for. You're
exposed to each other." At the moment Larry's wife, Beth, was
out on on the dance floor, perhaps in what most people would
consider an exposed position. Having just emerged from a dip
in the pool, she wore only underpants and red heels as she
moved to the heartthrob music in the tight embrace of a squarejawed car dealer named Konrad. Tall Beth's chin rested on
bald Konrad's shoulder and her eyes were closed. As I watched,
she pulled her face back and soul-kissed him.

"That doesn't mean you have to have sex with all the people in the building here," Edith said, "but you have to at least know that they are willing to bare their souls—such as you might experience *if* you had sex with them. And by so doing, you will get to know them internally, you know there won't be any surprises—"

"No surprises—you know, it's interesting to hear it stated like that," Jodie interrupted, showing a more reflective side than she had that afternoon. She turned to Skala: "You were probably thinking, someone like her—that's all she wants is surprises. But really, what she said is me all over. I like new experiences, but I don't like surprises. Does that make sense to you?"

"I believe so," Skala said. "You prefer your new experiences to be safe, without negativity?"

Jodie sipped some wine and swung her finger around at the few people remaining in the banquet room. "They're all like that, without negativity. That's why I love them so much."

The dance tune ended, there was some scattered applause, and Beth returned to the table and sat in Larry's lap. When Jodie had first introduced us, neither Beth nor Larry had believed I was writing a book. "That's what they all say," Larry had said, eyeing me up and down with a smirk. Like most fast-lane clubgoers they were impatient of denial and the sexual judgments deniers are apt to make in order to give themselves permission to go to clubs.

Konrad pulled his chair over and sat beside Beth. He had a shapely wife named Frieda, about a decade younger than his forty-five years. Frieda had gone back to the Annex with the rest of the crowd.

"The beauty of the lifestyle is that you get to have your catharsis and eat it too," Beth said now, with her arms around her husband's neck. Beth taught high-school English, and was pretty adept at twisting epigrams.

"How you feeling?" Larry asked her.

"All the good, horny things." She bit Larry's nose, then reached over and took Konrad's hand.

"You will not find me complaining about these good horny things," Konrad said, with a debonair Euro accent.

"For women this gives us a chance to go full circle," Edith said. "We get a closer understanding of ourselves—more so than men understand themselves. Women are actually much more analytical than men are. We look at things from all angles—that seems to be our need; we're very curious about all things—and in that need we feel our sexuality, our bisexuality, and when we come to allowing our need and curiosity to take over, we find out we like to help." The expression "like to help" was swinger code for a wife's being excited by her husband making love with another woman, and I believe that was where she was headed with her logic. Liking to help wasn't necessarily dependent on a wife needing to "confirm" her relationship with a potential rival, but it usually involved the same sort of bisexual closeness. "There are a lot of possibilities out there," Edith said. "Nonhurtful, pleasurable possibilities."

"It definitely enhances all those possibilities," Beth said. Theatrically she switched laps to Konrad, crossed her legs and put her hands behind her wet, blond hair, and threw her locks out across her bare shoulders. "I'm not unentangled from common sense," she laughed, stroking Konrad's shiny scalp. She tilted her head away from Konrad and looked at Skala. She was quite beautiful, and she knew how to set the light on her cheeks to accentuate that beauty. "My independence is intact here. I'm not giving up control."

"There are studies which show women are generally in control of consensual situations," Skala said.

"And it is *expected* here for her to be in control," Konrad said. "So that is something that will be very hard for him to convince anyone of." He indicated me with a tip of his Rolex. "Because it is so different here."

"The way I would handle it," Sol advised me, "first you look at the men—they're always supposed to be ready for this. Then you look at the women—unless they're neophytes you won't find many who aren't just as ready. Every swinger knows the saying—"

"You have to convince them to come but then you have to convince them to leave," Beth said. She leaned over to Leslie. "The fear every woman has is that she may get attacked in a swing club. But what's the other side of that fear? Could I— me—*could I really enjoy myself in a swing club*? That's even a more powerful fear. 'My God—I've turned into a slut. How could I have fucked two guys last night?'"

Jodie whistled, returning to her old self. "Two guys! I can *not* take the tease another *minute!*" She stood up, pulled her sleeveless sweater over her head and headed out of the hall, turning right in the direction of the Annex. Through the windowed wall I watched her greet some swimmers as she cut across the pool deck, stripping out of her clothes.

"I just spent time with some swingers who don't get into the big group thing," I said. "They do like to watch, though."

"For me, I like to have the release every so often," Beth replied. "We've got three little ones—four, six, and eight, plus I've got 120 students who make me feel as sexy as that chair. So once a month I really enjoy this. That's the total story— although I *can* do three weekends in a month," she laughed. "For some reason, usually February."

"Everyone is a sexual person," Larry reasoned, lifting Beth's legs into his lap and taking off her high heels. With both hands he caressed her painted toes as if they were strings on a lyre. "Everyone is an emotional person. If you feel good about your sexuality, then you can feel emotionally good about other people too."

"I'll tell you guys frankly, when I was young I wasn't into this at all," Beth stated to us. "The first time Larry said we should give this a try, I got here and I thought, Look at all these old people, yuck! I was twenty-five, but now I'm thirty-five, lemme at it! I wanted love and all the rest. Now I've got love—now I want all the rest."

"How long have you been involved like that?" Leslie asked.

"Since after I got over my depression from my third child," Beth said. "Three years now. We baby-stepped the first couple of months, then we had a group fantasy situation—all our friends—Konrad and Frieda, Sol and Edith." She looked around, probably for the other couples I'd seen her dancing with that evening, who had gone back to the Annex. "They all kept saying, 'Are you okay with this? Is this all right for you?' They were *so* nice, doing all sorts of things; I was the Queen of Sheba, and it was just terrific."

"When we drove home, I asked her, 'How did you like it?'" Larry related. "She says, 'It was all right.' So I asked, 'Well, did you *like* all these guys?'"

"I was still afraid to say how *much* I liked it," Beth recalled, "that he would think, 'I've created a monster!' Of course, you let go after that. But the first time it can be a shock; you have to try and feel each other out emotionally."

"Unfortunately," Sol said, "some guys, it's like, 'What do you mean you liked other men? I brought you here but I expected you to hate it!'"

"Right! So he keeps begging me, 'Tell me more, tell me more.' So I told him, 'You want to know? Here it is: It was *rea-l-ly* great. I had the best time. The men were *so* nice, it was so great. I never came so many times in my life.' Well!" she laughed. "He got so excited, we made love at a rest stop. That's his biggest fantasy since two years after we were married! Watching me."

"Every swinging man's got to like experiencing that,"

Larry observed. "If they don't, it's not going to work as a couple."

"Terry's trying to explain that biologically," Leslie said.

I told them I was coming up with a general theory to explain the lifestyle, from its soft end to its hard-core limits. In 1971 the science journalist Edward Brecher had reviewed Mary Jane Sherfey's theories on the sexually insatiable female and coined the term "Sherfey syndrome"—which he defined as "unlimited multi-orgasmic response in coitus with an uninterrupted series of males." He'd reported Sherfey syndrome as being the exception at swing clubs, but that it was experienced by normal, middle-class women without any ill effect on either their bourgeois marriages or their "sensitive maternal behavior." I had therefore derived a "syndrome" for husbands who were counterintuitively aroused by their wives' enjoyments—from soft-end flirtation to the extreme Sherfian response. I called it "sperm competition syndrome"—SCS. "It's a biological explanation for why swinging men get excited by watching their wives flirt or have sex," I said. "It has to do with increased sperm ejaculation and orgasm pleasure."

"That doesn't surprise me," Sol said. "Why would it be abnormal if every man who feels it is normal? It's alternative."

"The truth of biology is men are supposed to have this visual desire to come every twenty minutes in a different woman, and I'm sure that's true," Edith said. "For women it's more of a social desire. But women burn up the vibrators pretty good, too."

Sol stood up. "Blast off to the satellite?" he asked, hands at his side, imitating a rocketship.

"Ten, nine, eight—" Beth cracked, swaying her bottom to the left and right with each count. She pulled her legs from Larry's lap and jumped off of Konrad, stepped into her high heels, thrust her chest out and shook her breasts.

Arm in arm, the five rocked to the door of the banquet hall and followed Jodie's route to the other end of the premises.

"There's going to be a lot of naked people in there," I told Leslie and Skala as we trailed after our tablemates across the pool deck. We climbed the spiral stairs to the second-level corridor that crossed over to the Annex.

Ahead of us, at the far end of the corridor, Beth grandly pulled both wooden doors open at once. She held them for us gallantly until we got up to her and stepped through. One sweeping glance at the Annex would have made you conclude that the fantastic parade of couplings depicted on India's Tantric shrines could very well have been derived from life.

CHAPTER SEVEN

The Inside Story

The information on human females demonstrates
a certain insatiability for sex. This insatiability is
so strong, some suggest, that males must restrict
female sexuality, and most cultures do so in one
way or another.

MEREDITH F. SMALL, *Female Choices: Sexual
Behavior of Female Primates*

Watching his partner have sex with another man
excited the childless man once more. He could
barely wait for his friend to withdraw before taking over.

ROBIN BAKER, *Sperm Wars: The Science of Sex*

Given the cooperative pastimes of the couples at New Horizons, it is startling to think that Charles Darwin once concluded that females were sexually passive creatures, virtually forced to have sex with males. "The female, on the other hand," he wrote in 1871, "with the rarest exception, is less eager than the male. As the illustrious Hunter long ago observed, she generally 'requires to be courted'; she is coy, and may even be seen endeavoring for a long time to escape from the male."

The Annex aside for the moment, the illustrious Hunter probably would have gone faint at the sight of how sexually aggressive women can behave in even a modern European disco. And the Victorian Darwin almost certainly would have experienced a similar giddiness to realize that everyday married women frequent these haunts actively looking for adulterous sex. Over a period of several weekends in 1993, researchers from the University of Vienna studied women who showed up at a mainstream dance hall. They found that those in long-term, stable relationships were most likely to attend alone when they were ovulating, and they arrived for the evening wearing skimpy clothes as a prelude to infidelity. For most of the other women, the closer they were to ovulating, the skimpier their clothes. In other words, they were showing an arousal pattern we don't usually associate with humans but which Mary Jane Sherfey claimed was "homologous to the period of heat of certain higher primates." From the Northern Hemisphere to the Southern, virtually every research study has shown that during the two weeks around ovulation women have more sexual fantasies and are more likely to initiate sex and be unfaithful to their partners than at other times.

The term "male bias" is frequently used to slam scientists who have concluded that normal females are passive baby-making machines. Darwin—the supposed founder of the tradition of male bias in evolutionary biology—is, of course, also the genius who reasoned through the very processes of evolution. Life arose in its simplest form from nonliving matter, he concluded, and gradually achieved its variety through "numerous, successive, slight modifications." The modifications happened randomly, and if they resulted in a life form slightly better equipped to survive and reproduce in a competitive and changing environment, they endured. Thus, from life's first emergence in a chemical sea perhaps four billion years ago, probably as a tiny bit of nucleic acid able to clone itself (what we now call a gene), one successful modification was added to another, with organisms of greater and greater complexity diverging from that single common gene until tens of millions of species of plants and animals evolved on earth to take their own routes of genetic change.

Darwin called the two components of evolution "random variation," for the chance modifications made in reproduction, and "natural selection," for the crucial process whereby those modifications prospered or died off. Natural selection is widely acknowledged as *the* major force in biological evolution, and it is an exceedingly simple process. Stand naked in front of a mirror and behold its result. Traits that helped your ancestors survive and reproduce were "selected for," and you have them. Traits that hindered survival and reproduction were "selected against," and you don't. Today it is thought that the process of reproduction you engage in, sexual reproduction, probably evolved as a gradual improvement over the cloning process a couple of billion of years ago. Cloning is one cell turning into two; sexual reproduction is two cells turning into one. The combination of two sets of genes from a male and female of the same species to form a new individual gave the species a greater chance to vary its genetic makeup with each new generation and to adapt to ever-changing threats—which included staying ahead of enemies that wanted to eat it from without and parasitic diseases that wanted to feed off it from within. The pleasures of sex, and the hormones that drive animals to experience them, evolved to draw the two sexes irresistibly together to unify their genes and perhaps mix up the options a bit for the next generation. On a biological level, both the male and female orgasm arose to serve our reproductive success.

When Darwin first published his version of evolution in *The Origin of Species* in 1859, there was much gnashing of teeth in religious circles, but the capitalist-imperialist culture of his day was largely ready to accept a survival-of-the-fittest doctrine. Unfortunately for science, Darwin's time was governed by a certitude far more unshakable than the faith in biblical creation: it was the faith that females were much less interested in sex than were males. In fact, respected authorities argued that females didn't enjoy coitus at all. And so when Darwin tried to explain why only the males of many species possessed spectacular characteristics that actually hindered survival—like the cumbersome antlers of the stag or the long heavy peacock's tail—he came up with an hypothesis based almost exclusively on the male's point of view. On the one hand, Darwin saw males as so driven by lust that they had developed their costly accouterments in order to better compete with each other for females, either through direct combat or garish display. On the other hand, he saw females as demure, mentally dull, and as removed from lust as he considered Victorian women to be: they sat back, watched the show, and at the end of the day submitted not to "the male which is the most attractive to her, but the one which is the least distasteful." In a way, nature acted like a cattle breeder: the passive females accepted only battle-winning stags with the biggest racks, or the peacocks with the most impressive fans—that is, "supposing that their mental capacity sufficed for the choice." Generation by generation, this natural process selected for the exaggeration of those male characteristics signaling competitive health and virility. Since females wound up selecting for those characteristics, Darwin called the process "sexual selection."

There was, however, a group of hairy females whose spectacular difference from the *males* of their species he just couldn't figure out. "No case interested and perplexed me so much," he wrote, "as the brightly colored hinder end and adjoining parts of certain monkeys." He simply could not imagine that those flaming folds of exquisitely sensitive flesh were sexual swellings —that they, and the hormones which caused them, were driving the females with a "male-like" lust for twelve days at a time. Every bit as spectacular and "selected for" as a peacock's tail, the folds functioned to signal ovulation and to solicit sex for the female from multiple male partners—sometimes from every single male in the troop and, most delectably, if she could get away with it, from males outside the troop.

Darwin's inability to overcome his cultural conditioning in the matter of female sexuality is thought by some anthropologists to point to a frailty inherent in the entire field of evolutionary thought. It is why, to my mind, the implications of the sex lives of couples in the lifestyle have been pretty much ignored—except by mavericks. Theorizing and conducting studies to test their theories, scientists in the field of evolution can, in the end, act more like polemicists out to prove a cultural point. (As a nonscientist, I am not above this myself.) Darwin himself described *The Origin of Species* as "one long argument," and from his own day to the mid-1960s the evolutionary theory that only nymphomaniacs felt promiscuous desire held fast: it matched the culturally accepted behaviour of females.

At the same time female behavior seemed to match the theory that they were extremely selective about who they had sex with, that is, who they wanted to father their offspring—which was ostensibly the reason they had sex. Those who acted otherwise were considered evolutionary aberrants. Not until scientists themselves began living in a social milieu where respectable women started being openly promiscuous—as many previously had been in secret—did they say, "Let's modify our ideas about millions of years of evolution to accommodate this natural behavior." Often scientists were the newly aware women. "I was a young adult in the sixties," reflected Patricia Gowaty, a scientist who conducted one of the first studies of philandering female birds. "And I could look around me and see that there was a lot of social monogamy in people, but I could readily see this might not correlate with genetic monogamy because both men and women were having affairs. So I created a hypothesis about my own social life and the things that I could see around me." In this way mainstream evolutionary theory, no matter where it stands at any particular moment, can be said, like the media, to reflect, indeed to support, mainstream norms. Theory tends to change when it acknowledges a newly acceptable human behavior that has long been declared unnatural. Then scientists look back into the distant past, or at DNA, or at animals like bonobos, with new eyes. By the same token evolutionary theorists can tend not to notice unfamiliar or unacceptable behavior even when it is going on all around them. Perhaps that is why Helen Fisher, who went a long way to explaining female infidelity as natural, could theorize that Cro-Magnon people had sex only in the dark, at the back of the cave. Year to year, mainstream evolutionary theory changes, usually in tandem with some acknowledgment of present human behavior.

———————

Before discussing what mainstream theory presently acknowledges (and ignores), we should have a look at Mary Jane Sherfey's
theory of the sexually insatiable female. Much of what Sherfey
proposed has by now been accepted in the mainstream. But
few authors are willing to cite her or her embarrassing proposition: that it is natural—if culturally abnormal—for a woman
to want to attend "'orgastic parties', having relations with one
man after another, for precisely the purpose of gratifying [her]
capacity for numerous successive orgasms with coition."

   In the late 1930s, after a precocious girlhood spent wondering why no one could explain to her the precise reason women
menstruated (after all, cows and dogs didn't), Sherfey took an
undergraduate course at Indiana University taught by Alfred
Kinsey. At the time she was struck that the school treated his
course as academically insignificant—one credit, no roll call,
no grades. After she qualified as a physician and Freudian psychiatrist she attempted to find a hospital where she could
research the origin of menses and the problem of premenstrual
tension, but the male-dominated medical community showed
not the slightest interest in the subject; this, even as Kinsey
published the two statistical books that can be said to have been
the opening shots in the sexual revolution: *Sexual Behavior in
the Human Male* and *Sexual Behavior in the Human Female*.
In the prefeminist fifties, Sherfey opened a private practice in
New York and began researching premenstrual syndrome on
her own from an evolutionary perspective. This led her to
study primate females (the only mammal that menstruates);
which led her to study their extraordinary sexuality; which led
her to study the roots of human sexual behavior. Then, in 1961,
her studies led her to stumble on an obscure finding so overwhelming it changed her life: in the womb "the mammalian
male [was] derived from the female and not the other way
around"; and the female's clitoris was an internal *system* as
large and refined as the male's penis. Just as overwhelming was

the fact that no one seemed to be paying any attention to this finding that stood so utterly opposed to the standard theory of female sexual development. In a statement that encapsulates what might be called an evolutionary theory of the theories of evolution, Sherfey wrote: "I could only assume that this finding, which to me was a breath-taking, history-making discovery of the first magnitude with implications for everyone, had been ignored unconsciously because both the men who had made the discovery and those who had read the duly recorded data did not *want* this fact to be true."

It is hard for us to comprehend now, but from the time Freud published his theory of sexuality in 1905 to the mid-1960s, the clitoris had been largely assessed as a rudimentary erogenous zone (a "stunted penis," to use Freud's own phrase), a perfect preoccupation for an infant girl but a distraction from proper sexual fulfillment in an adult woman. Only neurotics and nymphomaniacs refused to give up playing with this fiery nubbin that sidetracked women from the "goal" of female adult pleasure—which was to achieve one "mature," vaginal orgasm to complement the man's single ejaculation. In Darwinian terms, evolution had "selected for" the single vaginal orgasm in humans. In Freudian terms, the normal development of a woman entailed the natural "transfer" of erogenous zones from the vestigial clitoris to the functional vagina.

According to the Freudian analyst Sherfey, however, this left women "in a strange dilemma of having a developmental theory that explains so much and conforms to so many life histories and felt experiences, yet one that has shown surprisingly little therapeutic effectiveness and has only a questionable basis in biology." As she came to an understanding of human embryonic development Sherfey also began to recognize that Freudian sexual theory had evolved to reflect culture, quite independent of fact. Not coincidentally, she realized, the vaginal orgasm matched the accepted view of females as naturally monogamous and satiated by one vaginal orgasm to one penile ejaculation—which matched the *perception* of women's behavior. Although men knew the mechanism of their own orgasms, *no one* knew the mechanism of the vaginal orgasm—and there was no proof it existed. That the physiology that produced the male orgasm developed from the clitoris was radical stuff for a Freudian to contemplate in 1961: it implied that a female's clitoris was important.

In Missouri, Masters and Johnson were studying human sexual response, and, in 1963, when Sherfey discovered their paper on the clitoral orgasm, she had a second epiphany. "It was truly a Eureka-experience for me. This was it! Freud was wrong. Men were wrong. Women were wrong. Common sense was wrong. There was no such thing as the vaginal orgasm as heretofore conceived."

Sherfey's writing now sounds hyperbolic to us. After all, does it really matter *where* a woman has her orgasm so long as the physiology is straightened out in sex-education classes and she is taught how to achieve one when she wants it? Considering how painful life can be in so many of its nonsexual aspects, the pleasure of orgasm might indeed seem like a gift worth cultivating but not shouting intellectual eurekas over. In fact, to a psychiatrist as well to an evolutionary theorist, it matters very much: the location and functioning of the orgasm bears heavily on female sexual capacity, which in turn affects the view of normal female behavior, the interpretation of history —including why millions of women have been murdered by jealous men unforgiving of their supposed harlotry—and, ultimately, the foundations of a culture that has operated mostly on the belief that female promiscuity is unnatural. Yet all the biological information coming Sherfey's way from Masters and Johnson and from her clinical practice proved that women weren't equipped to have just one or two orgasms, as most men were. Women could go on having orgasms for hours. Sherfey's patients were having "up to fifty orgasms in a single session." "To have the comfort of a label," she wrote, "I had considered them to be cases of nymphomania without promiscuity. From the standpoint of our cultural norm, this may be an accurate enough phrase. From the standpoint of normal physiological functioning, these women exhibit a healthy, uninhibited sexuality—and *the number of orgasms attained, a measure of the human female's orgasmic potentiality*."

To comprehend that potentiality, one has to think of the penis in terms of the entire clitoral system, instead of the tiny clitoris in terms of the entire penis. Unlike the penis, the clitoris is an organ whose sole purpose is pleasure. When aroused its hidden system is *thirty times* larger than the clitoris itself, and in its engorged state the amount of blood in the organ exceeds the amount of blood in an erect penis. Two broad roots and a pair of bulbous "caverns" create internal tumescence early on in the sexually excited female; while later, during orgasm, complicated muscle structures generate vaginal spasms that in turn push the slightly bulging cervix down like an elephant's trunk into the seminal pool deposited by the male—an active function performed by the female in her own fertilization. Sherfey explained how the many differences between female and male favor the clitoral system, with its five networks of veins fanning out on either side of the vagina all the way into the pelvis. However, *the* most significant difference for her lay in the postorgasmic activity of both systems. Whereas in males the engorged blood drains back from whence it came, resulting in a comparatively long recovery time, in a woman each orgasm is followed by an almost immediate refilling of the erectile chambers. This subsequent engorgement is in no way diminished from the first and produces even more arousal in the tissues. "Consequently, the more orgasms a woman has," Sherfey wrote, "the stronger they become; the more orgasms she has, the more she *can* have. To all intents and purposes, *the human female is sexually insatiable in the presence of the highest degrees of sexual satiation."*

Sherfey termed this experience *satiation-in-insatiation*, which she differentiated from the mere "satisfaction" society told women to settle for with a single man. Again, based on biological data, the work of Masters and Johnson, and her own practice, she argued for "the existence of the universal and physically normal condition of women's inability ever to reach complete sexual satiation in the presence of the most intense orgasmic experiences, no matter how produced. Theoretically, a woman could go on having orgasms indefinitely if physical exhaustion did not intervene." Thus, acculturated women who enjoyed one or even five orgasms might be "satisfied," she claimed, but they were not satiated, particularly during the two weeks around ovulation when her hormones made her most desirous of sex. "I must stress that this condition does not mean a woman is always consciously unsatisfied," Sherfey wrote. "There is a great difference between satisfaction and satiation. A woman may be emotionally satisfied to the full in the absence of *any* orgasmic expression.... The woman *usually wills* herself to be satisfied because she is simply unaware of the extent of her orgasmic capacity."

Sherfey granted that these marathon orgasmic sessions were usually masturbatory, but this was not because of any inability of women to transfer to a single, satisfying, "mature" orgasm. The problem, she posited, lay with the inadequacy of the male in a monogamous relationship: "Few males can maintain an erection long enough for more than three or four orgasms in the woman." And sex, she maintained, became more frustrating for the monogamous woman as she aged and had children; her "vasocongestion" capacity actually increased, as did her body's relative amount of testosterone, the hormone governing libido, which climbed ever-higher as she approached menopause. Overall, while men's capacity for orgasm and performance decreased, women became more inclined to experience, and more *capable* of experiencing, the fullness of their sexuality. As Sherfey noted: "These findings give ample proof of the conclusion that neither men nor women, but especially not women, are biologically built for the single spouse, monogamous marital structure."

Just what were women built for then? It is now well documented that a woman is equipped by evolution to promote the competition of several inseminates inside her, but in Sherfey's day no one dared speculate that the persistence of "insatiable" female capacity might have mating implications. For Sherfey, the implications were clear: women were built for a considerable number of men during *each ovulation phase*. The modern human female's complex and highly evolved structures, which produced insatiable capacity, must have been "selected for" to help her survive—otherwise, over time she would have discarded them as physiological traits. Sherfey assessed the sexual responsivity and hormonal changes of human females during ovulation and deduced that they were "too close to that of certain higher primates to be ignored. I would suggest (and will take to be true) that the use of the Masters and Johnson techniques on these primates, with sexual anatomy so similar to the human female's, will reveal the same condition of *satiation-in-insatiation*. Having no cultural restrictions, these primate females will perform coitus from twenty to fifty times a day during the peak week of estrus, usually with several series of copulations in rapid succession." Sherfey was roundly criticized for this observation on the grounds that she had discounted the "choosiness" of even the most promiscuous female primates, not to mention the spousal loyalty shown by the supposed monogamous gibbon. "If necessary," she went on, "they will flirt, solicit, present, and stimulate the male in order to obtain successive coitions, then take up with another. ... I suggest that something akin to this behavior could be paralleled by the human female if her civilization allowed it."

Sherfey rejected the notion that women were "naturally" more inclined than men to desire intimacy and privacy during the act of sex, pointing out that of 694 men and women observed in masturbation and coitus during the clinical trials of Masters and Johnson "women desensitize with appreciably greater ease than men: 85 per cent of performance difficulties from this cause occurred in men.... The most inconsequential psychosensory distractions easily impair the erection in all subjects regardless of how well acclimatized they are to the surroundings.... Analogous distractibility is not present in women."

Sherfey supposed that the rise of patriarchal civilization coincided with the "ruthless subjugation of female sexuality (which necessarily subjected her entire emotional life)." Based on an examination of Near Eastern myths and artifacts, she speculated that well into the Bronze Age societies existed that were ruled by women, and these early women would have been free to display "the fluctuating extremes of an impelling, aggressive eroticism.... For about half the time, women's erotic needs would be insatiably pursued": hence, Sherfey syndrome —the more controlled manifestation of which Edward Brecher would later observe described the behavior of some swinging women "when sexual inhibitions are cast off."

It is now generally accepted by anthropologists that the balance of power between the sexes—and thus the control of sexuality—rests on which gender controls the wealth in a society. Some scientists theorize that there may have been a prehistorical time, as recently as 10,000 B.C., when women did have at least equal rights with men based on their equal or even dominant role in accumulating wealth through food gathering and "net-hunting" of small animals—which in some societies might even have opened up ruling roles for women at all levels, from the spiritual to the sexual. But at some point in the transition from a hunter-gatherer existence to the development of agriculture, men, wielding the heavy plow women couldn't handle, got the upper hand on resources in settled communities. Desiring assured paternity, they enforced the state of matrimonial dominance that has characterized much of recorded history. Tales of prehistoric gynarchies and unleashed females like Lilith have indeed been around since the dawn of civilization. Sherfey offered up the body of modern woman to lend weight to the notion of a prehistorical reign of the human female's "intense, insatiable eroticism," an eroticism that "could be contained within one or possibly several types of social structures." She went so far as to predict that with the "scientific revolution...and the new social equality and emotional honesty sweeping across the world," our society could well be heading back to the structure from whence it arose.

We don't know that, of course, and we don't know if she was near the mark in her speculations about the unrecorded sexual past. Yet feminist North American civilization—where over one-third of women have had multiple sex partners by the time they enter university (a rate six times higher than when Sherfey posited her theory thirty years ago), and where the swinging lifestyle is established in hundreds of cities—is beginning to resemble one of the "social structures" Sherfey thought could have accommodated "aggressive eroticism in women." In 1997, the remains of a female warrior society thought to be the six-foot-tall Amazons of myth were discovered in Kazakhstan; they in turn were thought to be the remnants of the mysterious Minoan civilization, which the Greeks all but annihilated thirty-five hundred years ago in a battle with enormous females. Minoan art shows women driving chariots, fighting in wars, farming, sailing ships, and hunting with bows and arrows. It also depicts both men and women wearing very sexual clothing in daily life. Whether they lived in a culture of unbridled promiscuity is unknown, but it's worth pointing out that one of the most fastlane women at New Horizons, Jodie, outranked a couple of million men when she served in the U.S. military during the time of the Gulf War.

In the end, Sherfey did not argue that indulging inordinate sexual appetite was the way women *should* behave in our civilization, and she warned that if women threatened male virility, paternity, and the family, men would react violently and attempt to subjugate them in the manner of the patriarchs. The controversial point she stressed was that promiscuous female lust was innately part of a woman's sexual nature, and that this explained the behavior of some women "throughout historic time." As a psychiatrist her emphasis was on compassion, not promotion; evolutionary recognition, not cultural denial. "I urge the re-examination of the vague and controversial concepts of nymphomania and promiscuity without frigidity," she wrote. "It could well be that the 'oversexed' woman is actually exhibiting a normal sexuality—although because of it her integration into her society may leave much to be desired."

———

Sherfey published her theory in 1966 in *The Journal of the American Psychoanalytic Association*—the most respected in its field—and republished it in book form in 1972. As can be imagined, it was widely discussed and people breathlessly wondered if women would really behave that way if they ran the world and were given the total freedom to have sex with whomever they wanted. Evolutionary biologists soberly argued that, yes, women *could* behave that way, but most women wouldn't. A quick comparison of the "hinder end" of a monkey and the anterior side of even the most aroused female tells the story, they said. Ovulating women do not exhibit the irresistible sexual swellings of other primates that make them Sherfian creatures for a time. In human females ovulation is "hidden." Hidden ovulation was for a long time assumed to be the great divide between human females and nonhuman female primates. The various explanations given for the evolution of concealed ovulation rest on what might literally be called a motherhood issue: the helplessness of the human infant at birth. This, in part, say the theorists, accounts for the evolution of monogamy and human female choosiness—the natural way to be. Let's have a look at this theory.

At some point in evolution, probably about three million years ago, the pelvic changes required to accommodate the upright posture of early humans made it more difficult for females to bear their large-headed young. The solution selected for by nature was for the mother to bear offspring at an earlier stage of their development. The evolutionary difficulty, however, was that the infant was left so needful at birth that for at least four years considerable nurturing was required just to keep it alive. Also, if one assumes that women did not run the group of early humans or raise their children in primitive "day cares," infant helplessness necessitated that the father lend consistent support to the mother. If in a group of male-dominated *Homos* females were flying fertile sexual flags everywhere a male looked, and he was being approached by those females, he might be tempted to leave his defenceless "wife" and offspring, and go off and have intercourse willy-nilly. But if all the women in the group "hid" their fertile phases, he would be less tempted to stray and would stay home. A corollary to this theory is that females no longer experienced the hormonal rush and heightened sensitivity of periodically engorged flesh; with their sex drive thus diminished they became better wives and mothers. And so the human female became "continually receptive," like a turned-down flame on the back burner of sexuality, pleasuring her ravenous male when he wanted it and helping him resolve the dilemma of whether to stay or stray.

That leads us to one of the most resonant, persistent, and appealing explanations offered for hidden ovulation: it accounts for the origin of romantic love and fidelitous attachment between spouses. It goes like this: the male, wanting to father offspring and pass on his genes, would never know the precise week when he should have intercourse with his continually receptive mate, and so he would hang around and keep trying to have a baby by her until he fell in love, thus cementing their bond in time for the birth of their child. This presupposes that he and his mate would have known that sex causes babies—something many peoples such as the Trobriand Islanders in the Pacific hadn't figured out until the missionaries arrived (and many teenagers still haven't). However, if we take for granted that the early human male, with the approximate mental capacity of a modern five-year-old, was aware of the consequences of sex, the theory that hidden ovulation led to romantic love seems to work.

It may in fact *be* the origin of human primary pair-bonding. Almost everyone on earth falls in love, and even the most fast-lane married swingers believe so deeply in romantic love, the pair-bond, and responsible child-rearing in a nuclear family that they would toss me out of their clubs if I claimed they didn't. But we don't know for certain that the consensual non-monogamy they practice—including open eroticism, group sex, and all the rest—was not on occasion practiced by our distant ancestors even as they felt the attached, romantic love that supposedly arose from hidden ovulation. And we don't know that they would not have practiced it even more frequently if they had lived into their late thirties, forties, and fifties. As Timothy Taylor points out, many peoples of the world have practiced open sexuality—and some still do.

But if you visit the American Museum of Natural History

in New York City, you will see a diorama that stands as a model of our currently approved behavior and represents the monogamous outcome of hidden ovulation: a pair of *Australopithecines*, "Lucy" and her "husband," walking arm in arm across the three-million-year-old landscape as a loving couple. The scene has a lot of appeal for evolutionists, even those who believe Lucy might have been "occasionally" tempted by other males. "In a few years, she and her male might break up and start second families," Diane Ackerman wrote in *A Natural History of Love*. "But that emotional cataclysm would be the farthest thing from her mind as she travels with her lover."

Despite the fact that the museum presents this scene as "natural history" (with an assumed emphasis on the word natural) it is in large part coded fable, an example of the cultural wishful thinking we have allowed ourselves to cast over what we don't know about the past, based on what Ackerman approvingly calls "the version of relationships that has come down to us." Footprints of our chimplike, bipedal ancestors have been found, but there is no evidence to indicate that males and females walked together as couples, or that females didn't rule, or that they weren't as casually promiscuous as bonobos —the species evolutionists like De Waal and Taylor consider to be "the closest living analogue to the early *Australopithecines*." What we *can* read from the diorama, however, was possibly unintended. The hair of both creatures is shown thickest around the pubic region, where the eye is drawn—the reason for which pubic hair is thought to have evolved. "Look down here, I'm old enough to produce children," it virtually shouts. "Let's have sex." In addition, the male *Australopithecus* has a good-sized, thick penis for female pleasure and a strong rump for thrusting, while the female has good-sized breasts and fit-looking gluteus maximus. These characteristics are believed to have evolved because they gave both sexes visual hints fore and aft. We can presume that another *Australopithecus* would perceive their healthy bodies as flying the sexual flags as high as they could be hoisted, even if there were no telltale "swellings."

Notwithstanding the theoretical monogamous benefits of concealed ovulation, it should be noted that hidden ovulation is common among promiscuous primates, and the feminist anthropologist Sarah Blaffer Hrdy has theorized that it evolved to *facilitate* promiscuity. The female langur monkey in India has no sexual swelling, but when outside males show up to challenge the alpha male of their troop, the females begin mating with all the outsiders long before the old alpha is overthrown and a new one installed. The usual routine among langurs and some other primates is for the new dominant male to murder all the infants sired by the old alpha and Hrdy suggests that by "confusing" paternity through promiscuity and non-estrus receptivity, the females thereby save their young. Another explanation is that the langur females are simply thrilled by the prospect of sexual variety after being repressed by a single dominant male for so long. That would have sounded perfectly logical to Mary Jane Sherfey.*

Despite Sherfey, despite Hrdy, and despite no hard evidence that hidden ovulation led to a relatively low female sex drive and a high level of "choosiness," the standard model still held firm well into the 1980s. True, in the wake of changing female sexual behavior in human society a number of evolutionary

---

* A final point should be made: in humans ovulation is actually not all that "hidden." Astrid Jute, a biologist working at the Ludwig Bolton Institute in Austria, discovered in 1996 that the testosterone level of men rises markedly when they inhale an odorless cocktail of pheromones called "copulines" secreted by an ovulating woman. Men also rate unattractive women as prettier when smelling the stuff. In addition, a couple of studies have shown that women going to bars when near ovulation not only bare more flesh, but they tend to wear more jewelry. "These adornments, it seems, have the advertising value of a chimpanzee's pink genital swellings," the science writer Robert Wright has noted.

biologists had modified the model to acknowledge that human and nonhuman female primates were assertive beings, with sexual agendas of their own, but they tended to judge the naturally promiscuous behavior of female primates—human and nonhuman—by the size of male testicles, not female desire. Males who had a lot to fear from the competition of other sperm in the female's womb had evolved large testicles to produce copious amounts of ejaculate to swamp their rivals. Males who had little to fear from rivals had little testicles. Human testicles were somewhere between the relatively small proportions of the gorilla, who dominated a harem in his well-defended terrain and almost never had to deal with the infidelity of his consorts, and the relatively large testicles of the appropriately named *Pan satyrus*, the chimpanzee. Even in the case of those grandly endowed satyric primates, however, the theoreticians maintained that while females could be promiscuous (as it was noticed human females could be), they still invested far more heavily in offspring than males did; and thus, they had to be far more discriminating in their choice of males than males were in their choice of females—in short they had to be less driven to pursue sexual variety.

It wasn't until 1993, with the publication of *Female Choices*, that the anthropologist Meredith Small effectively rattled the standard model along Sherfian lines (although she never mentioned Sherfey by name). A few years before, she'd gone to the south of France to study a group of Barbary macaque monkeys living on a twenty-acre reserve. She wanted to test the standard model regarding female mate choice. "I knew that they mated with several males," she wrote, "but presumably they were more choosy when ovulation was imminent. I intended to observe the choices my females made and to discover why they preferred certain males over others."

What she found was female sexual responsiveness taken to its ultimate, Sherfian conclusion. "Yes, these females were making choices, but they seemed to choose every male in the group, one after another, and there was no selectivity during the time when ovulation might be occurring," she reported. "If Barbary females are supposed to be selective about which males would father the next batch of infants, I asked myself, why are they moving from male to male with apparent indiscriminate abandon...? The day I watched a Barbary female copulate with three different males in the span of six minutes, I knew that it was time to re-evaluate the current concept of female choice. Presumably the reason Barbarys didn't fit the standard model was because the model had some significant flaws."

Small's book came out just before Baker and Bellis published their physical observations of the "sperm wars" being waged in the reproductive tract of females, so she did not harness their explanations of the benefits of promiscuity for the female and the effect of infidelity on male ejaculatory response. But as Small studied the mating behavior of many primates—from the group-sex-oriented bonobos to the supposedly monogamous gibbons—a startling pattern emerged. Barbarys were not aberrations. "The only consistent interest seen among the general primate population is an interest in novelty and variety," she reported. "Although the possibility of choosing for good genes, good fathers, or good friends remains an option to female primates, they seem to prefer the unexpected."

Even female gibbons—long held as our moral equivalents in sex and thus our close kin in the primate world—were cheating on their lifelong mates. Indeed, at the risk of being beaten or killed by jealous males, most female primates would copulate with skulking, low-ranking males despite the fact that they'd just had the pick of the high rankers. This utterly violated sexual-selection theory.

"The stalwart females continued to stake out these low rankers and put up with abuse from other males," Small noted.

"This behavior is perhaps the clearest evidence of some sort of female preference, and the preference seems to be for variety. . . . In fact, the search for the unfamiliar is documented as a female preference more often than is any other characteristic our human eyes can perceive."

As I've mentioned before, the champion in the search for sexual variety in the primate world is the bonobo chimpanzee, whose behavior Small first saw on a video shown by Frans De Waal to a national conference on the apes. The video "silenced a room of three hundred primatologists and journalists," Small wrote. If you have ever seen a five-second clip of that film on television—the sum total regulatory bodies will probably ever allow on a non-X-rated channel—you have an inkling why. Watching bonobos have sex is very much like watching humans. "There is no escape, we are looking at an animal so akin to ourselves that the dividing line is seriously blurred," De Waal marveled.

It is probably for that reason that bonobos have appeared so often in the news since De Waal first began making colleagues such as Small aware of his research on the little-known ape in the 1990s. They are as close to us as our aggressive, violent other cousin, the common chimpanzee, but somehow they seem more human to people. And that is probably a good sign for swingers. If Mary Jane Sherfey had known about bonobos, she quite likely would have used them to reinforce her theories of female sexuality—at the same time modifying the juxtaposition of words like "impelling, aggressive eroticism." Because while the bonobo is maximally erotic, there is little that is impelling or aggressive about it. Tellingly, the sexuality of the bonobo was reported in journals as far back as the 1950s—but the embarrassed few who noticed must have decided not to spread the word.

Sex for a group of bonobos is so casual, yet so tied in with every aspect of their day-to-day existence, that to set it apart

from life, as we think we do in our own society, would be to
misread their use of pleasure, which can be summed up as follows: there is no fighting over sex, and sex is used to stop fights.
If they come across a choice bit of food in their native range in
Zaire, and the bonobos are unsure who will get it, they all start
having sex. Females grasp each other face to face and rub their
vulvas to orgasm. Both sexes gather round and play feelie.
Males "fence" each other with their erect penises. Females
felate males, males perform cunnilingus on females, and males
and females have intercourse, often face to face, which the
females seem to prefer, probably because the vulva is situated
between the legs rather than toward the back as with the common chimpanzee. All of this sex goes on at once, mind you,
and afterward the good feeling is so complete that the food is
shared with minimum conflict.

Again, tellingly, we seem now to be ready for a message
bonobos could have given us forty years ago had we been ready
to hear it. "Just imagine that we had never heard of chimpanzees or baboons and had known bonobos first," De Waal
wrote in 1995. "We would at present most likely believe that
early hominids lived in female-centered societies, in which sex
served important social functions and in which warfare was
rare or absent."

As Sherfey would have been interested to see, bonobo
society is clearly a matriarchy. "Females often dominate males"
is the exclamatory news primatologists now proclaim when
reporting on bonobos, a jaw-dropping fact considering that
"male dominance is the standard mammalian pattern" in all
but two species. As with humans, bonobo males are 15 percent
larger than the females, yet the males are frankly afraid of
pushing them lest they provoke a rare but collective attack.
Alliances are made among females on behalf of their young,
whom they nurse for four years, having sex all the while with
other females to cement these alliances. The females do exhibit

sexual swellings but they are proceptive most of the month and copulate in such a self-willed, ongoing fashion with so many males that it is obvious even the top-ranking females play no favorites with an ostensible alpha male—which they should be doing, according to the standard model. And while it is true that both sexes have a pecking order—and bonobos are no angels—their society is too egalitarian to say that top rankers arbitrarily "rule." It is a rare dispute that is not defused by sexual pleasure. Less than 2 percent of DNA separates us from the bonobo and only two and a half million years separates them from the hominids displayed in the New York diorama. One theory has it that since the time hominids branched off from their common ancestry line with chimps some six million years ago, the bonobo has evolved less from the progenitor of our species than has the war-making common chimpanzee—whose negative behavioral traits, including sexual jealousy and a propensity for political scheming, we have long regarded as the antecedents of our own.

It should come as no surprise that swingers have adopted the group-sex-oriented and casually lesbian bonobo as their mascot. But bonobos differ from lifestylers in that they do not appear to form nuclear families; in addition the males are sexual with one another, which, as I've noted, is taboo among swingers. Nevertheless, anyone who has ever heard of swingers and bonobos easily makes the connection. In *Female Choices* Meredith Small cheekily replicated a swinger ad in a mock "personals" section of a newspaper she called the *Simian Times*: "Swingers of All Sexes and Ages—join our bonobo sharing group, meet new folks, free-for-all fun."

Based on her survey of the entire primate world, and her anthropological knowledge of human culture, Small reached several conclusions regarding female sexual choice. All but one—a final end-page kicker—were in line with the cultural climate of the early nineties.

First, primate females were *choosing* to be promiscuous. It was part of their mating strategy: "From the point of view of the female, she should always be the new girl on the block. If a male's sexual excitement, and thus potency, is highest when he experiences a new female, it's to the female's advantage to *be* that new female. Females want novel males as much as novel males want them."

Second, the standard model of evolutionary theory was tied more to culture than to the facts: "The notion still prevails that females don't enjoy sex as much as males do and that females go about mating at a slow pace, refusing more males than they choose. This prediction of female behavior is supported, as I have shown, not with what females really do, but with evolutionary theory—females *should* be selective, nonsexual."

Third, there were social advantages to promiscuity: "The extended swellings of female bonobos and the fact that they have sex any time and anywhere is what makes the relationship between males and females equivalent."

Fourth, what primate females were up to had definite implications for humans: "Because we share with nonhuman primate females many of our broad patterns of behavior, we may also share our sexual nature."

Fifth (in perfect accordance with Sherfey), the high level of human female sexuality had throughout history placed a knife to the throat of assured male paternity, and this had caused women problems: "The information on human females demonstrates a certain insatiability for sex. This insatiability is so strong, some suggest, that males must restrict female sexuality, and most cultures do so in one way or another.... Part of that restriction may lie in convincing women that they are biologically less sexual and less intrigued by different sexual partners than are males.... The 'double standard' is really a statement about the power to control (or attempt to control) rather than about differences in male and female sexuality."

Small didn't think coercive "wife swapping" was the path-
way to female freedom. All she was looking for was a recognition of the sexual equality of men and women. And so, lastly,
she concluded her book with a startling bit of advice for
women: "The demands of parenting have selected for a particular social system and have given men more power over our
reproductive decisions than they should have. We should,
perhaps, follow the example of our bonobo sisters, who have
parlayed their sexual nature into equality with males."

Small's conclusions violated the standard model. But, as
Sherfey had said about Freud's clitoris-to-vagina "transfer"
theory, the standard model had "only a questionable basis in
biology" to begin with.

———————

As Skala, Leslie, and I took the same tour of the crowded
Annex that we'd taken with Jodie when it was empty, we
couldn't help noticing that the actual "sex part" of fastlane
swinging was neither impelling nor aggressive. It was certainly far less frenzied than, say, a pornograpic movie depicting Sherfian group sex where "intense, insatiable eroticism"
reigned—though the *feelings* described by those words were
obviously present in some of the participants. Generally speaking, these fastlane swingers—even the handful who were experiencing something homologous to Sherfey syndrome—were
quite as good-humored and sensibly garrulous with one another
as in the banquet hall. Most of the couples either knew one
another as club members or had appreciated what they had
seen on first meeting. Their eyes weren't glazed over with perverse self-abasement, nor did they seem to be straining to pull
nails out of walls with their teeth as they participated in their
polygon arrangements. Around the crackling firepit, on the
complicated Eros Seats, in the blue light of the white-curtained

Sultan's Tent, and on the Victorian couch of Miss Daisy's Academy, the couples did in fact look quite similar to the sculptures on Kajuraho's temples—although it should be remembered that those sculptures depict group sex in which everyone is smiling. Skala observed that the whole environment reminded him less of an orgy house than of a fitness gym where with great gusto everyone performs publicly and vocally, free from remorse. "This is quite fantastical," he said when we were back on the first level, where we beheld an arrangement of twisting backs and shoulders on the elaborate tiers of couches in the video room. Beth and Frieda were the objects of attention of Konrad, a "helping" Edith, and Sol—and seemed to have been so for some time. They had their arms around their lovers and every now and then they raised their heads in full consciousness and laughed. Meanwhile, Larry was sitting on the edge of the action cooing to his wife, Beth, even as she rocked slowly with Konrad.

By the time we walked back outside to the central area, the erotic masseur had set up his table and was pleasuring a woman with Swedish massage while her husband looked on. The husband was so delighted by his wife's enjoyments that almost the moment she got off the table he took her passionately on the couch of the firepit. When I walked back into the video room to check on our tablemates, Larry was hotly making love to Beth—more hotly than Konrad had. There was no question the polyamorous rite of "watching" was heightening the coupling of these couples. Their voyeuristic behavior points to a central paradox of males in the lifestyle: "Jealousy," as Brian Gilmartin put it, "becomes a sexual turn-on."

The almost universally shared reaction to jealousy by men in the lifestyle is particularly hard to understand because it seems to violate how all men are biologically programmed to react to spousal infidelity. Until quite recently, from a biological point of view, it was actually *easier* to understand how women could accept their swinging husbands than it was to understand the reaction of men to their swinging wives. "If indeed a man's great Darwinian peril is cuckoldry, and a woman's is desertion, then male and female jealousy should differ," Robert Wright wrote in *The Moral Animal*. "Male jealousy should focus on *sexual* infidelity, and males should be quite unforgiving of it; a female, though she'll hardly applaud a partner's extracurricular activities, since they consume time and divert resources, should be more concerned with *emotional* infidelity.... These predictions have been confirmed—by eons of folk wisdom and, over the past few decades, by considerable data."

The data is actually confirmed in the lifestyle—for women. One of the foundational convictions of longtime swingers is that friendly sex between lifestylers poses no real threat of emotional infidelity to a marriage; thus, in lifestyle theory, the greatest threat of "social sexuality" should be lessened for wives. And according to their own testimony, it is. "These people," Gilmartin reported, "do not see deep, long-lasting friendships with their swinging partners as competitive with the *committed* type of love characteristic of a sound marriage. Friends who see each other very often are regarded as 'loving' one another, but in a *noncommitted* way." In the culture of veteran female lifestylers, then, a husband's "noncommitted" sex is appreciated by her as part of the all-around social warmth attendant to swinging in a safe environment; when it is interpreted by her as posing an emotional threat to her marriage, she either talks to her husband and calls a halt to the proceedings or, as mentioned, she embraces the rival woman bisexually and "confirms" that the threat is unwarranted. Either way, she usually (not always) resolves the issue.

For a man, however, his wife's lack of "love" for a sex partner should not mitigate against his automatic reaction. "What drives men craziest is the thought of their mate in bed with another man," Wright observed. "They don't dwell as much as women do on any attendant emotional attachment, or the possible loss of the mate's time and attention.... Husbands tend to respond to infidelity with rage; and even after it subsides, they often have trouble contemplating a continued relationship with the infidel."

But not swinging husbands. They enjoy the feeling engendered by a wife's sexual "infidelity." This, I suggest, is partly because they have learned to experience an automatic reaction they can use for their own pleasure—"sperm competition syndrome." SCS could explain the biology behind the pleasures swinging men get from sharing their wives. The 1.5 million men in the subculture appear to be able to accept and capitalize on what every man seems to be programmed by evolution to accomplish when he consciously or unconsciously suspects a partner has been unfaithful. "We're hypothesizing that men may actually ejaculate sooner when they perceive a potential risk of sperm competition," Tom Shackelford, a researcher at the University of Michigan, told the curious millions watching the documentary "What Do Women Really Want?" on The Learning Channel in 1997. (Although he was probably not referring to swinging men, who usually know how to control and savor their quickened urges.) Men, Shackelford continued, "may actually ejaculate more forcefully; the ejaculation may subjectively seem more intense, the orgasm may seem more intense, and the sexual relief following ejaculation may be more intense. All of this having been selected as a counter to potential sperm competition." It was as if a suspicious male suddenly enjoyed (or endured) a biological syndrome, since his ejaculate was also awesomely rich in sperm cells.

Probably every "cuckolded" straight man has experienced SCS and felt the urgent drive to engage in sexual activity with his "betraying" partner. But in our society, as Wright pointed out, the straight man usually experiences this sexual imperative as rage or self-torment. The syndrome can produce a range of behaviors: a man can start out asking hectoring questions then progress to masochistically demanding to know every last detail of a liaison—"Did you go down on him? How many times did you come? You let him *what?*" SCS can end in reconciliatory sex, violence, rape, or even murder. "'My gut reaction to this,'" confessed one husband to author Dalma Heyn on his discovery of his wife's infidelity, "'was so deep, so violent, I felt my stomach being pulled out of me. I'm surprised, sometimes, that I didn't kill or maim one of them, because I was nuts.'" Men almost never admit that their physiological response to encountering their partner having sex with another has a red-hot core of sexual desire to it. But when we understand the biology of why men universally obsess over the details afterward, we can see that something fundamental to human evolution is transpiring inside his body.

As I've reiterated in this book, the most venerable criticism of the lifestyle is that it is merely a means for men to have sex with women other than their spouse. Without doubt, almost every swinging man enjoys that pleasure, but if you probe a little deeper into their sexuality these men will tell you that being with their wife while she is being intimate with others is one of the most powerful draws of inviting another couple into their marriage for a night. As Elliot had told me at the Eden Resort: "It was like I was watching a movie star in a love scene. I can't believe how *beautiful* she gets. So hot!" Female swing-club owners concur: "It's a favorite fantasy of guys in the lifestyle, in my experience," Chris Cosby of C.A.S.T. Couples in Houston, Texas, told me at a Lifestyles convention. And Patti Johnson, who runs San Francisco's Bay City Socials, and who believes that the lifestyle is built on "matriarchal principles" that are geared as much for the female's pleasure and desire for male attention as for the male's desire for multiple partners, said, "It fits together nicely, like a puzzle; a woman gets to be treated like a queen, and a guy gets to feel he's married to a queen, with all the guys wanting what he's got. They get really charged with all the flirtation." Long before much was known about sperm competition, the observant Gay Talese, author of *Thy Neighbor's Wife*, described this counterintuitive reaction of even neophyte swinging men to their wives' encounters at an orgiastic swing club in California: "Men who noticed that their wives aroused other men became in many cases aroused by them themselves and strove to repossess them."

In a manner unseen in straight society, lifestyle husbands have become connoisseurs at transmuting the natural urge to wipe out the competition into the pleasurable urge to—as Robin Baker put it—"duke it out inside the female to win the right to fertilize the egg."

Let's look briefly at how SCS works; why swinging husbands would consciously use it to eroticize their marital sex lives; and how it fits in with the willing promiscuity of wives who are comfortable in the lifestyle. SCS gives a whole new meaning to Iago's advice to Othello: "Look to your wife, observe her well with Cassio."

Until recently it was thought that the number of sperm a man deposited in his partner, and the force of his orgasm, depended on how recently the man had ejaculated. If a man masturbated on, say, Wednesday, then made love on Friday, he'd ejaculate less sperm with less force on the Friday when he made love. It was also assumed that all the sperm in a man's ejaculate had one purpose. After a "routine" ejaculation of between 100 million and 300 million sperm cells, the seminal pool on the floor of the vagina seeped into the cervix and the sperm swam through the uterus and then to the fallopian tubes where they endeavored to meet up with an egg if one were floating by. If a woman had sex with two men, it was thought that the sperm from both partners would simply swim in their usual manner to the ovum, and one sperm cell would blindly win the race. The general consensus of biologists was that a fellow was equipped with enough sperm so that if he got lucky with a naughty wife, it would be a fair race between him and the cuckolded husband, and vice versa. Essentially, the theory of human sperm competition was viewed from a philandering man's perspective: there was just no evidence that females could aggressively and promiscuously promote such competition in their bodies.

Then, in the early 1990s, Baker and Bellis persuaded cohabiting students at the University of Manchester to use condoms and deliver to the lab each day the semen the males had ejaculated. The couples recorded the intimate details of their lives on questionnaires. The researchers examined the behavior of the males' sperm when it encountered another's, analyzed paternity tests, and conducted surveys of the females to find the prevalence of multiple mating within five-day periods.

In 1995 Baker and Bellis published their complete findings in *Human Sperm Competition: Copulation, Masturbation and Infidelity,* which demolished the notion that sperm were merely programmed to swim to the ovum, that females were "naturally" monogamous, and that males' ejaculations and inseminate were not governed in any critical way by millions of years of female behavior. They discovered the smoking gun of "natural" human female infidelity. "There's Kinsey," pronounced Patricia Gowaty in an interview in 1997, "there's Masters and Johnson, there's Baker and Bellis. They're giants in the world of sex research. I think they're heroes."

Their "disturbing" conclusion was that these sexual adaptations were so fundamental that they could only have been shaped by evolution. The "innate" male fear of female licentiousness appeared justified. In our evolutionary past, monogamy had probably never existed as a biological "norm" for our species. Nor did it exist today. "Every one of us," Baker wrote in his popular book *Sperm Wars*, "is the person we are today because one of our recent ancestors produced an ejaculate competitive enough to win a sperm war." Embedded for millions of years in the genes of every man is the absolute conviction that his partner could be having sex with someone else within days, hours, or minutes of having sex with him. The longer the time she spends away from him, the more convinced his *body* becomes—the body being a more accurate measure of evolutionary tendencies than a wishful mind. What I have termed SCS, and the increased pleasure in ejaculation it causes men, is the naturally selected manner in which males combat spousal licentiousness. Whenever a husband prepares to have sex with his wife, he unconsciously weighs the odds that she has been, or will be, unfaithful to him: "To increase the chances of winning the sperm wars that might follow, he needs to introduce more sperm. And this is just what he does." Unconscious in straight men, cultivated and enjoyed by swinging men, SCS is a product of nature.

Suppose a straight couple are living together in ostensible monogamy, seeing each other every day and having sex a couple of times a week. Every time they make "routine" love the man will deposit some 200 million sperm cells, depending on how much his "loading muscles" squeeze out from the two sperm tubes rising out of the testicles and on the number of orgasmic spurts he employs to deliver the sperm and seminal fluid from the prostate. According to the old view, all these sperm were, by design, fertile egg-getters. But Baker and Bellis thought there could be another reason for the profusion. They discovered that less than 1 percent of a male's vast number of sperm were programmed for this job. More than four-fifths— "kamikaze sperm"—were designed to actively hunt down and kill the sperm cells of other males in the female's vagina, cervix, and womb. And just under one-fifth—"blockers"— were designed to obstruct the path of another male's sperm.

Hence the billions of sperm a male's testicles produce every month—enough to fertilize every female on the planet—most of them warriors ready for combat in the bodies of philandering women.

According to Baker and Bellis, a male would be totally unaware of the different war divisions in his inseminate, nor would he be able to control the number of "troops" he was ejaculating. At work was a blind evolutionary process governed by genetic inheritance: this process had selected for both the composition of a male's sperm based on the probability of having to fight a war, and the amount of sperm cells the male's body instinctively knew it must deliver to the female based on the immediate likelihood of that war. The routine delivery of millions of sperm, which could survive up to five days in the female, served as a kind of screen against surprise attack by a rival. Baker called the act of routine sex "topping up."

Returning to our straight couple, suppose the man's wife goes away for three days on a business trip with some colleagues that include an ex-boyfriend. Consciously the husband thinks she's a loyal wife, but his genetic inheritance tells him differently. The night before she returns he feels the urge to masturbate, out of boredom he thinks. But his body is telling him to expel "old" sperm and shunt to the front of his sperm tubes younger sperm ready for battle. Normally, after three days without sex, he would inseminate her with the usual number of sperm. Their time apart, however, signals to the husband's most basic instinct that an enemy could be at the gate, and his body begins preparing for war. Eventually, the single cannon shot of that war will be an act of increased pleasure.

Let's suppose the man's wife has indeed not been loyal, and she comes home with her reproductive tract secretly filled with the sperm of her ex-boyfriend. According to Baker she will then be unconsciously driven to do something very curious (something lifestyle wives, almost without exception, and without much resistance from their husbands, do as well). "When she gets home, she works very hard to have sex with her partner." Whether or not she really desires to get pregnant, her unconscious mind is telling her the following: that "she wants to have her egg fertilized by her ex-boyfriend only if his ejaculate is also the most fertile and competitive. In other words, her body wants to promote *sperm warfare* between the two men...."

As the couple make love and he approaches orgasm, his body begins to "load" sperm into his urethra—600 million sperm, not 200 million, regardless of whether he has masturbated during her absence. His loading muscles are more forceful than usual, shunting to the front nearly the full length of the two sperm tubes, and he spurts in a surprisingly pleasurable orgasm that, according to Tom Shackelford's hypothesis (and you can confirm it with the testimony of any swinging husband), feels stronger and longer-lasting than the ones he experiences in routine sex.

Since his wife's body is full of her lover's sperm, the two "armies" set at each other, exactly as she had unconsciously planned and he had unconsciously prepared for. Now her orgasm comes into play, evidence that she is fully equipped by evolution to participate in the competition.

By varying the timing of her orgasm, she can favor one set of sperm over the other for uptake into the cervix. If she orgasms before her husband's insemination, her cervix will descend and absorb acidic mucus, which will hinder the passage of the alkaline sperm. She will be as unconscious of planning this timing as her husband will be of planning the number of sperm he delivers. As Josef Skala explained to me, if she has unconsciously chosen to favor her extramarital lover's sperm with the timing of her orgasm, a greater proportion of her husband's sperm will leak out of her body after sex as "flowback."

Let me point out here, as Baker does, that this competition

can entail the inseminates of more than two men in a woman. "Once a woman's body contains sperm from two *or more* different men, those sperm compete for the prize of fertilizing the egg....It is indeed a war—a war between two (*or more*) armies." [Italics mine.]

To illustrate for his readers the natural drive of men and women to establish sperm competition in a group-sex encounter, Baker set up a fictional scenario involving two couples that he called "fair exchange." He assessed the behavior of the two couples as being congruent with one of the ways people were programmed to behave—that is, as "a recognizable part of the rich mosaic of human sexuality—a part, moreover, that promotes sperm warfare."

In Baker's scenario, one of the wives initiated the "swapping." "Eventually, as they lay together, it was the serious stroking and kissing of their bodies by the other couple that took them across the threshold from embarrassment to intense sexual arousal. The intercourse they had, while still being caressed by the other couple, was the most exciting either had ever experienced....Watching his partner have sex with another man excited the childless man once more. He could barely wait for his friend to withdraw before taking over." He had orgasmed minutes before and would now orgasm again. He would have been experiencing sperm competition syndrome.

In this fictional vignette the couple "never repeated the exercise." In fact, many couples in the lifestyle indulge in the exercise no more than once a year when they feel drawn to experience the "intense sexual arousal" it causes them. Or, if they are fastlane swingers, they may seek it once a week. They may frequent clubs like New Horizons or they may have a small circle of discreet friends who never go to clubs and who hardly "swing" at all. But if we look at all lifestylers in this biological way—from the inside out—we can at least begin to comprehend why they do what they do and the reasons they say it gives them pleasure. It is easy enough to declare the lifestyle abnormal, but millions are in it, and we should weigh the good arguments that the behavior could have a natural basis. It involves the programmed urge of both males and females to promote or fight sperm wars in females, the casual female bisexuality and group sex so prevalent in our close relatives the bonobos, and the voyeuristic pleasures of males who—as assured of their partner's emotional fidelity as their partner is of theirs—know how to enjoy the hot reaction of their bodies to spousal "infidelity." Indeed, the new revised latest edition of the standard model is actually catching up to swingers. Now females are thought to be "semimonogamous," "mildly promiscuous," and capable of "multiple mating." No one, however, has yet dared to put a number to the adjectives "semi," "mildly," and "multiple," and, thus far, at any rate, Baker and Bellis have not reported on the three big fastlane swing clubs—Connections, Number One, and Adam and Eve —in their university town of Manchester, nor on the dozen other big clubs in Britain. Perhaps if they paid a visit they might discover that thousands of mainstream marrieds have an unreserved idea of what number we should read into that word multiple.

———

An hour after Skala, Leslie, and I had first come upon our tablemates in the video room, they were all more or less played out and singing vibrantly in the showers. An hour after that the Annex was empty. All the fastlane couples in the club who had been fondling and titillating—they'd all changed back into their fantasy outfits or Bermuda shorts and sneakers and gone back to the banquet hall. By one-thirty in the morning most of them were sitting around tables chastely gossiping and laughing and drinking soft drinks and eating whole-wheat sandwiches prepared by Connie and her dad. In a few days they would all return to society as law-abiding middle-class taxpayers.

"What's your opinion, Skala?" I asked.

Skala took a bite of his ham and cheese sandwich and chewed and didn't say anything. Then he sipped some of his drink. Then he said, enigmatic as Vishnu: "Their pleasure is derived from being aroused."

I waited.

Then he said: "Their arousal is most important to them. That's the essence of their sexual pleasure, and maybe their lifestyle. The older women are most sexually arousable and pleasure oriented, and the men look at the women and if the women are aroused that gives them their pleasure. I have not seen many male orgasms here tonight. They seem to know their orgasm kills their arousal. Not for the female but for the male. The actual coming is not that important to the males— they seem to like to stay in that state adoring the women. The Grecian urn. Or your Hindu sculptures.

"It's just my first night," he said. "I'll give you another opinion tomorrow."

CHAPTER EIGHT

The Rules

Every study we looked at emphasized the overall
normality, conventionality, and respectability of
recreational swingers.

DUANE DENFELD; MICHAEL GORDON,
"The Sociology of Mate Swapping"
The Journal of Sex Research

Before I arrived at New Horizons I knew that roughly three-quarters of lifestylers were not disposed to anonymous, pile-on sex. According to the studies I'd read that Edgar Butler had cited in *Traditional Marriage and Emerging Alternatives*, roughly one-third tended to "emphasize the social aspects of swinging," another third tended to "desire and emphasize close emotional relationships with their sexual partners," and perhaps one-tenth were at least "fairly selective" in choice of partners. Overall, most swingers preferred the kind of encounters I'd seen take place at the Eden Resort, where couples got to know one another (even if in a short space of time) before becoming intimate. What I learned from my first couple of days at the Northwest Celebration, however, was that even the couples in the hard-core quarter of the lifestyle liked to spend hours in sexy display in elegant environments like the banquet hall—where they elaborately seduced each other before segregating into friendly cliques and entering the Annex. Group gropes between couples who paid at the door and jumped in a pile with no socializing beforehand—as had occurred in the seventies among hard-core swingers in big clubs like Plato's Retreat in Manhattan— seemed to be largely a thing of the past in the lifestyle, at least according to what the hard-core swingers at New Horizons were telling me. It was a claim I would verify in that most fast-lane corner of the continent, Southern California.

To be sure, open eroticism is still the main fare at clubs, and you can see most levels of spouse sharing practiced side by

220

side every weekend at each of the hundreds of clubs in North America where "on-premises" swinging is permitted. Some swingers watch, some dance close, some make love, and almost certainly they are congregating by the score in a house dedicated to their activities right in your hometown, maybe even on your block. The fact that you don't know about it (unless the police decide people shouldn't be doing it) brings me to the point of this chapter.

Swinging within the lifestyle subculture almost always occurs peacefully, according to the same middle-class rules most people live by, without violating the bourgeois sensibilities of the people involved, and without any documented harm to society. Further: although swingers seem to turn the world upside down, they are acting in accordance with the attitudes and values that make up North American culture.

Now that sounds like an outrageous observation—but I take no credit for it.

Back in 1971 an anthropology professor at Northern Illinois University completed a three-year study of heartland swingers and stated it categorically: "It is our position that swinging is absolutely not deviant behavior in terms of American cultural patterns."

Dr. Gilbert Bartell titled his book *Group Sex*—an activity that to him did not require a redefinition of cultural patterns in the Nixon era. To Bartell, the behavior of the couples he investigated (more than a hundred of them, most of whom had voted for Nixon) was "not tantamount to 'sickness.'" While the press accounts of mainstream swingers declared them "bizarre," Bartell deduced the opposite: "The sequence of learning, action and relearning swinging is supported, not by alien influences, but is legitimized and reinforced by feedback from respectable, even staid, institutions within the American system." At its sociological essence, Bartell believed, swinging was the appropriation by the middle class of what the media constantly advertised as the chief privilege of celeb-rity: the license to indulge in royal revelry, which was refused to commoners. The people the media sold the dream to *were* the bourgeoisie, and the bourgeoisie, therefore, *were* the swingers. "We impose different standards on different members of society," Bartell wrote. "Movie celebrities can perform in one fashion, but a good housewife must perform in another. How does one adjust to this conflict between one's movie model and one's own activities? Our female interviewees told us that one way to resolve this conflict is to swing."

Bartell averred that he personally considered casual swinging sex "repugnant," but as an anthropologist he observed that even while engaged in their rites, swing couples preserved "essentially normative middle-class values," among them the ideal of a spicy, emotionally monogamous marriage. At a stage when most long-married people were giving up the thought of ever being hot for each other again, or were committing adultery to experience that heat with others, the lifestyle provided couples with "an increased sexual interest in the mate or partner." The majority of Bartell's respondents reported that "swinging created for them a better relationship, both socially and sexually."

It did not surprise Bartell that for this accomplishment swingers were decried in the press as "'a pathetic, sometimes ridiculous product of our society's frantic search for pleasure, youth and good looks—coupled with the need to preserve the niceties of house, family and job.'" That commentary from the *Chicago Daily News* fit in with his theory of the interplay of social and cultural forces that caused and censured swinging at one and the same time. The *Chicago Daily News* often featured in its entertainment and gossip sections paens to the hot lives of stars like Elizabeth Taylor and Dean Martin.

Not much has changed since Bartell's day. If you had perused the mainstream media around the time of the New

Horizons convention you would have found celebrities still being praised and promoted for behaving like swingers in the same outlets that were labeling middle-class swingers pathetic and ridiculous for behaving like celebrities.

Our patterns of seduction and scolding would be merely funny if it were not obvious that the judgments of offended journalists are among the reasons swingers find themselves harassed and arrested for doing exactly what the rich and famous are applauded for doing. I'd like to offer some examples that show how unfair this process is and why swingers should be spared the humiliation inflicted on them by the media. Swingers follow social rules, which they take seriously; when they adhere to the rules, they usually do not do themselves (or anyone else) any harm.

———

Let's start with the left-hand, right-hand seduction-and-condemnation of swingers in a glossy men's magazine: *GQ*.

Middle-aged men thinking of attending the New Horizons convention that summer of 1996 would have found inspiration in an April article called "The Last Swinger," about Tony Curtis. Perhaps the most blatantly orgiastic star in Hollywood, the seventy-year-old actor "showed us how to live life with a capital *L*." "Tony Curtis! He's fucked them all; he's fucked everybody, and here we are, another night on the town with old T.C., because guess what? He *still* fucks!"

The reader encountered "the sly old satyr, unsated" over his lunch date at the Los Angeles restaurant Spago with the actress Jill Vanden Berg, "this strapping 25-year-old triumph of a blond," outfitted (like many of the wives at New Horizons) in "five-inch spike heels" and "a skintight dress of pearlescent vinyl whose high hem continually gooses her epic ass." Describing Curtis's recent heroic times with strippers and actresses and secretaries, the writer, Tom Junod, offered a hymn of praise to how Tony had "had enough lovers to qualify him, in his own estimation, as 'the greatest cocksman to ever come down the pike, man.'" Tony was "dedicated to the art of eating pussy." He was "alert to every instance of appetite, however idle." "Offering the world instruction in the art of *celebrity*," Tony's philosophy of life was, "Take it."

> Tony steps onto the dance floor alone, and the girls just flock to him, strippers especially; he dances in a thicket of them, five or six at a time, until at last Jill stands before him and starts bumping and grinding, doing a dance that is an announcement of erotic intention, and then they go home, Tony says, and they *play*.

Sound familiar?

Yet in *GQ*'s estimation such play was not permitted for average, middle-aged folks. In its 1993 article on swingers punnishly titled "Strange Bedfellows," Judith Newman informed us that the thousands of playcouples at a Lifestyles convention she attended seemed like ridiculous figures in "a painting by Hieronymous Bosch, Bosch by way of Wal-Mart." From her opening reference to a fellow as an "iguana" with "serious love handles" to her final disparagement of a "plump and dowdy" plumber's wife, the holy trinity of fashion—age, shape, and class—was used as a major argument for why we should feel revulsion for these unfashionable transgressors, for whom "swapping mates is simply adventure on the cheap."

> As my friend Melissa, a Los Angeles television producer whom I sneaked into the dance, succinctly put it when she first saw those acres and acres of flesh: 'Moo.' As a rule, swingers are not,

to put it delicately, in the first bloom of youth. Most are in their mid- to late-forties. These are people who, like some American Legionnaires, can't stop living out what they see as the most dramatic, exciting moments of their life, moments that happen to have taken place in the sixties, when they had a body fit for jockstraps and halter tops.

After interviewing a Lifestyles Care Team couple identified as "Gwen" and "Stan," Newman mocked lifestylers for the dignity with which they'd treated their spouses: "A woman is invariably 'a lady' in swingers' parlance, which is sort of like calling Elizabeth I 'the Virgin Queen.'" She pitied the déclassé conventioneers because they tried to live like the stars while preserving the niceties of home, family, and jobs: "I considered the homes in the suburbs and the grindingly dull jobs. I thought about the lousy paychecks and crying babies and malls." And she was horrified that these unassuming burghers could enjoy so much sex and not be terrified by the wrath of avenging angels: "Wait a second, I thought. No more discussion of AIDS? *That's it?*" she asked herself at a Lifestyles seminar on STDs, part of her five-hundred word tirade against the reckless ignorance of all swingers. Yet when profiling its celebrity swinger, Tony Curtis, *GQ* handled the subject of STDs by not bringing it up. Not one of its seven thousand words warned of the bad karma that the former heroin addict and his partners risked incurring by having as much sex as the swingers who'd made Judith Newman "feel an urgent need to be elsewhere."

Women's magazines practiced the same Janus-faced ethic, glorifying the promiscuity of the stars as they reinforced proper monogamous happiness for average, married females. In the case of *Cosmopolitan*, the chief preoccupation in the months leading up to the New Horizons convention was "Holly-wood's Sexiest Women"—an article that fostered the fantasy of achieving the irresistible sexual power these gadzookian dishes had over others. "These are the fields where I learned oral sex," Kim Basinger told us, indicating an entire town and its surroundings, which she'd purchased by dint of her sexual powers. "Women are cynical about being used as sex objects—which is a shame, because it's fun to use your sexuality."

"Just looking at her makes me want to have sex with her," the producer Menachem Golan said in agreement.

"I went wild," Jane Fonda, the former group-sex-oriented star, told us on the same page.

"I was wild," Melanie Griffith said, baring her soul. "I could do anything I wanted and did."

On and on it went—bosoms bulging from low-cut gowns fit for a lifestyle party—one female icon after another pruri-ently bragging from the rarefied Hollywood heights about the swinging edge to their sex lives. Meanwhile, a few pages in, *Cosmo*'s advice columnist, Irma Kurtz, offered the following warning to a lady who confessed she had "kind of enjoyed" the kiss of a woman in a group-sex encounter: "Each time a new partner is added, chances of contracting an STD increase expo-nentially. Sex, by the way, is meant for *couples*. We are not group sex animals. So forget about the exploits of a few free spirits." And on another occasion, when a happily married woman wrote Kurtz to say she and her husband "want to become swingers," the potential playcouple were rudely casti-gated: "I think swinging is detrimental, dangerous and just plain tacky. You say you 'want something more.' It seems to me that when two people who love each other and have good sex decide to include strangers, they are settling for something a lot less than what they already have: the true intimacy that commitment creates."

It is not at all strange that the editors of these magazines

could publish these contrasting assessments of swingers without even a passing acknowledgment of their own class bigotry.
As we have seen, preserving the privilege of the few and keeping the masses hungering for that privilege by denying it to
them is one of the ways the media profit all around. But, in
addition, mainstream media bosses appear to honestly believe
two things: one is that elite swingers, being few, don't threaten
the fabric of society, while plebeian swingers, being numerous,
do; the other is that elite swingers, having attained status by
virtue of some special power, can be trusted to be safely orgiastic, whereas common swingers, having attained nothing
besides lousy paychecks that they spend at Wal-Mart, have to
be treated like sheep.

To my mind, the media in these cases have ignored what
they would normally call a "holy-shit story": ten thousand
gatherings a year are held in North American swing clubs
packed with spouse sharing couples, yet one doesn't hear of
violent confrontations taking place in any of them. The media
have dismissed all the evidence that middle-class swingers can
be trusted to behave like the promoted archetypes Curtis and
Basinger. At the very least, that evidence suggests swingers are
as deserving of dignified treatment as gays and lesbians, whom
the media stopped humiliating as degenerates some time ago.

The social facts the media have not reported are succinctly
phrased by Edgar Butler: "Swingers aren't any less well-adjusted
or more unhappy or less psychologically fit than any average
cross-section of conservative, middle-class, middle-aged married people," he told me in his campus office at the University
of California at Riverside. "It's no longer academically permissible to study them seriously, but I've seen no new evidence to modify my view." He directed me to his textbook, in
which he'd cited one of the most extensive (and last) studies of
swingers—Brian Gilmartin's National Science Foundation-
funded survey: "About 85 percent of both husbands and wives

feel that swinging is not a threat to marriage or love between spouses. None of them reported that their marriage became worse since they began swinging, and the majority feel their marriages have improved.... Many swingers reported that rather than dampening their ardor for each other, swinging often caused an arousal of sexual interest for each other. Many of them often engage in sex together immediately after returning from a swinging party."

Since he first began investigating the phenomenon in the mid-1970s, Butler has studied the lifestyle by attending Lifestyles conventions and interviewing its participants and leaders. An international authority on the subject, he's been greatly disturbed at the way swing couples have been vilified by a society that forces them to live what Bob McGinley had called "secret dual lives." Given that the vast majority of swingers come from the ranks of right-of-center, white-collar suburbanites who are avowedly anti-drugs, pro-law-enforcement, and who drink no more than the general population, Butler sees the lifestyle phenomenon as *part* of mainstream society, not separate from it. He's no promoter of swinging, but his inclination is to defend all minorities against human-rights violations. That is why, as chairman of the sociology department at a prestigious university, he risked ridicule and took an unpaid position on the Lifestyles Organization's board of directors, taught the facts about alternative sexual lifestyles in his classes, and included an eleven-thousand-word chapter on swinging in his sociology textbook.

"If you look at the data, HIV/AIDS hasn't surfaced among swingers in a way to justify using it as evidence of their instability," he told me. "It's not used as a medical argument. It's used as a moral one. The behavioral patterns of that subculture are guided by the same bourgeois rules which govern straight marriages, except they're expanded to allow for all kinds of sexual expression within a bourgeois marriage. Of course it's a different lifestyle—no question—that's why it's a subculture. But the rules they follow are designed, from their perspective, to enhance what we call a traditional dyadic relationship. They'll tell you they swing in part because it makes them hot over each other. They do it for a lot of reasons—sexual, egotistic, social, playing out a fantasy—but they also say they do it for the marriage. And the studies I've looked at of long-term swingers back them up on that claim. They do feel surges of warmth, closeness, and love for each other after swinging. The rules of their subculture allow them to do that in safety and with some measure of security."

As Frank Lomas once told me: "Swing couples don't play with fire so much; they build a hot one in the fireplace and keep it going behind the grates."

———————

Saturday morning the playcouples at the New Horizons convention had to take a test. It was administered at a seminar called "The Lifestyle and You"—a group discussion that in its own casual fashion addressed the rules of swinging.

By then the clientele at the club had changed somewhat from the mostly hard-core attendees that had arrived Thursday. Now crowding into the glassed-in seminar room above the pool were representatives of the other three-quarters of the lifestyle. Here were the soft swingers who only watched and massaged in the manner of Chuck and Leah at the Eden Resort. Here were the "interpersonal swingers," the Elliot-and-Lindas, who most of the time did not have sex with couples unless they felt some emotional bond. And here were the "recreational swingers," the Carla-and-Eds, who were "more fast," but who shied away from having sex with more than one couple at a time, and who got most of their fun from dressing like the stars and, in Butler's words, socializing in "fairly stable groups." These were the official "types," although most academics like Butler refer to all as "recreational swingers," to differentiate them from the small subset of the lifestyle known as "utopian swingers"—the movement's left-wing ideologues who believe in group marriage, whom I would meet at my next scheduled convention a week hence.

About fifty of the generically named recreational swingers were greeted by a retired small-town police officer listed in the brochure as Bob, and his homemaker partner Judy who took the floor as Bob rolled the doors shut. Judy had a remarkably lineless face for her fifty-five years and was quite pretty, although, clasping her hands at her lap and wearing billowy pants, sensible flats, and a floral blouse, she reminded me more of a grammar school teacher than the exuberantly loud and laughing glamor girl I'd seen on the dance floor last night.

"We all know that partying is what the world thinks the lifestyle is, but we also know that what's underneath the fun makes all the difference," Judy told us, raising her intertwined fingers to her broad bosom in an almost prayerful position. The architects and engineers, pharmacists and teachers, nodded their agreement.

"Whether this is your first experience or whether you've been in it for a very long time," Judy said, "we both feel, Bob and I, that the issues are actually the same. What it comes down to is that you both put your relationship first. Maybe you both don't want exactly the same thing out of the lifestyle, but at least you're both devoted to each other, and what you do want doesn't hurt your partner's feelings or damage the relationship. We're not here to have secret love affairs, sneaking off for rendezvous with someone else's partner."

This statement reflected a norm I knew to be almost universal in the lifestyle: swingers may practice open eroticism, but they definitely do not have open marriages. They would never give each other permission to have an affair, preferring to treat each party they went to as a separate event and each erotic encounter as something to be negotiated, monitored, and shared. Whether they merely danced close and socialized or got together with others, playcouples believed so firmly in the "traditional dyadic relationship" that two academics, Rebecca and Charles Palson, once declared swinging a "conservative institution." Butler as well has always maintained that "most swingers consider themselves as monogamous." They practiced "faithful adultery."

"Now—all of this requires honest communication," said the big-gutted Bob, playing Judy's tag-team facilitator. From his toes to his bald pate he looked the part of your stereotypical country cop, with a gentle Western drawl to match. "Do you reassure each other—do you reassure both partners of the couple you're with?" he asked. "Also, is everybody willing? And what about when you get home? And what about before you leave home? And what about if this is your first time partying? All those ways to prevent hurt feelings through open communication—being honest with your partner—is why we do this seminar. Because if one just goes along with the other without saying anything, you have one miserable person in that relationship."

And so we began the test: everyone had to fill out a three-page questionnaire, which was about the last thing you'd expect swingers at a New Horizons convention to take time out to do. I glanced through the sheets Bob gave me. The first page was titled "What turns you on/What do you think turns your partner on?" Couples had twenty-six "activities" to rate for themselves and their partner, from: "1) not interested/turned off"; to: "5) really turned on, enjoy this every chance I get." The activities themselves ranged from soft swinging ("flirting," "group nudity," "erotic pictures"), to interpersonal swinging ("threesomes") to hard-core limits ("sex orgies"). According to the nonscientific standards of this questionnaire, a number discrepancy of more than two—between what you thought your partner wanted and what he or she really wanted —put you in the "danger" zone. If what you enjoyed every chance you got was in fact uninteresting and a turnoff for your partner, you both had a big problem.

"What are your sex preferences and tastes?" the second sheet asked. It focused even more specifically on problems presented by differing agendas, with preference ratings from "1) I like it" to "5) I hate to do it, but do it to please my partner." Finally, the third sheet was titled "Sex Personality" and dealt with intimacy issues, such as how you thought your partner assessed you ("warm," "passive," "frigid"), how much time you spent talking about swinging, and communication cues you and your partner employed to signal boundaries while interacting at parties.

"Shhh—no sharing, and *no* peeking!" Judy called from the front of the room, holding up a finger like a schoolmarm at the couples who had begun to banter. "That'll kill what we're trying to do here." She raised her chin and pursed her pertly lipsticked mouth as she surveyed the swingers, who set to working studiously for the next ten minutes.

Though these sheets of Bob and Judy's seemed unsophisticated, they were, according to Bob, a means of making the partygoers aware if they were breaking rules that applied to two broad categories of the lifestyle: how a playcouple related within their marriage, and how they related to others while swinging. An uninquisitive reporter attending an environment like New Horizons would not perceive these rules since, as in most subcultures, they were invisible. But at their emotional core, the rules were no different from those that circumscribed flirtatious behavior among long-married couples at any suburban gathering. In fact, the emotional issues that dominated a straight marriage held fast in a swinging pair-bond.

"Generally," Butler wrote, "swingers agreed that for successful swinging, a couple had to have a viable relationship based upon love." At home that meant constant communication, respectful language, and keeping arguments free of personal attacks; at a party the number-one rule was *reassurance*. No matter how enamored marrieds allowed themselves to become with others on the dance floor, or lost in passion in bed, spouses—by touch, word, or after-sex discussion—must always strive to comfort each other with the knowledge that their pleasure was part of a comarital experience, not a progression to an extramarital love affair. Ignoring the rule of reassurance led to a feeling of betrayal no different from what straight couples experienced when they got wise to an adulterous spouse. Abiding by this rule meant putting the marriage first at all times. That is why Butler could claim that "swinging marrieds probably represent the least revolutionary of the emerging alternative lifestyles" that he examined in his book.

To nonswingers, of course, it seems incredible that one could enjoy sex with an intriguing extramarital partner and not feel anything beyond "noncommitted love." But veteran swingers say they have learned how to put a cap on a romantic experience. "You go off privately with someone," Jennifer Lomas once explained to me, alluding to her preference for closed swinging, "and you have a fantasy affair with a beginning, a middle, and a fond farewell; you just compress it down to an evening so no one gets hurt. There's no midweek calls— 'Oh, I love you, I have to see you again...!' There's an understanding: this is happening in the lifestyle. The art of it is you feel admired and affectionate, so it's erotic, but you let your husband know—it's not a threat, it's a fantasy with a friend."

It should always be borne in mind that these are long-married, middle-aged people who are able to function this way. Most swingers will tell you that couples under thirty or couples just falling in love are incapable of combining all the fun of a short-term extramarital fling with all the social, economic, and emotional benefits of traditional fidelity—which the social rules of the lifestyle allow. Couples in their thirties and forties, swingers say, are much better equipped than younger folks to accept that their beguiling diversions are, in a literal sense, as fantastic as a Hollywood dream. Middle-aged swingers easily step in and out of their fantasies simply because they have been around the block a few times and know how to control their hearts. Because their fantasies are bookended by a loving marriage, they are recognized as plausible only during the experience of the fantasy—not beyond. The entire "play-couple philosophy" is structured around "sharing fantasies," in Bob McGinley's words, and it requires the maturity to be able to strictly circumscribe the experience of the fantasy. Forbidden fantasies derive their texture and pleasure from their seeming impossibility, but swingers believe it isn't that much of a compromise to experience them in the safety of a sanctioned environment, with the approval of their spouse. The lifestyle party provides the venue—sans the lying and hurt that an affair can cause. Overall, the rule of engagement couples follow allows them both to display the kind of emotion to extramarital partners that keeps encounters erotic and express love within the marriage to keep the encounters nonthreatening.

The other outstanding issue addressed by Bob and Judy's questionnaire was coercion. One of the few marital rules actually written down in the lifestyle is the rule of consensuality, which in theory protects lifestyle spouses against the possibility that either the husband or wife might draw the other into an activity not previously agreed upon. "Everyone has the right of refusal," states the boldfaced type in *Etiquette in Swinging*, the handbook of the North American Swing Club Association. "The actual sexual activity engaged in by swingers can be as varied as the people involved. Everything, however, is ALWAYS consensual." The sociologist Jerold Meints has termed this "the explicit rule" of swinging, and it is emphatically enforced by patrolling overseers at clubs like New Horizons, or by hosts at house parties, who are always on the lookout for partners who seem unhappy in a particular situation and who will expel a couple, or pull them aside for interrogation, if they detect they are a potential source of discontent to each other or to the party. A new couple who show up at a gathering—no matter how outrageously dressed—can count on being left alone sexually until they declare they are interested. Virtually every academic who has reported on the behavior of swingers asserts that this rule is almost never violated. The anthropologist Bartell attended dozens of parties with his provocatively dressed wife at which, he said, "swingers *assumed* we were neophyte swingers, anxious to start swinging." Yet even when he and his wife disrobed in the midst of an orgy in order to fit in, he discovered he could "observe without participating.... Seldom did we find it awkward to avoid swinging." It startles most observers to witness how the most unsophisticated husbands at a place like New Horizons behave as models of knightly decorum toward women. Even if dancing in a negligee with a man in the midst of a bacchanal, a woman had only to inform her interested partner that she didn't have sex in mind for the boundary to be clearly respected for the rest of the evening. She could flirt with, tease, and posture to any man who caught her fancy but it was forbidden for the fellow to respond with uninvited touching of any part of her body that would be normally out of bounds at a straight party.

"May I have your attention!" Bob announced at the front of the room. "Everybody had a chance to finish...? Okay, guys! Go ahead and start sharing answers!"

At Bob's okay the crowd exploded into gossip, the decibel level creeping up as excited husbands and wives compared what sounded like an hysterical catalogue of desires. I took advantage of the general uproar to have a peek at the questionnaire of the woman on my left. She immediately covered it up, her cheeks glowing red as if with every available drop of blood drawn from her shoulders to her scalp. "I wouldn't show this to my psychiatrist," she laughed, "and I don't even have a psychiatrist."

"Pia's terrified of what she wants," her husband cracked. "She's terrified she'll get it."

"How long have you been in the lifestyle?" Leslie asked my standard question for the weekend.

Pia looked at her watch. "An hour?" She giggled and sat back, trying to pull down her short leather skirt. "We just drove up. This is our first time to a club. How about you?"

"We're sort of around the lifestyle," Leslie said. "My husband's writing a book."

Pia was a nurse, and her husband, Earl, was a physician. As Leslie, Skala, and I had noticed, the health professions were well represented at this convention. "Have you guys been to the Annex yet?" I asked.

"Actually, we just had the tour," Pia laughed. "What a place! Wow! It's like a theme park!"

They'd been raised in a small town as Christians, were now in their mid-forties with two teenagers, and had been together since ninth grade, married twenty-seven years. They'd each had one adulterous affair in their lives—and their marriage had almost broken up over it. "Whose suggestion was it to come here?" Leslie asked Pia.

Pia looked at Earl, cocking her pretty, teardrop-shaped face. "I'd say mutual, wouldn't you?" she asked, but then turned back before Earl could answer. "I suppose my reason's on my homework sheet," she laughed again, folding it into quarters on her lap. Eventually I would discover that she was conflicted over her bisexual and group fantasies, which she hadn't even begun to admit to herself until she'd turned forty.

"One of the things my terminally ill patients always tell me," Earl said, "is this: 'The only thing I regret is not doing what I really wanted to do in life. If I'd'a only stopped and smelled the roses.'"

"You'll find lots of roses to smell here," Leslie said.

"Okay! May I have your attention again!" Bob called. He rapped the table in front of him with his ring. "We'd like to—Okay! Hey, folks, *folks*!" he shouted, trying to quell the banter that had been growing ever louder, threatening to break into an open party. "So—did you guys get each others' feedback?"

"Yeah, Donna's attitude to men is very unbiased," a fellow cracked. "She wants *all* of 'em."

"Well I should have known," Donna said. "Only answer private questions in private."

"Okay," Bob said, "what we'd like to find out now—Have you listened to what your partner was saying? Any major surprises—anybody like to share?"

"We had a hundred percent compatibility!" said a non-swinging woman, Dr. Jean Henry, holding up sets of questionnaires in both hands. She would shortly become the associate director of the Center for Research on Women's Health at Texas Woman's University near Dallas, and was now following the same convention route I was on, comparing the subculture on the Coast to the one in the Lone Star State, where there were no fewer than twenty-one NASCA-affiliated clubs and dozens more unaffiliated ones. One of these, the Inner Circle, had been raided two evenings before. In her master's thesis Jean had focused on "female self-image" and, as I'd learned during an interview with her at the pool, she would have liked to have received a grant to conduct an official study of lifestyle women. But, as usual, no one besides the police wanted anything to do with middle-class swingers, so she'd driven up here on her own hook as part of her summer holidays.

"You guys come to a *full* agreement—well that's *fan*tastic!" Bob praised Jean and her partner, Clark Ross, who ran a wilderness travel agency. "Anybody else have a hundred percent compatibility in that regard? It doesn't mean that you had the exact score as each one. The important part of the test's that you knew what the *other's* score would be. That's the real crux of things."

"I'm compatible with *both* my partners last night!" a woman named Sonia called.

"Now you got everything," Bob said. "Was there anybody that experienced a big discrepancy, where they had a five of something and you had a one?"

There was a lot of talk in the rows as people went back to sharing scores and fantasies. But no one was brave enough to stand up, as in an encounter group, and confess a problem. Not yet.

"Not that you have to share here if you don't want to," Bob said, acknowledging the reticence. "Important thing is that couples share with each *other*—so they understand, each couple. Everybody likes to party, sure, but communication's what we're talking about. Communication is an enhancement to this lifestyle. It's not a detractor. Because one of the things the owners were trying to accomplish by establishing this whole beautiful environment was to make it more comfortable for people, so they could feel fun and luxurious, yes, but there's places all around to get off by yourselves and stop and say— 'Such and such just happened, how do you feel about that? How do I feel about that?' You know, it doesn't matter if there's all this fun on the outside, if what's on the inside—"

"I've got something to say on that," said a very pale and frail-looking fellow in his early forties named Kenny, a transparently decent guy who worked in computers in Portland. He had arrived yesterday afternoon with his wife, Naomi, who could have been his twin in lean weight and five-foot-ten height. The previous night, at the "Happy Hooker and Joyous Gigolo Dance," they both had been dolled up appropriately. Now they were dressed as if for gardening on a Saturday afternoon, in runners, shorts, and T-shirts. "I don't think any-one's been more fearful at times than I have been myself this weekend," he said, at which his wife took his hand.

"Have you guys ever been to a lifestyle occasion before?" a woman asked from the back.

"Well, yeah, but never like this here," Kenny said. "I met people from all over the place and from all different levels here, and I believe the process can be too much for some of them sometimes. Coming into this is like the kid in the candy store. You rush in and find out that you go into sensory over-load and you start to shut down, you go into shutdown. So here you are in a sex club, and your sex is shut down. And of course when that happens, you look around and everybody else seems to be doing just fine. In fact, more than just fine," he laughed nervously.

"There've been times we're driving home I think that way," a fellow to my right said. "You're not alone in that."

"And do you talk about it?" Judy asked the guy. "Do you communicate?"

"Well, obviously—we're back here," he said.

"I think men should be shown just as much sensitivity as women are shown," Judy said. "I don't think they get shown enough in this environment. That's one reason I prefer closed swinging in the cubbyholes, or a little, safe group of three or four. Because I want to give attention, and when you're in a large group it's a very difficult task."

"There was actually a point made in a discussion we were having that women get paid way more attention than guys do," Bob said. "What do you think of that?"

"That's absolutely true," Kenny's wife said. "Because we spend so many years being thought of that way, we expect it."

"It's kind of fun, actually," said a heavyset woman, "but I know what you mean. Of course, we do dress for attention."

"Well, that impacts me," Kenny said, "because everybody

was so into it, I felt left out. After a few tries, I tried to move ahead and get turned on, and all of a sudden reality set in. And so I thought, well maybe watching those videos—or maybe there's something about me that's wrong? I know you're not supposed to be afraid here, but this is one man that does get fearful in that situation. I do get sensory overload, and I do shut down. It's just part of it, we've been working on this and we do want to come back. But we left here last night and I said we're not coming back. But—here we still are."

"And how do you react to him when he feels so vulnerable?" Judy asked his wife.

"To me it's more important how he's feeling," Naomi said. "So I just didn't let anything happen. When it's the other way, if I'm feeling vulnerable or jealous, I just tell him, 'I'm having a problem with this woman. It's not a big deal, I'm just letting you know it's there.' And if I can get that feeling out then usually what happens is that it comes together for me. Either he'll say, 'Okay, no problem,' or I'll see there isn't a problem, or she and I will start talking and confirm. So it's reciprocal."

"So you check to see if the other partner is okay, is comfortable, is coping, is happy, is enjoying it," Judy said. "There's that nurturing that goes on—the caring, the communication. I feel the same when I meet a really attractive man. I feel like I've got to communicate with the woman first. Because I have to find out, he's giving me all this attention—how does that sit with her? How many feel that's the best approach?"

As in a school class, everyone raised a hand.

"Because you never know, say they're new: Is this their first time? If it is, it's really scary for her. I think for everyone it has to be really scary that first time."

"That's the first thing that hits you is being scared," said Sonia, the one who was compatible with her two partners of the night before (one of whom had been Judy). Like my tablemates Edith and Beth the other night, and like many of the women at the club, both Judy and Sonia were freely bisexual. "You went in a car," Sonia continued, "and you went in holding hands and you went and sat down and when a guy came over and asked you to dance, you think right away, Where is this going to go?"

"How long did it stay scary?" Pia asked beside me.

"Actually, for me it worked through pretty quickly," Sonia said. "I had a very nice first experience. I think it depends on that. He was very sensitive. But it's more on Allen," she said, referring to her husband beside her. She mussed his hair. "If I didn't know that if I said, 'Okay, we're leaving,' that we would really leave, then I don't know about this. My feeling is that if a couple doesn't have that, then there's no way they can continue to swing and make it work—it's not going to work. They've got to keep that sensitivity, that communication—then they're really free to have a great time. But that has to be there from even the first time they're thinking about getting involved."

"I'm just curious," my partner piped up. "How many women here initiated their first swinging experience?" About half the women raised their hands. Most of them were in the fastlane.

"How many had husbands initiate it?" The other half raised their hands.

"You can really almost tell who it was that would initiate the lifestyle in their relationship," Judy explained. "They're always so bubbly."

———

Most of the media reports I read of swingers before I entered their world that summer admitted that consensuality rules reigned at parties: "No means no is the good news at the convention," the British *Elle* observed at Lifestyles '95. But almost all stated that women were in the lifestyle only because their husbands forced them into it. "Apparently a lot of the women have come here to keep their men happy," *Elle*'s writer, Lucie Young, claimed. When a woman explained to Young by the pool that entering the subculture had been jarring initially but that she had gone on to embrace it ("'It was difficult at first, but by the second day it's like right on'"), she was dismissed as self-deluded: "Her biggest fear was that her husband would have sex with someone who satisfied him better than she could." Immediately after this judgment, however, Young noted: "Girl-girl petting is one of the major activities around the pool. Virtually all the women here define themselves as bisexual." Virtually everyone was heterosexually available as well, Young pointed out, adding, "The rules, such as they are, are established by the wives and girlfriends." Contradicting herself time and again with this catalogue, Young, with flat British contempt, resisted the temptation to get a handle on what was happening before her very eyes—heterosexually and bisexually—and on why, for some wives, "by the second day it's like right on." Like many journalists, she couldn't accept the subculture's total celebration of sexuality because she couldn't get beyond the indisputable fact that in a lot of cases it is the husband who first suggests the idea of going to a lifestyle party, with the wife taking her own time to get used to the idea.

If you talk to veteran swinging wives who are completely out of the closet, like Jennifer Lomas, the business manager, Cathy Gardner, the mortgage broker, and Sherri Cooper, the social worker, they will tell you that the full weight of social conditioning keeps most women from initiating the idea of attending a swing club; therefore, it *is* usually the man who first makes the suggestion. Yet, they argue, the vast majority of women—whether straight or bisexual—are not "forced" into the lifestyle by abusive husbands.

Their logic is as follows: they differentiate between being encouraged by their husbands to attend a lifestyle event, enjoying it, then embracing the culture as a happy mode of marital living, and being abusively coerced into entering the lifestyle and not enjoying it at all.

They explain that middle-class women in our society are raised to regard spouse exchange as "detrimental, dangerous and just plain tacky," while men are raised to find it alluring. However, once in the lifestyle, they say, most swinging wives (not all) consider themselves liberated from the social brakes that kept them from enjoying the abundant dressing up and permissive sexuality of the subculture. The lifestyle allows them the freedom to behave like the forbidden goddesses of Hollywood. Moreover, given that the rules of the lifestyle are "established by the wives" and preserve the stability of traditional marriage, Lomas et al. maintain that swinging women are able to act out their erotic fantasies with an exuberance equal to, if not greater than, that of their husbands.

There is considerable backing from academics to support them in this claim. "I think in this particular culture, in our society," Jean Henry told me at New Horizons, indicating the women splashing in the pool with a variety of partners, "I'm not so sure that women have been left behind. In a way, I think, now it's more acceptable for women to actively say 'I like it,' instead of having to pretend that they're going into it under duress, or because the male in my life wants me to do this."

Dr. Ted McIlvenna, the director of the Institute for Advanced Study of Human Sexuality, a graduate school in San Francisco, has canvassed hundreds of swingers over the years. Just after the New Horizons convention he told me that once lifestyle women, especially middle-aged women with incomes that allowed them to be independent of their husbands, "found that safe context, they took charge, as if it were the most natural way for them to express themselves. They went out, they bought the clothes, they did the planning, they did everything to go back into that social milieu because it was a milieu that endorsed their sexuality." A year and a half later McIlvenna would set the *Los Angeles Times* back on its chair when he told a reporter: "Women are taking a more prominent role in these swing clubs. They call the shots. More women are working, and with that comes more power, affluence and associations. In the old days, men screwed around, and the women stayed home. Now women are out there." The media can persist in claiming that women are in the lifestyle only to keep their husbands happy, but if reporters decide to make the calls, experts from numerous institutions will tell them a different story.

Obviously there is more to the lifestyle than just the act of sex: we are talking about a milieu. "We've found the majority of the people involved seem to be in it for the culture and the open socializing, not necessarily for the physical engagement," Jean Henry told me at New Horizons. "Sexuality in the lifestyle is far more broadly defined than what you see over there." She pointed to the Annex. "Sexuality helps define women to themselves in our culture as to whether you are attractive or not. This lifestyle is a way for women to get a feeling for being sexually attractive, i.e., 'I am more feminine and I am a more effective woman because these men want to have sex with me, and, therefore, I have a power and an allure to my husband and to others, which I can carry with me.'"

Regarding this issue of self-image in the lifestyle, Jennifer Lomas pointed out that as middle-aged women express their fantasies within the subculture, they begin "to see themselves as hot stuff—and they have a lot of fun with that." This is somewhat explained by the fact that for a lot of males within the lifestyle a healthy fifty-year-old woman is actually *more* erotic than a twenty-year-old: her total package of sexuality— even if Rubenesque—seems warm and frankly expressed as opposed to the icy hauteur paradigmatic models are apt to vacuously exhibit on a dance floor in a straight nightclub. That is why one of the most oft-repeated sayings of veteran lifestyle women is: "You have to convince them to come but then you have to convince them to leave." That is why McIlvenna says: "The men initiate, the women perpetuate." And, as Butler's colleagues Lynn and James Smith found in their study of swingers: "Women are better able to make the necessary adjustments to sexual freedom after the initial stages of involvement than are men, even though it is usually the case that the men instigate the initial involvement."

In my interview with Cathy Gardner, a handsome, forty-nine-year-old grandmother who attended clubs at least twice a month with her husband, Dan, she took the point of view of a libertarian in order to turn on its head the notion that females remain in the subculture to please their husbands. "Aren't some women being coerced to *not* be in the lifestyle?" she asked. "I'm happily married for so many years, I *love* my lifestyle, so I naturally ask the question: Who is doing the coercing? And my answer is, society, religion, television, they're training people all the time, in a way making sure women act a certain way. I think people like me are actually rebelling against being told to *not* be in the lifestyle."

The forty-one-year-old Jennifer Lomas held a similar view: "When I think back on how we first got involved in this, it's clear to me now how my upbringing was saying no, no, no, how it wouldn't even let me get to first base on the thought. That's the point that everyone picks up on as to why swinging is supposed to be a man's game. They say, 'Well, if women love the lifestyle so much, how come they're not the ones dragging their husbands to clubs to begin with?' The answer is it happens sometimes—actually more and more as society is changing, and not just with bisexual women. But the real answer is that women are brought up so that you're supposed to find one guy and live happily ever after, or, absolute maximum, play around on the side. Nobody ever told me until I got into the lifestyle that two people could get married and have sex with other people and be happy. But for men, it's almost the reverse message. Get married and sow your wild oats. That's why they usually take the lead. Then, like me and Cathy Gardner," she laughed, "the women take over."

In the case of the forty-five-year-old social worker Sherri Cooper—another handsome grandmother, but a bisexual—she had been the one to take the lead and persuade her husband, Danny, a carpenter, to become involved in the lifestyle. "Commentators walk in here, take a look around, and say, 'These can't be normal women, they're all unhappy or crazy,'" Cooper told me at a convention. "That's what they say, and that's what people believe. I always wonder, would they go to a convention of lesbians and say the same thing? They look at me like I'm from another planet when I tell them 'This was my idea to come here.'"

Increasingly, bisexual wives who have heard about the lifestyle are initiating involvement in the subculture. Yet, as Jennifer pointed out, and as was evident at New Horizons, "as society changes," even some straight women are taking the lead.

However, the typical journey of couples who end up firmly in the lifestyle most closely resembles that taken by Jennifer and her husband Frank: it was Frank's idea. After Frank first suggested swinging he became what sociologists refer to as an *encourager*. Encouragers make up the vast majority of men in relationships in which wives perpetuate swinging. "Male encouragers," Butler wrote, "reject the double standard on idealistic grounds, mainly egalitarianism; they feel swinging will be a positive experience for themselves and their wives." Frank's ongoing encouragement led Jennifer to enter *the enthusiasm stage*. "The wife finds she no longer feels guilt about participating in comarital sex," Butler reported. "She is actually beginning to relish it to an even greater extent than her husband."

That is the claim of many swingers when they speak to sociologists (and reporters). The lifestyle has its dropouts; there are what sociologists call *user males*; yet the warning message in NASCA's *Etiquette in Swinging* and on its Web site makes it clear that the subculture only wants people who fit certain criteria to get involved with swinging. It is the same warning delivered to couples in screening interviews before they are allowed to visit a club. "Swinging is not for everyone.... A positive feeling about yourself, your mate and relationship is important. People who are jealous, play social games, have a poor opinion of the opposite sex, are deeply religious or have relationship problems are among those who are not likely to enjoy swinging."

As the saying in the lifestyle goes, "Swinging never made a bad marriage good," and most swingers believe that. Indeed, after years of investigating a subculture that is far more rule-bound, discriminating, and controlled than it appears, Edgar Butler, Jean Henry, and Ted McIIvenna have found that the least-told story is how pleased happily married couples *in* the lifestyle are *with* the lifestyle—even though it may have taken them some time to get to that stage.

For Jennifer Lomas the transition from straight to swinger wasn't instantaneous by any means, and it wasn't without complications. As Jennifer described it, her journey into the lifestyle followed a predictable pattern in which she and her husband eventually experienced comarital sex. Some couples never get to that point and stay "soft" for the entire time they are in the lifestyle. Some try it and find it an upsetting experience they never want to revisit. For Frank and Jennifer the journey took years. It involved, as she would tell me, a process of overcoming justifiable fears; retracing false steps; receiving positive reinforcement from people she respected and trusted;

and, finally, establishing a context of permission in the right environment. Eventually she felt comfortable enough to enter a new culture—the lifestyle.

To Jennifer's mind, one of the lessons of her tale for neophyte swingers was that there is a right way and a wrong way to step into her world. The right way allows couples to take a look around and have the rules explained to them, so that they can decide whether they want to stay, return some other time, or never come back. We should listen to Jennifer's story.

———————

Like a lot of lifestyle women, Jennifer is ebullient and prone to using a lot of body language when speaking. In looks and personality she is one of the more attractive lifestyle women: tall and shapely, redheaded and tanned, and full of expository asides about the joys of open sensuality that she has come to accept as part of her life. Yet she is no compulsive-looking seductress: in the daytime she generally wears sweat socks and sneakers, shorts and a plain blouse, and very little makeup. After asking the loquacious Frank to excuse us so I could have a couple of hours to hear his wife's side without interruption, Jennifer and I sat down in the interview lounge of the Lifestyles Organization. Here, as an LSO employee between 1989 and 1995, Jennifer had grilled hundreds of first-time couples for any hint of abuse before she allowed them to attend a swing party at the organization's mansion; by the time a neophyte couple had left the room she'd explained to them the lifestyle's rigid rules. She'd since moved on from her job at LSO to take a position as business manager of Laser Tech Engineering and was as little shy of relating stories about the reactions of her co-workers and friends to her being an out-of-the-closet swinger as of her sex life.

"We were married, I think, ten years when Frank first

brought this up," Jennifer began. "I was in my late twenties, never had another man; Frank never had another woman—since we were married anyway. Our sex life was great. I was completely happy. Great job, great husband, we hiked, bowled, skied—the California good life.

"One day, he's coming home from work at the bank, he sees a smut magazine on a stand, *West Coast Swingers*. He takes a look." Here she put one hand behind her flaming hair and put her other hand on her hip. "You know," she burst into laughter. "Tarty stuff. So he really wanted it, but he was raised Baptist; he was so embarrassed, he thought about stealing it. Anyway, he buys it, and he brings it home and shows it to me. 'Look at this, honey. Can you get over it? Look what she's wearing. Do you think that guy's a turn-on?' Blah blah blah. 'Yeah, well, so?' I said. 'They're swingers.' Because it was filled with really crude people and creepy captions."

"You mean like, 'Bi wife and well-hung guy want to meet other couples'?" I asked.

"Yeah, yeah, the full treatment. It was nauseating. I was totally typical. I didn't want anything to do with it; I was totally disgusted by the whole idea. And, of course, my first thoughts were, 'There must be something wrong with me, why do you want other women?' He said, 'I don't want other women myself—I want it with you.' And I thought, Yeah, right! He said, 'No, no, no—look at all this erotic stuff going on. You don't think that guy's good-looking?' 'Yeah, well, forget it, throw it out,' I said.

"Actually, Frank and I talked about it for a very long time," Jennifer went on. "He was very patient. We were talking at least three years. And, you know, during that time we started to play the games, just between us. He was buying lingerie and dresses for me and posing me for pictures and falling over backward at how I looked like his tart fantasy. I guess, for me, it came to a point where I started having a good time with the fantasy, just at that level. You know, 'what would you do if' business. 'In the happiest wife's dreams, many men pass through,' as they say. I sort of let myself go in my mind."

"Why did you decide to turn the fantasy into reality?" I asked.

"I can't remember what exactly it was that turned the key for me," she said. "I think it was because he just seemed to be getting off so much on *me* as a fantasy that I finally felt reassured. I think it was probably then. And I said, 'Okay, just for a look.'

"Well, we had a *really shitty* first experience," Jennifer told me in laughter. "I was disgusted. We went at it in the worst way. We answered an ad. We were so naive, we didn't know *what* we were doing. You want to know the rules, Terry? Don't answer an ad to first get into it. Rule numero uno *uno*! There's clubs literally everywhere that hold Friday-night dances where there's no swinging and you can meet couples and talk with them and find out if it's for you. If you want the on-premises club stuff you go to their party house on Saturday and you know everybody's screened in an interview. Ads you don't know why they're doing it that way."

"Maybe they're just afraid to go out in public," I said.

"That's a big reason, actually. But you just don't know if there's another reason. Well, we found out there was. Frank and the guy talk on the phone and on a Saturday night we go to their condo. Big fantasy. This is it. I wore all the doo-dads," she giggled. "And they open the door, and of course the picture they put in the ad was about ten years old. And the lady's got a sixties hairdo. But anyway, at least they didn't meet us at the door naked. Plus, they were actually very civilized once we got to talking. These were our first swingers, right? So just the fact that they didn't jump us was a bonus in my book.

"So we're there and we're drinking some wine and they're sitting over on one end of the couch and we're on the other end. Three videos later I'm fishing around in my mind for a good excuse to leave without hurting their feelings—then they start kissing each other, and then he's undressing her and himself—oh God, not a pretty picture. On top of that, he couldn't even get it up for his own wife."

"You sat there and watched them?" I asked.

"The room was pretty dark, thank God. So Frank, he says something like, 'Well, I just want to thank you folks for allowing us to share this intimate time with you'—something gracious. And all I'm thinking is, This is not exactly the highlight of my life. I felt for them, but that wasn't the point, you know. The least they could have done was put a footnote in the ad—'Taken 1962, add pounds, subtract hair.'

"So—I can tell you something about the lifestyle at the beginning. If you go in blind and ignorant like we did, and answer an ad, that's what you wind up with. Neither of you know what you're doing. It's all strange—and you wind up in a Three Stooges movie."

She shook her head and sighed. "I mean, I think Curly's pretty cute, but—"

"Did that upset your relationship?"

"No, no, that wasn't even a thought," she said. "By then that never entered my mind that there was a problem with our relationship. But it sure killed the fantasy for me for two years. I wouldn't even get into the games properly.

"Okay—so one day he comes home from work and says, 'Jennifer, Jennifer! This guy at work—.' Apparently he heard of this sophisticated party club. 'Everybody's really together and intelligent and professional,' he says. 'They've been hanging out for years. If there's any unfit people they've been weeded out.'

"I put him off for a while, then I thought, Well, if it hadn't've been so ridiculous the last time, it might've worked out. I honestly did in a part of me enjoy the fantasy of being sensual with other people. It wasn't like a ravenous desire, but whenever I would think of it, it would be something pretty—*not* like a swinger ad. So, as they say, I 'allowed' myself to say yes. It's very important to keep up appearances to yourself that you're just going along.

"Well, this was a great party. And everyone's nice looking, well mannered—and I was talking with the women and the guys just like at a straight party. There were environmentalists there and doctors and people from all stripes. Really non-threatening. There was no sex at all going on, but the outfits were pretty interesting. So we spent a couple of hours talking with this couple about what it was all about, and the dos and don'ts, and their experiences good and bad. The talk was really right. Then we went to their apartment and—oh wow! All of a sudden I understood, I enjoyed it. They were both so terrific, really relaxed and playful and full of laughter. And they had massage oil, and fragrances, and it was like, if we consummate this, we consummate it—if not, not. Of course we did," she laughed. "We giggled the whole time! It was so light. It was a turning point for me. We really hit it off with this couple as friends.

"And that was on one weekend. They in turn invited us to a party on the next weekend, where we met another group of people that also were all our age group, our same income, that had a lot of things in common. And then they invited us to a third party. And then we started meeting a whole crowd of couples that we had something in common with, who we could go bowling with and then go to the lake with and go skiing with. And it started making sense. Today we still know a lot of couples from that first party."

"So it took you five years," I said. "And then in just a few weeks you were all the way 'in the lifestyle'? No transition from soft swinger to recreational?"

"Right, it was a mental paradigm shift. Once you meet a

crowd of great people who you can be friends with, that's the way it happens sometimes. I guess, for me, it was that here were all these married people so totally comfortable with who they were as sexual, emotional people—they were so relaxed and playful about their desire for variety—right in the open. I hadn't met too many couples where one or the other hadn't cheated on their spouse. Lying and cheating and backstabbing and going in back doors. Here you could flirt, know you're attracted to men, so why not be open about it and pursue it in the lifestyle? We practice safe sex, we get tested every six months on top of that—so why not? It's just generally so exciting. What it does is give you butterflies again, like, oh God, I wonder what's going to happen tonight, and you take extra special care to do your hair and makeup, and wear a special outfit. It's kind of like a dating process all over again, but you still have the comfort of going home with your spouse. The security of your inner relationship that's perfectly fine, but you get to have this inner excitement. For me the variety is *wonderful*. No one's the same. Some men are more intimate, some are more passionate, but there's really no end to the excitement of being among people who accept that this is socially acceptable—it's fun, it's friendship, and it's great sex. I think it's the way life should really be lived. And if it's no longer fun you just get out of it. It's not like a sex cult where couples come looking for you to haul you back or else. We know a few couples who dropped out who we're still friends with."

"Why did they drop out?" I asked.

"In two of the cases they got into swinging with relationship problems, and I think swinging magnifies problems if you already have them. They both wanted it but it got to a point where they realized, we've got problems and this is making it worse. The worst thing you can do in this lifestyle is try to swing when you're not getting along. So you have to stop. It can become interpreted as a payback for an argument, or a rejection. It basically violates the rule that you're in there as a couple. Once you do that, and you're not in there as Mr. and Mrs., but as Mr. doing his thing and Mrs. doing hers, it's not really the lifestyle anymore. It becomes more like singles swinging or adultery or a marriage of convenience. It just got too hard for them to cope and they dropped out. Another couple I know, the husband became very prominent, so they dropped out because they became afraid it would ruin his career with clients. Which it hasn't done for me and Frank since we came out."

"You're out of the closet to everyone?" I asked.

"Completely. Work, family, and friends. I don't have any terrors about being discovered. I came out when I went to work here at Lifestyles in 1989, and I'm never going back in. I took a big pay cut just because I really believed in the lifestyle and wanted to be around lifestyle people all the time. And, of course, now that I'm back on a standard career track and no longer work here, that means several things. I work with all guys, and it's pretty standard that every man that meets you thinks you want to have sex with them. Every woman thinks you want to have sex with their husband. If they don't get to know me, they pretty much consider me a threat to the stability of the world. So I always have to wind up having to have this little talk with everybody: 'I'm in a lifestyle. It's between Frank and me, you don't have to worry, we don't cheat on each other. We're in control of ourselves as anyone else.' I went through that stage at Laser Tech for about a month or so, and things are very cool there now. It's kind of like what being gay was like in the early sixties.

"But here's something very interesting that's different from being gay. After we get through that stage, and they see I'm quite normal, they become really, really curious, especially if they see Frank and me together and see how happy we are. They start to ask a lot of questions. For instance, I have two totally straight girlfriends that I used to work with at Barclays Bank. And at first they were shocked: 'He let's you, you let him, how can you stay married?' Well, we keep in contact, even though we've gone our separate ways, and when we get together for our once-a-year dinner and our catch-up, nine times out of ten they've finished telling me their whole year in five minutes and they want to know how many parties I've been to, how many men I've been with, what holidays have I been on. And they go, 'Oh my God, Jennifer, you're living a fantasy life, you're so lucky, oh I just can't believe it.' I go, 'Well, yeah, it's a fantasy but it's still real. It's just an alternative for some people.'"

"What about your family?"

"My mother's great about it. Her exact first words were: 'What goes on behind closed doors is none of my business.' But she also said—we brought a whole crowd to the house to meet her and my sisters, eleven couples—and Mom took me aside and she said: 'Jennifer, you have the nicest friends. These are very decent people—wonderful people. I'm amazed.' All my sisters have accepted it. I have three. One's a schoolteacher, very serious. It's funny. I was always in her shadow. And now it's reversed. She envies me and would like to become more like me. Not necessarily in the swinging lifestyle, but to be more self-accepting and outgoing."

"Are any of your friends out of the closet?" I asked.

"Just one or two, like Cathy Gardner, and that's it. As I say, I think it's probably fairly rare, mostly because of the job situation. They all have kids—some of them have grand-children—some kids know, some don't. We're thinking our-selves of having children pretty soon now that I'm at that age. It'll be a serious move. Some things will change, not everything, but we'll have to make different priorities. That's not to say we have to stop totally, either. I think we'll be going to parties less frequently but I don't think we'd get out of it. All of our friends stayed in the lifestyle; I can't imagine just, like, ending it—boom."

"Are you going to tell your kids?"

"Frank and I were just talking about that. I think they'll ask when they're ready, and I'll give them an honest answer. There's no reason to deny it. I'm not doing anything wrong, and it's very obvious that we have a very loving, caring relationship. I don't think they would ask if they weren't curious or ready for the information. It's no different from being a lesbian mother, say, except, for some odd reason, in our society I'm supposed to be much, much worse than any lesbian that walked the earth."

"I guess because there's thousands of lesbians out of the closet and not very many swingers who are out," I said.

"Exactly—and you have to ask, Why is that? I think the numbers of swingers are about the same as for lesbians. I'm not advocating couples come out and go marching. What I do believe is the public should be educated that we have rules, and it's just plain bigotry for the press to be writing about us as if we're freaks and for police to be raiding clubs and arresting people like they did in Texas, or closing down clubs. It really is bigotry. The majority of swingers are just like normal straight people at a party; they talk to people and get to know them, and then maybe focus on people who they're really interested in. And if it happens, it happens.

"I have to tell you, for Frank and me we've always had such a good, strong relationship that it's never been a problem for us. We've always had an eye out for each other, and we know our dos and don'ts. *Do ask! Don't disappear!*"

———

When the dos and don'ts were strictly adhered to, they allowed swinging marrieds to enjoy all manner of dress, flirtation, and

sex practices. The rules Jennifer followed made her feel justified in posing questions to her critics: "Why are we not allowed
to be uninhibited? Why stop, if it's controlled and it's not
harming us?" At its enticing core the lifestyle may have been
about the real possibility of spouse sharing but, in varying
degrees leading up to that act, it was just as much about dressing like sexy stars, flirting in the style of those stars, and watching others on parade and in action. As Jennifer told me, "It's so
liberating to be in this community and nobody is judging you.
I can dress tarty as Madonna and do anything I want, and not
feel judged. I can watch everybody else and not judge them."
If, as they say, adulterous extramarital sex is about breaking
the rules in secret, with no rule other than adhering to the
bond of secrecy, then the lifestyle was about living by rules so
that the same excitement could occur openly within marriage.

If you take the viewpoint of a sociologist, rather than a
moralist, it's obvious that swingers were doing exactly what
the likes of *GQ* and *Cosmo* glamorize Tony Curtis and Kim
Basinger for doing. In the media's eyes, playcouples were
guilty of taking their privilege "on the cheap," of replicating
Lifestyles of the Rich and Famous even though they no longer
had a prayer of being rich or famous. You had only to look
around New Horizons to see what the media had wrought: the
club was a veritable five-star resort. At any hour of the day you
could see couples playing like the stars in the giant heated pool
and others relaxing side by side in the luxurious Jacuzzi at the
foot of a molded rock grotto underlit in blue and green and
flanked by potted palms. The huge, windowed wall at the
head of the pool gave you a view into the banquet hall, with its
crisply set tables crowded with conventioneers sipping soft
drinks or eating their five-dollar snacks while Vivaldi's *Four
Seasons* played softly over the speakers. Spectacularly framed
by the windowed north wall that ran the length of the entire
club, the flowers, lawn, and forest of the grounds stretched

away like a duke's demesne. In every facet of its ambiance, New Horizons contrived to imitate the kind of hideaway that catered to the needs of the world's sequined and tuxedoed icons, who enjoyed their well publicized trysts on the other side of the moneyed world from small-town Washington. Collectively we pay billions to the media for a peek at the exploits of the rich and famous. Why can't you, swingers ask, if you are comparatively poor or anonymous or nowhere near beautiful, indulge in those exploits for a few days, and then go back to work?

The most astonishing thing about the Saturday-night climax to the convention was that only about a tenth of the couples wound up going back to the Annex. The real fun to be had was at the dinner and dance surrounding the Blind Fondle Contest —a self-parodying affair in which patrons strained to capture the public private lives of all those TV and movie celebrities who had been married five or six times or were prone to attending awards ceremonies in slinky slit gowns and keyhole halters. I have been to a lot of lifestyle bashes where the glitter was garish and the outfits had been worked on for months, but in terms of blatantly accentuated body shapes that bore no relation to our cultural ideal, nothing matched the parade that flounced into the banquet room at eight. To be sure, half the people were skinny or shapely, muscular or even gorgeous—made for magazines—but it was the big folks who riveted attention merely because they were so happy and glamorously proud.

Sitting down to their prime-rib dinners, men and women alike cast self-confident smiles about them. It was supposedly "the night you can chase your pagan fantasies," but the establishment had supplied no toga wear and, in any case, the self-willed swingers preferred the least-dressed look featured in

Madonna's book, *Sex*, with its teasing glimpses of mock celebrity orgies that playcouples lived or watched for real. The most ample shapes were slipped into sexy wear that pushed what they had up, squeezed it out, netted it over tightly and draped it in lace. Shadowy fabric vectored the eye to points you were not supposed to stare at. As an underwear ad at the time had it: "There's a side to every woman that's very Marilyn." But here the ante was frankly upped. Making a grand entrance a lady of pedestrian figure showily stripped out of a red silk robe by a potted tree near my table. Head back, hand held demurely in the air, wearing bikini underwear, she clicked shamelessly across the dance floor, trailing her cape, to cheers. "Olé!"

"You ever see in *People* magazine where they have the ten worst-dressed women?" Sonia from the seminar asked Leslie. "Where they set up these examples where they're torn down for looking horrible—maybe the neckline's too low or the hemline's too short?"

"You mean if they're not suitably built to wear the outfit?" Leslie asked.

"If they're bulging out of the outfit," she replied. "If they're bulging out, if they're not a skinny rake, and they dare to show some flesh that's overflowing the costume, then they'll point the fingers at them as looking ridiculous, and how could they even dare to go out in society like that, unless they're young and beautiful models. But here she's accepted—they don't look anything like the models, but it's fine. It's beautiful. Don't you love it? They're so *gorgeous!*"

After a rich ice-cream-and-cake dessert, the music man, Stan, whom Jodie had engaged on our first meeting, put on the beat and we watched the show.

The dancing gave Skala an intuition that there was another level to this party. Being of ancient Bohemian stock he discerned a racial memory coming on: except for the jockstraps, teddies, body stockings and spiked high heels, he felt as if we could be in Pilsen at the height of the Middle Ages, at the licentious peak of Fat Tuesday, when the townsfolk behaved like the erotic gods their pagan ancestors had worshiped—except here the gods were tabloid. In Europe it was called "Kermis" —here it had no name—but it was still a night of steak, beer, and pillowy beauty that many in our anorexic age would not accept as being deserving of the word erotic.

At the tables the wives sat on their husband's knees, breasts spilling out from merry widows and bedroom bodices. Allure established and sustained, they kissed neighboring guys, flounced onto the laps of female friends. No one had sex but it was still a skewer in the eye to *Cosmo*'s delicate sensibility. *Tacky?* Not to these guys. They had utter contempt for bulimic guilt over an ounce too much of this or that. *Dangerous and detrimental?* Only to institutionalized forces. It was like Woodstock—not a shot was fired, but it seemed to strike terror into the heart of the establishment.

"Blind Fondle Contest! Blind Fondle Contest!" Ron called at the mike, and the men clambered behind the painted plywood wall with the little doors. Their wives, lining up for a feel and a guess at whose scrotum belonged to them for life, soon broke the rules and reached all the way through, squeezing buttocks and thighs in more than dexterous inspection. There was supposed to be some scoring and a prize at the end, but the judging collapsed when Jodie and one of her friends ran behind the prop and began trying to get the men a little more prominently displayed through the trap doors.

Following the chaotic "contest" the hall was made disco-dark and every couple poured onto the dance floor beneath the swirling spotlights. All of a sudden Pia, breathless with titillation, her cheeks cadmium red, revealed one of her fantasies. You couldn't keep many secrets on this night, but this one was so tame it was laughable. "I'd love to dance naked!" she told us—and this was certainly the place for it. Earl helped her undress and she proceeded to have a blast on the ballroom floor with Larry, our Thursday night tablemate, who was tall and strong enough to lift her. She rode his hips while he boogied, her arms waving at the lights above her head and her breasts stretched taut.

In the midst of it all I watched Jean Henry and Clark Ross dancing civilly with each other out on the floor—good sports. The music and hilarity of the crowd was too deafening to have a meaningful conversation, but I'd already posed a big question to Jean the other day by the pool: How did she go about explaining the sudden popularity of this?

"Cultural psychology," she'd told me. "What's the overall culture that permits this? It has to do with cultures that develop within the culture. It doesn't explain all of it, but you have to weigh what's so-called forbidden and what might be becoming permitted. I think that's a cyclical thing. We could be moving in a new direction."

Clark offered me his layman's opinion. "Also, you have to look at the domestic needs of women," he said. "How many of these women are in that domestic mode? I don't think very many of them are. How many of them have independent incomes? Most of them."

"But they all have that emotional anchor with one man on an ongoing, long-term basis," Jean said. "So that may be satisfying that need—that kernel. You've got that anchor: I have my family, I have my long-term emotional bond. Whether they're fooling themselves or whether it's real, it's there. They're also satisfying the cultural definition of relationship as well. If you can get approval within that, you can go do whatever you want."

"Look at the other side of it," Clark said. "Instead of asking 'why?' Ask: *Why not?* How could you explain why not?"

————

An hour later Skala, Leslie, and I took a break in the lobby and watched the swingers through the glass wall. At least half the partiers were now stripped down to fiesta underwear, or less, and were shaking their bodies, gyrating in their bare feet, kicking the night through what they perceived as the goal post.

"I might phrase where they're coming from very simply," Skala told me as we watched them from the couch.

"How's that?"

"There's a line in *Passion Play*, by Jerzy Kosinksi. The hero, Fabian, he takes his girl to a swing club. It's called Dream Exchange. She asks him something like, 'How can they do this in public? Who are they?' He gives an answer. I don't remember it exactly. Something like they're just normal people, I think. Maybe it's just as simple as that. It's always been this way for some people."

On the drive down to California the next day, I stopped off at a bookstore in Portland and found a copy of the paperback and the exact quote.

"'Who are these people?' she asked.

"'Just people, their appetites traveling without break between desire and gratification.'"

CHAPTER NINE

Loving More

We also believe there are more of us out there: people who would flourish in the lifestyle, but who haven't discovered it yet.... *Perhaps you are one of us?*

RYAM NEARING, *Loving More:*
The Polyfidelity Primer

Audrey and her two spouses, Lewis and Mitch, climbed onto stools and invited the hundred men and women sitting on the floor to share their "saga in polyfidelity." As I'd heard stated and restated in a variety of tribal drum sessions and seminars over the past three days, polyfidelity is a term used by idealistic lifestylers to describe "a new relationship form." It means exactly what it says: polyfidelitists are faithful to many. Like swingers, they make love with more than one partner, but, unlike swingers, they have more than one partner to whom they are faithful. This weekend marked the tenth annual gathering of these polyamorous folks, and it was held in Harbin Hot Springs resort, a "sacred healing place" in the dry mountains above the Napa-Sonoma wine valleys. The conference was called, definitively, "Loving More."

"We are a work in progress," Audrey, a corporate lawyer, explained, meaning that she, her legal husband Lewis, and her co-husband Mitch were in the process of getting some of their approved lovers to move in with them—which is what most of the people here were up to as well. In fact, the redwood walls of the rustic meeting hall fluttered with letters pinned there by both veteran and neophyte poly couples announcing their aspirations for "more." As in this purple sheet with a smiling face that I noted down: "Loving Dyad Seeking to be More: We are looking to develop a close, loving, committed polyfidelitous life-long partnership with others. Talk to us!" Or this one: "We are looking for a very special man to be part of our lives and relationship. I am 23, 5'6", attractive, and manage a law office. My husband is a 35 yr. old accountant. We're both into Science Fiction fandom. Our daughter is an adorable, well-behaved five year old. Please call me at....If a man answers, COMMUNICATE. Warmly yours, Regina."

Standing by the sliding door to the patio, haloed by these winglike personal ads, was Ryam Nearing, one of the chief organizers of the conference, now bouncing her naked baby, Zeke, on her hip. The wholesome-looking Ryam had a primary spouse named Brett Hill—the confirmed father of little Zeke—plus a legal husband, another co-husband, and one co-wife. Polyfidelitists give their group marriages funky names like "Jubilee" and "Sanity Mix"; Ryam's Hawaii-based tribe was called "Syntony Family." Perhaps because it was meant to be a model for the world, the Syntony Family was considered by many polyfidelitists at the conference to be the most puritanical expression of their subculture. "In Ryam's family you really can't have sex with someone until they're in the family and they move in," Audrey had told me outside on the porch. "It's like no sex before marriage. I mean, Ryam and Brett have the poly version of Ozzie and Harriet." At the moment handsome Brett was down at the lower hot tub giving a seminar just as popular as Audrey's: "Tips on Finding Other Poly People with Locals and Online."

"Everybody's relationship is a work in progress," Audrey affirmed on her stool. "So, what we're going to be relating to you over the next two hours is our own particular experience in this lifestyle. It is not a judgment or a statement that this is the right or wrong way to do it. We hope, in turn, that you will respect that this is our way of doing things. All of us in the poly lifestyle have a lot of humility and awareness that family expansion is an organic process."

At this the whole room nodded somberly. Unlike the bawdy ambiance of that other spouse sharing convention I'd left behind last week at New Horizons, here gravity and childlike sincerity ruled the day. In terms of age the poly people were about ten years younger than the New Horizons crowd; in terms of fashion they walked around nude or wore earthy sarongs, tie-dyed T-shirts, and muslin dhotis. The fact is, no one at Loving More would have been caught dead wearing a garter belt or silk jockstrap, and whenever I'd overheard some of them loving more than one, it was through the flap of a tepee where inside they were calling spiritual words to their partners such as you would never hear in Miss Daisy's Academy: "Thou art God! Oh my love, you are God to me!"

They also quoted their favorite author a lot. For instance:

"As Heinlein said, 'The more you love, the more you can love,'" Audrey's husband Lewis, a forensics expert, interjected. "I was always a big Heinlein fan. Is there anyone here who isn't?" he laughed, knowing there wasn't. Robert Heinlein wrote the 1961 science-fiction bible of the poly people, *Stranger in a Strange Land*, which took the viewpoint of a newly arrived Martian to make the case that sexual competition and sexual jealousy were the ultimate causes of the wars, murder, and mayhem on Earth. To solve the world's problems, the novel's alien protagonist, Valentine Michael Smith, establishes the Church of All Worlds and teaches his followers to open their marriages and say "Thou Art God" when they make guiltless love in groups on the grounds of his idealistic commune. Not unexpectedly, the media declare the communards detrimental and dangerous and Smith is physically torn to pieces by a mob of Christians storming his free-love paradise.

"I have all kinds of things from Heinlein posted on my wall," Lewis said. "'There's no limit to how many people you can love.' 'If there was enough time, you could love the vast majority.' That's why this type of marital structure has always made complete sense to me."

"I am very deeply in love," Mitch, a computer consultant, affirmed, taking the hands of his spouses. "I have always been searching for ways to love more. Now I've found these two and I'm very happy. I'm out from the shadow."

Most everyone in the room knew what Mitch meant by that. He'd just published two articles in *Loving More* magazine —the ideological organ of the poly people—revealing that he was a refugee from San Francisco's Kerista Community. Founded in 1970, Kerista had been one of the most successful sexual-sharing communes ever to be modeled on Heinlein's utopian vision, with dozens of adults involved in an open group marriage and various business enterprises that had grown to produce communally shared revenues of eighteen million dollars. Yet Mitch had described how, by 1991, the money had disappeared in bad business moves, and Kerista had "turned into a cesspool of insensitivity, megalomania, debauchery, and childishness." His most disheartening conclusion was that even at the best of times during the twenty-one-year existence of Kerista, the worst had never been absent. I'd read Mitch's "Dark Side to Community" that morning over a breakfast of scrambled tofu and granola, and I realized that, like many swingers, polyfidelitists can cut short the incipient snarkiness of outsiders when they admit to being aware that every one of their brightly lit dreams has, as Mitch said, its "shadow" side. They seemed flaky, but only at a quick glance —in the manner that a peek into the New Horizons Annex could leave you with the impression that swingers were anarchic and uncivilized.

"Okay, it's early, so to change the energy and increase the spirit of fun before we get started," Audrey said, "I'd like everybody to stand up. We would like our friend Marguerite, who I've discovered loves to sing, to help us do a fun little song that kind of embodies some of the philosophy that's helped us. We're going to start doing it, and you just kind of 'monkey-see-monkey-do.'"

A dark-haired woman in a flowing muslin dress and plastic

sandals walked to the front of the room. "I sing this song with children, so I'd like to invite all of your inner children here to participate fully, including the hand motions," said Marguerite. "It's fun. Actually, it can be as deep as you want. Some of you know this song. It's called 'The Magic Penny.' It's really about this: The more love you give away, the more you get! We're going to do the little children's hand motions so that you can practice giving more love away and getting more love back. You can really get into it by actually giving away love to the individuals around you in the room. Ready?"

"Ready!" everyone shouted, eager as six-year-olds.

"Okay, here we go."

> *Love is something if you give it away*
> *Give it away, give it away*
> *Love is something if you give it away*
> *You end up having more*
> *It's just like a magic penny*
> *Hold it tight and you won't have any.*

At the end of this song everyone hugged the polys in full circumference around them. I offered hugs to the non-poly Texans Dr. Jean Henry and Clark Ross, then found myself in the arms of a ruggedly handsome old man named Lloyd, whom I held onto because I really liked him. Back in 1971, when most swing clubs were still living-room affairs, Lloyd had been on the executive committee of Sandstone Ranch, the encounter-group oriented "love community" in Topanga Canyon, whose members included individuals of such stature as Max Lerner, the syndicated left-wing columnist; Betty Dodson and Sally Binford, the pioneering pro-sex feminists; Daniel Ellesberg, who'd leaked the Pentagon Papers to the *New York Times*; Alex Comfort, author of *The Joy of Sex*; and Edward Brecher. Lloyd had kept the sexually politicized spirit of those swinging days alive in his heart, as I'd found out the very first hour of this conference when he stood up before the two hundred assembled polyfidelitists and said: "At the end of World War II, America invented the nuclear bomb and the nuclear family. The nuclear family is more dangerous!"

Now, after several encounter sessions in which we'd sat beside each other relating our "personal myths," Lloyd said to me, "Brother, I know you'll be gentle and loving to this lifestyle. You don't have to see us as we see ourselves, but you have to *hear* us. We are only trying to expand the narrow passage through which the race can't fit anymore."

Poly people really talk like that.

———

To get a handle on how the day-to-day lifestyle of spouse-sharing polyfidelitists differs from that other "lifestyle" led by playcouples, you have to understand the bottom-line distinction between "utopian swingers" and "recreational swingers." As defined by sociologists like Edgar Butler, poly people are to recreational swingers as, say, Trotskyites are to liberal democrats. They are radical theoreticians who believe the lifestyle is much more about changing the world than it is modifying a single marriage. "Recreational swingers have no great overt revolutionary feeling that the establishment needs to be overthrown," Butler wrote. "They violate norms but nevertheless accept them as being legitimate. However, utopian swingers are nonconformists who publicize opposition to societal norms and [make] attempts to change them." They "advocate some form of group marriage or communal life, an idea rejected by almost all swingers."

Frank Lomas pointed out for us the conservative desire of swingers for their own bathrooms, and in this they are historically congruent with mainstream swingers since World War II.

Most of them have grown from the rows first sown by that suburban Johnny Appleseed, the traveling salesman Leidy, who promoted recreational sex within a primary pair-bond. Although many utopian swingers like Lloyd started out as recreational swingers—and still cross the line on occasion—we can trace their more serious approach to multipartner sex to a different source, the free-love communes of the nineteenth century, in particular the Oneida commune in New York.

Founded in 1848 and lasting for thirty years, the Oneida commune's utopian premise was stated by its leader, the radical Christian preacher John Humphrey Noyes: "In the Kingdom of Heaven the institution of marriage which assigns the exclusive possession of one woman to one man does not exist, for in the resurrection they neither marry nor are given in marriage but are as the Angels of God in Heaven." Noyes specifically applied that premise to the sexual relations of the three hundred men and women at Oneida, who all accepted his idiosyncratic religion, called "Bible Communism," which held that since divine love was non-possessive, possessive love was the original sin. At Oneida, therefore, romantic love was viewed as a sinful emotion—entailing as it did a feeling of we-two-and-not-you—and monogamous marriage was an evil institution based on economic selfishness—we-four-and-no-more. In order to live in "universal love," the communards practiced "complex marriage" in a huge brick mansion, where everyone had sex (though not group sex) with everyone else. In an odd reversal of sinful behavior, however, the proscription against feeling exclusive love for one's sexual partner was constantly violated by the communards.

For all its frailties and faults, Oneida was a financial success, and it lasted until the law took a dim view of what was going on in the mansion. In 1879 Noyes was declared a public enemy by the locals and fled to Canada under threats of prosecution. After this the complex marriage of the religious commune, already teetering, collapsed completely. But the secular dream of universal love and sexual sharing lived on among nonreligious anarchists, sex radicals, and communists, who carried it through the Depression and the war in their bohemian lairs. From this emerged a subculture in the late forties and early fifties whose cool adherants believed in beatitude, partner swapping, and social revolution: the beatniks.

These were the modern archetypes of the poly people—the first of the New Agers who would discard Christianity almost entirely in favor of wistful interpretations of Buddhism, Taoism, and native traditions. Made famous by Jack Kerouac in novels like *The Dharma Bums*, the beats were hairy intellectual types, and they all viewed the North American supermarket world as needing a radical shake-up. Sex was satori, and the capitalist monolith that promoted monogamy was, to the beats, hard, aggressive, militaristic, and, in an odd way, atheistic. To make love in groups was to help bring down the system by undermining the conventions that controlled and regulated human sexuality.

Being pleasure oriented, the swinging rebels occasionally visited the parties thrown by the *MR.*-inspired swinger magazines, but by the early sixties you could tell by the dress and talk of the couples in attendance that some just wanted to sexually share within their traditional marriage, and some wanted to show that sexual sharing was an act of revolutionary love. Heinlein had recently published *Stranger in a Strange Land,* and its proposition "Martians don't own *anything*" struck a tremendous chord among the beats. No one knows for certain who formalized the utopian faction of swinging by inventing the term "polyamorism," but it seems to have entered the vernacular of some whole-earth hippies during the "love-in" era of the late sixties, and, by virtue of the "ism" suffix, it declared that multipartner sex was a distinctive doctrine, an ideal with a goal, as opposed to just a swinging sex practice. The goal of

threesomes and foursomes became Peace on Earth. Make Love
not War.

Technically, "recreational swingers" practiced a bona fide
form of polyamorism, but because playcouples were strictly
bourgeois in their value structure, most polyamorists did not
consider themselves swingers. Today polyamorists would
group-gestalt you into a corner if you labeled them swingers
without qualification. They are "in the lifestyle," and use those
words all the time, but polyamory is an ideology—"loving
more than one"—with the emphasis on the word "loving."
They have departed from Noyes in their belief that you can
sexually, spiritually, *and* romantically love more than one.

Polyfidelity takes the polyamorist lifestyle one ideological
step further, actually, back in the direction of Oneida but
without the Christian predicate. The term polyfidelity was
invented by the secular Kerista commune in the eighties to
describe the most politically mature form of polyamorism,
which Mitch described in *Loving More* magazine as including
"group marriage, shared parenting, total economic sharing,
a group growth process, and a utopian plan for improving
life around the world [by] community living." In the case of
Kerista, polyfidelity also involved a lot of group sex among the
generally bohemian-looking communards, who formed group
marriages, dissolved them, formed new ones with different
partners, and then merged to "encompass all but two people
in the community." Yet because Mitch "genuinely loved" his
lovers, "all [his] familial relationships were indeed primary
and equal," and, therefore, the "experience was in keeping
with [the commune's] strict polyfidelitous ideology."

Strict communitarianism is still pretty much what polyfidelity means to its adherents—which explains a lot of the
millennial seriousness you encounter at poly conferences:
utopians consider their poly-swinging lifestyle as a beacon on
the hill to the rest of humanity. They might be pleased that

millions of bourgeois swingers have derived a system of rules that enable them to transcend societal norms and affectionately make love with others without jealousy—something their hero, Heinlein, would have approved of as a step in the right utopian direction—but they are highly critical of swingers who feel there is no need to complicate things by falling in love with their lovers and sharing bank accounts. Look at us, they seem to say: we go the whole hog, romantically loving many spouses, pooling our resources, and moving in together on our inner-city communes and truck farms in the country.

Given the sorts of difficulties you'd expect in living a poly-fidelitous life, it is not surprising that there are only about one-tenth as many utopian as recreational swingers. Drawn on a chart with circles and double-headed arrows criss-crossed and connected, group marriage resembles something like a compli-cated football play that must be executed every day—not just at parties. "A third person triples the number of relationships to be fulfilled and maintained compared with what a couple has," Butler wrote, "and a fourth partner brings the number up to twelve. Love, trust, and communication are reciprocal behaviors that must thus be expended in a number of different relationships." In California, the median life span of a tradi-tional dyadic marriage is five years; only 7 percent of group marriages last that long.

Yet the very heroic complexity of poly life makes it an alluring ideal. Today polys have as many centers of family intimacy in North America as swingers have clubs. On Gabriola Island in British Columbia, in Jackson Hole, Wyoming, in San Francisco, New York, Toronto, Denver, and other centers of New Age awareness, polys gather around real or symbolic campfires, beat drums, meditate, and discuss shamanism, "the new sexuality," goddesses and gods, matri-archy, ethnobotany, "reclaiming history," pagan rituals, and white witchcraft. When recreational swingers attend their gatherings—as they are often invited to do in advertisements placed in swing publications—they find the language of polys to be eerily different from their own. Poly talk is ecstatic in metaphor, often Martian, part of the dialect established by Valentine Smith's Church of All Worlds, to which a thousand polys belong. When poly people make love they "blend" and "quicken eggs" and "share water." When they appreciate what you are saying they "resonate" your words and "grok" your soul. They refer to their families as "nests" and their parties as "intimate networking."

The fact is, polys are making some headway into that supposedly "other" lifestyle of playcouples. Polyfidelity lecturers regularly make the swing-convention circuit, proselytizing their views to couples whom they feel are already partway there, and whom they urge to sit down after a night at the club and discuss ways to extend their erotic play to true love. Stan Dale, head of California's Human Awareness Institute and a founder of the Loving More conference, was the keynote speaker at the Lifestyles Organization's 1993 convention. As mentioned, Dr. Deborah Anapol, one of the founders of *Loving More* magazine, often lectures at Lifestyles conventions. As does Dave Hutchison, head of the Liberated Christians, which embraces swinging as the first step straights might consider taking on the road to poly commitment. Bob Miller and Carol Roberts, who attended the convention at New Horizons, are board members of the polyfidelitist organization Family Synergy; they, too, lecture at Lifestyles conventions, trying to pull the two movements together. "Some of our members are 'evolved swingers,'" states their brochure, "attracted to Family Synergy because of its focus on deeper relationships." Indeed, on page one of every issue of *Loving More* its editors, Ryam Nearing and Brett Hill, espouse the poly "ecology of love" mission statement that you'll find stacked in piles at the literature tables of Lifestyles conventions. "We affirm that loving more than one can be a natural expression of health, exuberance, joy and intimacy," the poly leaders write. "We view the shift from enforced monogamy and nuclear families to polyamory and intentional families or tribes in the context of a larger shift toward a more balanced, peaceful and sustainable way of life."

Straights coming across such sentiments in poly literature beside the cash register at their local New Age bookstore might suspect that the poly movement has a distinctly "feminine," if not feminist, feel to it. That's the case across the board. Of the seventeen contributing writers in *Loving More*'s summer issue, eleven were women. The emphasis in all the articles was on love and relationships, personal growth and relating, self-awareness, and intimacy through "family expansion." *Loving More*'s logo features three hearts in a row running perpendicular to the tagline "New Models for Relationships" (in contrast to the bitten apple of the North American Swing Club Association).

And that brings us to one other important feature of the poly people. If there are questions as to whether women "drive" the swinging lifestyle, there should be fewer questions about who runs the poly movement. Women seem to. It was women, Butler wrote, who "tended to put talk into action... developing a real, multifaceted relationship that evolved into a group marriage."

When you attend their rites you find that many poly women reach back beyond their "science fiction fandom," their beat and love-commune heritages, and see themselves as descended from prehistoric "copartnership societies," in which women may either have ruled or lived as full equals to men. There was certainly one thing you couldn't help noticing at the Loving More seminars, from the opening talk to the closing ceremonies. Many of the poly leaders were high-level female professionals in the straight world, and many of their expanded families were polyandrous—that is, the husbands outnumbered the wives. In most of these group marriages, the women had activated the expansion.

———

Take Ryam, for instance. She literally wrote the book on polyfidelity: *Loving More: The Polyfidelity Primer.* The day before the lecture by Audrey, Lewis, and Mitch, I'd sat with Ryam and six-month-old Zeke by the hot-spring pool, just after she had conducted her ninety-minute "Women's Circle."

Ryam is a conservative lady. It was a hundred degrees in the eucalyptus shade, but she was covered neck to sandaled feet in a bib dress. She had plain brown hair, a bright, healthy face that never sees makeup, and the strong, sure hands of a new mother. In that summer's issue of *Loving More* she'd printed a proud family picture of Barry, Allan, Brett, herself, and Ruth sitting demurely at a picnic. They were all around age forty and the men looked as straight as preachers. Brett had his hands on Ryam's shoulders, Barry had his hands on Ruth's, Ryam and Ruth were holding hands, and Allan—in the middle— had his hands on his thighs. "For many people, their first area of interest in polyfidelity is the 'sex part,'" Ryam had stated in her *Primer.* "Can it be a healthy desire and ecstatic experience to be physically and emotionally intimate with more than one person at a time? Can you experience the feelings of special-ness, passion, and in-loveness with more than one? Based upon the direct experiences of many people, the answer is 'Yes, of course!'"

"A lot of people in this movement—especially women— say, 'Okay, well, I've always been this open, loving person,'" Ryam explained to me, hoisting the squirming Zeke to her shoulder. "They know that about themselves from early on. But, as with me, I didn't really have the words for it, I didn't know there were other people doing it. There's something about being more open in the way you view relationships that's almost never talked about in polite society. Like I say in my book, it's usually portrayed as illicit, insane, or illegal, and always temporary. But cheating is okay so long as no one finds out."

I asked her if she'd found herself drawn to having more than one husband from childhood, as a sort of sexual orientation.

"I think there are a lot of people," she replied, "not so much that they are 'drawn' to it, but that they have a tendency that way, and suddenly they meet a couple who give them words for it, introduce them to other people doing it. For me it was in the late seventies with my husband Barry; it was sort of like, 'Oh, I've discovered I'm poly!' I finally came to that realization. So we had an open marriage for a few years, but we found it wasn't quite what we were looking for. We wanted something more stable and with bigger roots for a family. So at the time I was in love with Allan, and we brought him in and we were in a polyfidelity triad for thirteen years. Three years ago, Brett entered the picture. I got into a loving relationship with him and we went from being a polyfidelity triad to being a family of four."

"You and three men."

"That's right. And a year and a half ago, my legal husband Barry met Ruth and she joined—so that's all of us who live together now. I think it's not people *becoming* poly, it's sort of like a blossoming; everything was already there, but now they know. It's a realization kind of a thing."

"So then it's not just another orientation?" I asked.

"Well, I think all humans are poly. I don't think humans are biologically monogamous. I suppose, if you're talking about orientation, it's the orientation to go against the grain and be natural about it. It's the orientation to be who you are naturally. Why not? It's natural to love many brothers and sisters and cousins. It's natural to love lovers."

"Jealousy's natural too," I said.

"Oh yes, of course, but there's a word we use, 'compersion,' it's the opposite of sexual jealousy—it's where you have positive feelings when you see your loved ones enjoying their relationship with each other. Poly people had to invent that word because they invented the relationship in which it came to be."

I pondered the significance of that for a moment. There really was no word in English, or in any other language for that matter, to describe that "warm emotion" Ryam experienced watching Barry happily in love with Ruth. Could it be because no one in the history of humanity had ever felt such an emotion, and so it had remained unnamed? Would it ever enter the language as a "natural" feeling that was experienced often enough to need a word to describe it? Throughout her book, Ryam had stressed that "polyfidelity is a *new* marriage form." It was biologically normal, she said, but it was not based on economics or religion or the dominance of one sex over the other, as other forms of monogamous or polygamous marriage had been in the past. "Instead," she wrote, "polyfidelity is based on individual choice...an egalitarian family that comes together voluntarily....A new form for a new millennium, polyfidelity is in its infancy at this very moment. It encompasses the highest evolution of the sound ideals of individual choice, voluntary co-operation, a healthy family life, and positive romantic love. It embraces sexual equality, a nonpossession orientation towards relationships, and a widening circle of spousal intimacy and true love."

"What did you talk about at the Women's Circle?" I asked.

"Well, a lot of people said they were intellectually and emotionally poly for a long time, but the direct experience of it brought up all kinds of negative feelings they'd never been raised as children to deal with—not with the fairy tales we read. And we talked about how the only way through it is to live it, to work with it. There are ways to make it easier, and we shared techniques and ways of looking at the world from this fresh perspective with each other. And we gave each other support that we're not crazy because we live this way. These are our natural instincts; the natural instinct is to love more than one person. We as women know this about ourselves. So what we've found in this lifestyle is a very attractive arrangement to feel close and warm. When it's working it's a very high, loving way to live."

"So you have to invent new fairy tales to tell little girls?"

"That's right—nonmonogamous fairy tales," she said, smiling, kissing Zeke.

I pictured one of those fairy tales. Sleeping Beauty, Cinderella, Prince Charming, Tarzan, and Aladdin all in one poly house.

The poly world would probably say that without compersion you couldn't get them to live happily ever after.

———

While waiting for the start of a Human Awareness Institute seminar called "Opening to Intimacy: Authentic Connecting," I thought about a basic poly belief that employed a metaphor from *Stranger in a Strange Land* to encapsulate their lifestyle: unless the world learned to "share water," we were doomed. Sharing water is the central allegorical rite of the Church of All Worlds, derived from the brotherly ritual of Heinlein's Martians, brought to earth by Valentine Michael Smith from a desert planet where water was in such scarce supply that, rather than fighting over it, the aliens made apportioning it a daily act of loving communion among all beings. Literary snobs scoff at the sci-fi symbolism of Heinlein, but nobody can deny that, writing in 1961, he was decades ahead of evolutionary psychologists in his central theme that men have fought wars since the beginning of time because they couldn't share women.

A brief retelling of *Stranger in a Strange Land* helps clarify this poly-mix of metaphors so crucial to utopian lifestylers. Valentine Michael Smith (whose first name should not be lost on you) was an orphaned Earthling born on Mars and raised by Martians. Some decades after World War III, a pod of the four smartest and most worthily monogamous couples on Earth were sent on the spaceship *Envoy* to colonize the red planet, and were not heard from again. The Earthlings met a fate very similar to that which befell the mutinous crew of the *Bounty* in 1789: fifteen men left Tahiti with twelve women and landed on the isolated Pitcairn Island. When the group were discovered years later, only one male was left alive: within a short time they had murdered each other over the women. In the case of the Earthlings on the *Envoy*, after Valentine's birth his mother and her lover were murdered by her husband, who then killed himself. We are led to believe the others were murdered as well.

Interestingly, Heinlein's native Martians were immune to fighting over sex because they were all born female and then matured into males. They were also advanced enough to be in almost continuous touch with God through a super-mundane, LSD-like experience of total understanding they called "grokking." The Martians raised Valentine with the knowledge of grokking but with no knowledge of sexual jealousy. That was the way he was delivered into the hands of a rescue party from Earth when he was in his twenties. Christlike, sexually innocent, he winds up on the estate of a famous writer named Jubal, who is surrounded by female secretaries. Valentine begins to teach them all the ritual of sharing water, which immediately becomes synonymous with sharing sex, the hoarded commodity that had led to war on the *Envoy*. After grokking every bit of intellectual book knowledge on earth, Valentine, like a latter-day Siddhartha with the last name of an Everyman (Smith), decides to learn what the real world is about. He and his lover Jill eventually wind up in Las Vegas, where Jill gets a job as a stripper. Though ridiculous, this is a crucial juncture in the story, at least as far as understanding both wings of the lifestyle in North America. Remember the excitement of husbands at watching their wives with other men in the Annex? Remember the joy women took in being the glamorous objects of men's attention and their thrilling "urge to help" when their husbands engaged other women? It's all here in Heinlein's book—exquisitely heightened because Valentine, whom everyone now calls Mike, is telepathic, and he can at one and the same time read the thoughts of the men in the audience, project them to Jill, and invite her into his mind so she can perceive his arousal at the other women stripping on stage with her.

The poly people eventually gave a name to that sensation: erotic compersion.

"She posed, and talked with Mike in her mind.... '*Look where I am looking, my brother. The small one. He quivers. He thirsts for me.*'

"'*I grok his thirst.... We grok him together*,' Mike agreed. '*Great thirst for Little Brother....*'

"Suddenly she was seeing herself through strange eyes and feeling all the primitive need with which that stranger saw her.... But she was amazed to find that her excitement increased as she looked through Mike's eyes at other girls."

After this encounter, Mike begins to broadcast his philosophy among humans, founding the Church of all Worlds, based on the philosophy of loving more in groups amid ritually shared water in warm tubs—the first mention of hot-tub sex in America. Nests of Mike's church begin sprouting up all around the world, but when the media does their job on the swinging man from Mars, the righteous world reacts. Cheered on by reporters, they mob the gates of his commune screaming "*Blasphemer!*" Stoned, beaten, and impaled, Mike tells humanity with his dying breath, "The Truth is simple but the Way of Man is hard.... Thou art God. Know that and the Way is open."

Contemporary context is everything here. The year 1961 was the height of the Cold War: the nuclear doomsday clock was set at a couple of seconds before midnight and the equivalent of a million Hiroshima bombs were locked and loaded and on hair-trigger firing orders. How did we get ourselves into that fix?

For Heinlein the core problem was not the biological truth of our sexually competitive nature but our inability to transcend that nature through sharing. "All human behavior, all human motivations, all man's hopes and fears, were colored and controlled by mankind's tragic and oddly beautiful pattern of reproduction." The tragic part of the story for Heinlein was that whenever humans made beautiful love, they immediately wanted to possess the body they loved—even if it meant killing the body and all the competitors who wanted it also. Everything men did—from earning wages to becoming rulers and setting out to conquer the world—seemed to be done with an eye to getting and possessing sex partners. Everything women did, from dressing provocatively to damaging a rival's reputation through a clever slur, seemed to be motivated by their desire to attract a man to "quicken eggs" and make sure the family's wealth stayed at home—even if that wealth was excessive and people went hungry elsewhere. *Stranger in a Strange Land* argues, as do poly people, that if nuclear bombs are ever used in an all-out war it will be because of the dog-eat-dog dynamic of sexual competition. In this Heinlein and the poly people have considerable backing from evolutionary theorists.

Trace the history of war through the centuries from the Trojan War onward and you will find that "as for motives, sex is dominant," as Matt Ridley wrote in *The Red Queen*. The first war recorded, in Homer's *Iliad*, began with the abduction of a beauteous woman, Helen. If territory, resources, and power were gained by men in war, it made the victors more attractive to mates and eliminated rivals in the process. In both preliterate societies and our own, men compete to accrue and display resources to attract partners and, once mated, husbands and wives join hands to gather and profligately use even more resources to promote the welfare of children born within their dyadic relationship. To scientists, there seems to be no way out of this Darwinian dilemma: productive and destructive, it is the *causa movens* of all action. "There is now overwhelming evidence that there is no other way for evolution to work except by competitive reproduction," according to Ridley. The free will of which we humans are so proud is just another mechanism "to satisfy ambition, to compete with fellow human beings... and so eventually to be in a better position to reproduce and rear children than human beings who do not reproduce."

Polyfidelitists, on the other hand, really believe that there is a way to rewrite this unforgiving script. Why not, like Valentine Smith, teach men and women ways to share sexual and emotional love within an "expanded" family that does not cramp the ability of people to love each other "more." Wouldn't that take the edge off at least one cause of our woes?

In this the poly people are not as far as they believe from the thinking of playcouples—who merely don't make a big deal about proselytizing the truths they personally perceive. When asked, however, they tend to offer the Loving More philosophy in earthy terms. As the Lifestyles Organization's director of publicity, Steve Mason, told the *Los Angeles Times* in 1998: "We've often thought that the best way to solve all the world's problems is to turn the United Nations into a swingers' organization. How do you drop a bomb onto people that you've just had an orgasm with?"

Yet polyfidelitists are more impatient than the merry Mason, who feels sexual sharing at clubs, parties, and conventions is progressive enough for most people. Like other millennial thinkers, however, polys believe we are at a crucial juncture in evolution and that something *more* must be done *now*, before desperate conditions born of sexual competition destroy us. Ryam Nearing concluded her book with a ringing one-page testament called "Polyfidelity and Saving Humans," in which she challenged people to break out of the "divide and conquer nightmare" of isolated family living. "We can cocoon into our homes and approach the next millennium as insulated as possible from the dark ages mentality that we'd hoped was dead and buried but now appears to be resurrecting.... *Or we can stand as expressions of choice, of creativity, of psycho-spiritual exploration.* ... Polyfidelity is one part of the answer. It is one part of the potentially positive future we can envision. *It is one part of the dream that we can live now, continuing to develop it as we go along, and always sharing it with others who may be looking for love, belonging and a mission.* In the interest of human potential and on-going evolution, let the strength of social diversity of which we are a part, prevail."

Phrased that way, it sounds like a millennial dream—and only a dream. But polys actually train people in fulfilling that dream. They teach people techniques for overcoming instincts and living in a house with those they might rather put a kitchen knife into, never mind feel compersion for. "Before people can successfully live in a group marriage," Butler wrote, "they must learn the things that one learns in an encounter group; they must value intimacy and know how to encounter people in an intense situation, with person-to-person interaction that is disarmed and open."

About an hour after my talk with Ryam, Chip August, a senior facilitator at Stan Dale's Human Awareness Institute, pressed a button on a boom box and the kind of music that swells during the cathartic parts of a tearjerker movie filled the main meeting room of Harbin Hot Springs. Eighty naked people sat on the rug with their legs wrapped around the waist of a person they had never touched before today—and didn't like much either. They had all followed Chip's instructions to mill about the room and purposely search out a partner they had been "avoiding," "were angry at," or "somehow would *never* choose for a partner." Amazingly, within a minute they had all zeroed in on a target. Even in a crowd of polys it seemed that people could instantly identify a person who after two days on a life raft they would probably beg God to be delivered from. They had then taken a minute to explain to their partner why they had bestowed this backhanded compliment on them. It was a gestalt exercise known as "truthing."

"I chose you because you reminded me of my first husband."

"I chose you because you kind of cut in front of me in line during breakfast."

"Now," said Chip, when they were done, "reach your hands out and lovingly begin to stroke your partner's face. And as you do so I invite you to ponder this: what happens if you open your heart to this person and say 'I love you'?"

In the musical seconds that followed, hands reached out like branches from a forest of peeled human souls, and the image looked to me to be a potential cover for *Loving More* magazine. The words "I love you" were whispered throughout the room.

Chip, a mountainously large man, beamed like the Buddha he sort of nakedly resembled. Halfway through this ninety-minute workshop, the personal growth of the attendees seemed to be heading them right down the path to the seminar's promised goal of having them live perpetually beneath a "shower of love drops." "I want to suggest to you that you can live in love," Chip had stated when all had first taken their clothes off. "Whenever I present to people the option of living constantly in love they say, 'Oh my God, that's a dream, you can't feel that way moment to moment, I would have to quit my job.' I want to suggest to you that it is possible, and that in this next hour and a half of space you can feel it is possible. Everything we're going to do here is about living at choice. Loving others is not a function of them, it's a function of you."

Before you heap laughter, scorn, and ridicule on what could too easily be dismissed as New Age nonsense, "I invite you to consider the possibilities," as Stan Dale often said at his HAI gatherings. Seven months before, Dale had taken a toned-down version of his "authentic connecting" workshop to the People's Republic of China, where he was a national hit from Beijing to Guangzhou. He was interviewed by the head of China TV for an hour and a half, speaking to hundreds of millions on "love and intimacy, sexuality and relationships." After presenting his HAI workshop at Shandong University, he was awarded an honorary professorship. If we consider the mission statement of HAI, "Creating a World where Everyone Wins," and the subversive possibilities of millions of people expressing themselves with sexual freedom in a national structure where they don't even have the right to open their mouths about "alternative lifestyles" for Tibetans, it is a miracle Dale and seventy of his acolytes were invited back the following September to whistle-stop their workshops from Shanghai to Beijing. Chinese elites with some real influence in government have actually sat down on the carpet, stared into each other's eyes, and touched each other's faces. "Tell me why I am crying," the head of China TV had asked Dale, tears pouring down his cheeks. In the past thirty years, forty thousand people have gone though HAI's weekend retreats, and most of them have emerged swearing it could teach backbiters and butt kissers to "love more" in their workaday lives. According to the HAI brochures, rituals such as the one that was taking place before me promoted "personal growth and social evolution, replacing ignorance and fear with awareness and love." In the years before the Soviet Union collapsed, Dale was over there on three occasions giving his seminars to glasnost-leaning bureaucrats and academics. "Consider the possibilities."

"You may notice there are tears in that face before you," Chip said, and, indeed, some were now crying. "With your partner's permission, stroke their hair. You are stroking God. Notice what happens when you take a breath. Open your heart. Think the thought: I love you. Touch your partner's hair lightly. I invite you to realize that ten million years of evolution have brought you both to this point. You don't have to believe in the concept of evolution to believe that all of our lives have a starting point, and they have led to this moment—now—and I am stroking this being before me. A perfect God-being. Ask: If not now—when? If not here—where?"

He told everyone to stare into each other's eyes without looking away. "Many of us live our lives as if we are traveling in an elevator. When we feel it is our floor, we get off and say good-bye to the other people. But we can stay in the elevator and take that journey upward."

A gorgeous young woman of perhaps twenty-five with a God's eye painted on her cheek, who was sitting with a loudmouth in his fifties, one of the few cigarette smokers at the conference, called aloud, "Oh yes!" It wasn't sexual. She was expressing some emotion she felt at grokking someone she probably perceived as an arrogant, unhealthy, overage womanizer, the one she had chosen for a partner because she disliked everything about him.

"Now, partner number one, cup your partner's face in your hands," Chip said. "Can you see the soul in that person's face? Give your partner little baby kisses all over their face."

All kissed their partners, smiling blissfully.

"Now, partner number two," Chip said, "give sweet-daddy-and-mommy-kisses. This isn't about turning someone on. Tell them, 'I love you, Little John.'"

The room was filled with softly murmured "I love yous."

"Feel the love."

Beat. Music rising.

"Now, both of you kiss at once."

Sitting on my stool beholding this amazing sight, I tried to picture backstabbing Communists from the faculty of Shandong University and the bureaucracy of China TV following these instructions, choosing their worst enemy and giving them sweet-daddy-and-mommy-kisses. I had to consider the possibilities: maybe one of them would have some restraining influence over starting a nuclear war because of Taiwan. No wonder an organization called the Ethical Humanists had once elected Stan Dale "Humanitarian of the Year"; no wonder he was one of the world's thirteen recipients of the Mahatma Gandhi Peace Medallion.

I had interviewed Dale just before I'd driven up to Harbin. He lived in the clean, airy California town of Belmont, south of San Francisco. On his wall was a drawing of Gandhi given him by a lifer at San Quentin prison. On another wall was a computer drawing of two nude airborne lovers embracing—with the man's erect penis coming into view after a few seconds of staring. On the mirrored table was a Japanese sculpture of a Nō dancer—a male dressed as a female—called "Looking For Her Soul in the Mirror of Her Face."

Stan was about seventy, with two spouses—Helen, whom he'd been married to for thirty-nine years, and Janet, who'd been living with the Dales for two decades. He had the vandyke beard and arched brows of the sixties "guru" Allan

Watts, whom he distinctly resembled. He received his training in Japan during the Korean War—not from a Zen master, but from the aged female head of a geisha house, at which he lived for seven months. The geisha gave him a stone and told him to discover the beauty of the universe in it. When he found it there three days later in a moment of satori, she offered him an adage to live by for the rest of his life: "If God wanted to hide, He would hide in human beings, because that's the last place you would think to look."

"I learned reverence in the geisha house for all people and all things," Dale told me in his sonorous, almost hypnotic voice. It was the very voice that played the Shadow on radio in the 1940s, and then narrated the *Green Hornet* and *Sgt. Preston of the Yukon*. Later, in the sixties, Dale was the host of the first phone-in radio show, in which a burdened public called in to talk about love, relationships, work, and sex. It was just an idea that had occurred to Stan one night in 1968, at WCFL-Radio in Chicago, when he was "Stan, the All-Night Record Man": Why not open up the phone lines across the nation and let people talk? Within a couple of days he was averaging a hundred thousand calls a night. That prompted him to hold his first "Love, Intimacy, and Sexuality" seminar—for which he coined the term "love-in," another first—which drew a thousand people just by word of mouth. He formalized his experiential seminar into a workshop, got a doctorate from Ted McIlvenna's Institute for Advanced Study of Human Sexuality, and he was now the longest-reigning encounter-group facilitator in North America.

"What is the lifestyle, Stan?" I asked.

"The lifestyle is very simply more than two people who love each other," he replied. "Notice I use the word love, not necessarily 'have sex.' No previous words suit who and what we are. What is funny is that I support all these different labels for the lifestyle, because the lifestyle goes the full 180 degrees, and I would *like* people to be a little less sure about what it is. On the one hand, swingers." He put his hands together to his right. "On the other hand, us." He did the same with his hands on his left. "But I support swingers. We're not swingers, but I support them."

"Why does everyone hate the lifestyle? From over here," I said, putting my hands together on my right, "to over here?"

"Because early on, powerful people found that the best way they could impose their power was through sex," he said. "To make certain behaviors wrong, evil—if they could control people with it, they knew they could control the masses. It wasn't even a conscious thing. As soon as that started happening they had the power. If you're interested in procreating, and somebody said, 'Oh, there's only a certain way you're supposed to procreate,' then they've imposed their fantasy on you—which is proof of the awesome power of fantasy if there ever was one."

He emphasized this concept of fantasy because it was very important to his seminars—and he didn't mean sexual fantasies per se. Stan's main thesis was that people have to choose to replace the "fearful" fantasies of their "social" and "biological" minds.

His talk at the 1993 Lifestyles convention had dealt with that subject: it had been called "Overcoming Fearful Fantasies." Fear, in Stan Dale's *Weltanschauung*, was "the basis of all human problems" and "the most destructive power on earth." It was brought on by the anticipation of losing, which we are always on guard against, and which causes us to be ridden with anxiety and depression as we fantasize the loss. "Utopia," however, "lies just between the ears."

It was simple stuff, really; replacing the negative fantasies with positive visions, much like Olympic athletes are trained to do these days. But what was not so simple was the primitive cause of the fear: loss of a mate to a sexual competitor. We want to win at life to get and keep a mate, and if we lose at life we can lose the mate to a winner: crucial stuff to our genes' agenda—what Dale called "the procreative imperative," which he said was the source of much meanness and much love. What could we do to get rid of the meanness? We could "decide *not* to forsake all others," he wrote in a book called *Fantasies Can Set You Free.* "The marriage myth tells us that the reward for marital servitude is a special kind of devoted love that is ours alone; that essentially we *own* it, as we might hoard a casket of jewels and defend it to the death against robbers. But misers live narrow, suspicious lives, fearful and shut in behind darkened windows lest thieves discover their treasure."

"Here's the fantasy we're given," Dale told me now. "Some guy comes along and says he spoke to God and God said this is what you're supposed to do. Women you cling. Men, well, hey, God's a man, so he understands men.

"What our workshops are about is choice," he went on. "If you want to be monogamous, and *choose* to be monogamous, then be monogamous. If you want to swing, if you *choose* to swing, then swing. I happen to think there's more down both those roads—there's the knowledge that sex isn't a particular moment that begins at A and ends at B, then you go do something else in the alphabet and then you come back to A and go to B—and so on. Learn all the letters and then choose. Most people don't think they have choice. There's a billion people in China who have been told that. Somehow I've managed to convince the *powers* that be there to let me come in and tell everyone they have choice. Each moment they can choose, not because someone said they spoke to God or Mao. Choose your own fantasy. Sometimes the choice is complicated, and sometimes it's pretty funny."

"I'm really proud of Mitch and how he and I have worked through this last thing," Audrey told the crowd at her poly-fidelity seminar. She was referring to a love affair Mitch was having with a woman Audrey couldn't relate to at all. Audrey liked Mitch's other lover very much and had formed a poly women's group with her. She really liked that woman's husband, too. And then there were the two women Lewis was having affairs with. One he'd met at the Ancient Ways Neo-Pagan Festival, and she had just got married to someone else. Audrey liked her, although "that was kind of a tertiary thing." There was the question also of whether her own boyfriend could get along with Lewis; he would almost certainly be able to get along with Mitch, if not Mitch's girlfriends. "Actually, it could be a really beautiful thing to behold if they were included," she said.

"Sounds like swinging to me," Jean Henry leaned sideways and commented in my ear.

To tell the truth, after over an hour of this, I didn't know which persons Audrey was thinking of including in her triad. Although they did have a methodology for dealing with different "qualities of jealousy." There was the standard jealousy the "male primary" felt for his wife, and vice versa. Then there was the female primary's jealousy over her secondary partner for his tertiary love affairs, and the different qualities of jealousy he would cause her by becoming jealous of his girlfriends for their affairs. They also had a rotation schedule they'd worked out for sex.

I knew that bourgeois swingers would say that the way they themselves lived seemed simpler. They had one partner, they loved that partner, and they had sex with other people once in a while whom they liked and fantasized about loving. But, though it's easy enough for me to make polyfidelity into a "Who's On First?" routine, the poly people were dead serious: they wanted to change the world for the better by multipartner means. Like Dale said, it was a matter of choice.

"Okay," Audrey said, "we're going to close by having everyone stand up and form a circle, or hold hands with those around you, but a circle would be really nice. We'd like to invite you to just take in what you heard, the joys, the pain that we have felt, and hold a vision for yourself of what you'd like to take, and sing along."

All the polys held hands, forming a circumference around the room. People in long gowns, naked people, long-haired hippies, short-haired execs. Lewis hit the button on the boom box and Audrey closed her eyes and leaned her head back as everyone began to sway. "Together," Audrey shouted. "Oh yes, together."

> *Love is but the song we sing,*
> *And fear's the way we die...*
> *Come on people now*
> *Smile on your brother*
> *Everybody get together*
> *Try and love one another right now.*

One hour later I was driving down I-5 in 110-degree heat to swing central, firm in my prejudice that swingers and polys were after something similar. After all, the word "love" comes from the Sanskrit word *lubhyat*. *Lubhyat* means desires.

CHAPTER TEN

Beyond the Pleasure Principle

The lifestyle has nothing to do with overthrowing society—although that's not a bad idea.

ROBERT MCGINLEY

When I first arrived at LSO headquarters after the "Loving More" conference, Bob McGinley had predicted that the *New York Times* would be "on that line wondering what the hell has happened to society." With the success of the conventions, the growth in the number of NASCA clubs, and the wide open attempt by millions of suburbanites to combine their values and fantasies, McGinley had a sense that the lifestyle was about to be taken seriously. On the other hand, it might be taken too seriously for the likes of some.

As the whirl of activity at the Lifestyles Organization accelerated in preparation for McGinley's 1996 convention at the Town and Country resort, there were real machinations going on behind the scenes to wipe out the openly erotic lifestyle in California. It was the job of the Department of Alcoholic Beverage Control, the state's most powerful agency, to enforce regulations that prohibited "conduct involving moral turpitude" on licensed premises. The agency now believed those regulations applied to private hotel rooms as well. Under the conservative administration of Governor Pete Wilson, the aptly monikered ABC was planning to apply the letter of the law to licensed premises where swingers gathered. The government had definitely reached its trigger point with playcouples, and was about to scatter buckshot over multimillion-dollar hotels, resorts, and clubs from Sacramento to San Diego—either revoking liquor licenses or threatening to revoke them if a hotel dared to hold a gathering at which behavior "contrary to public welfare and morals" *might* take place. Eventually, during the summer of 1997, it was the *Washington Post* that called McGinley to find out what the hell was happening to society.

By then the pebble in McGinley's pocket had grown to the size of a boulder.

———————

Twelve days into my sojourn at LSO, Luis De La Cruz, the facilities director of the Los Angeles Music Society, walked in through the travel agency, waved as he passed me in the photocopy room, then turned into McGinley's glass-walled office. Luis and his wife Theresa had volunteered to curate the Lifestyles Erotic Arts Exhibition and they were responsible for making the show the largest of its kind in the world. In the past year, however, Luis had been uttering direct intellectual challenges to those in authority who were not pleased with the exhibition. Luis claimed that the real aim of the Erotic Arts show was to get people to throw off the thinking imposed upon them by political rulers and religious leaders. Not surprisingly, Luis's principled pronouncements about the political goals of sexual freedom drew the attention of the authorities, and those principles—according to a Federal judge—were what the 1996–97 war on the lifestyle was ultimately about.

"We've got two TV crews who want to cover the convention now," McGinley told Luis and me in the board room. "One's HBO and the other's German TV, so they'll both be doing something on the Erotic Arts Exhibit. I made sure I got a 'fair treatment' clause in the contracts."

"That'll actually be nice for the artists," gentle Luis said. "I don't think they'll have any problem with that."

"They'll be doing interviews with them standing beside their work. So it'll be a nice promotion for the show—and for them, and for us. All across North America and Europe."

"That's wonderful, Robert."

While they turned to arranging the moving trucks to transport this year's several hundred artworks to the Town and Country, I looked Luis over, assessing what a valuable asset he was to McGinley's plans. Although he was not a swinger, if you mentioned the swarthily handsome man to the women here at Lifestyles you would see eyebrows shoot skyward and hear sighs uttered. Luis's photogenic qualities aside, McGinley was pleased that Luis was very effective at getting the Erotic Arts Exhibit taken seriously by critics in mainstream media. Luis was a man of considerable stature in the "straight" world of painting and sculpture as director and curator of the Newport Harbor Art Museum and the Los Angeles Art Association. In the last year, that uppercrust world of "nonerotic" art had focused on Luis. In the next year I would watch the focus turn to McGinley, the convention, and swinging itself.

It had all begun eleven months earlier, when the Fifth Annual Sensual and Erotic Arts Exhibition had wrapped up at the end of the 1995 convention. Luis, Theresa, and McGinley had decided to extend the show by moving two hundred paintings, sculptures, and collages to the Desmond Gallery, located in a mall on Los Angeles's Sunset Strip that contained such fashionable outlets as the Virgin Megastore. Following its high-society wine-and-cheese opening, the show was to have had a one-month run; McGinley even hired a guard to prevent kids from wandering in and beholding, say, a painterly rendition of group sex, or some sculpture of a woman riding a terra cotta phallus as big as she was (the latter the work of Lee Thomas, a former novice in a convent). But the mall's owners, 8000 Sunset Ltd, which had approved the show, shut it down three days later, citing their right to protect the mall's image.

Luis and McGinley gave some interviews to Los Angeles reporters, and then *Penthouse* magazine got excited over the censorship issue and featured an eleven-page story on the show (amply illustrated, of course) for its 1.1 million subscribers—which caused a laughable irony for Canadian readers. Those north of the border who flipped through *Penthouse*'s January 1996 issue would have discovered that this article on the censorship of erotic art was itself censored by the Canadian authorities. Three-quarters of a computer painting depicting a loosely roped woman frolicking with disembodied penises in a desert canyon was blacked out. "Art liberates," De La Cruz explained in *Penthouse*. "It's also a catalyst to other thinking.... And that's exactly what medieval kings and priests wanted to stop —free thinking—and the way they did that was to oppress sexuality, amongst other things."

The point was, said *Penthouse*'s writer, Susan Reifer, explaining Luis's philosophy, that where sexually free art goes, people follow. "When erotic art, which originates in the hidden recesses of an artist's imagination, is released to the public, a chain reaction begins," she wrote. "The viewer who recognizes his or her secret—his or her fantasy brought to life on the walls of a gallery—may begin to think more freely about sexuality, as well as art. The artist whose work is heralded in the light of day may begin to loosen the bonds of self-censorship so subtly imposed by social mores."

"The transformation of people's liberties is amazing," Luis said in the article—stating what was essentially the goal of McGinley's playcouple philosophy.

The supreme irony was that the Lifestyles Organization, Robert McGinley, and swinging were treated with dignity by the magazine. Why would that be odd in what was really a mainstream skin rag? Because, just three years before, *Penthouse* had, with the ringing righteousness of a crusading exposé, featured a sexually explicit story on its cover, "Swinging Sex Clubs' Dangerous Comeback." "What on earth is going on here?" Ellis Henican wrote. "Don't these people know this is the 1990s? What about AIDS...? Are these people nuts?"

They were "whistling past the graveyard." And who was the mercenary Pied Piper leading these swingers to their deaths? "His name is Robert McGinley," the "Ross Perot" of modern swinging. "Yes, they even have their own trade group."

Now, in 1996, *Penthouse* was calling the Pied Piper of sexual death "Robert McGinley, Ph.D.," head of "a free-thinking advocacy group," which, parenthetically, "still throws some reputedly wild parties." The issue had become "free expression" in the face of "repression."

At the time, McGinley was thrilled by *Penthouse*'s change of heart; it was the first positive press he had received in a dozen years, and he would mark January 1996 as the date the mainstreaming of the lifestyle had begun to show results. But he also intuited that the good press could prove a trigger point for the authorities.

———————

McGinley's name was called over the intercom and I recognized the voice of Debbie Espen, his forty-three-year-old daughter, who worked full time in the Club WideWorld end of the business. Two of McGinley's other children were part-time help at the company as well: David took promo pictures for Lifestyles brochures and Dan was a handyman at the club. They weren't swingers but they looked up to their father as a hero.

"Dad? Are you there? Your lawyer's on the phone."

"Excuse me," McGinley said. "It's over that club raid again." He meant the one in Texas where the DEA agent, his partner, and eight other swingers had been arrested and the Inner Circles Club shut down.

While McGinley was saving the Inner Circles I asked Luis why he was involved in putting on explicit erotic-art shows at a swing convention.

"Well, I tried to put it on somewhere else, but you saw what happened," he laughed.

Luis went on to explain that he and Theresa had first met McGinley in 1990 through Theresa's sister, Cathy Gardner, and her husband, Dan, the out-of-the-closet swingers who were good friends of the Lomases. At a club dance that Cathy and Dan had invited them to attend, Luis (and all his credentials) had been introduced to McGinley. A couple of months later, at another dance, McGinley asked Luis if he would consider curating a show of erotic art at the upcoming convention at the Hacienda Hotel in Las Vegas. Assessing the people around him as normal, yet extraordinary in a way that was condemned as abnormal, Luis realized there was something profound taking place "on a level of pure perception." As intrigued by the hatred swingers aroused as by the movement itself, he said yes.

"I've always wanted to cut down the insider-outsider aspect of life," he told me. "Both within the individual and in society. I don't think '*they*' recognize that '*we*' are one of '*them*' —'*we*' make those designations internally, excluding parts of ourselves, which allows us to make those designations externally, excluding others.

"For instance," he went on, "I told *Penthouse* the whole show was about 'taking down fences,' because the real essence of the show is about making the art acceptable. What's the fence keeping it from being acceptable? It's that there's definitely a conscious intent on the part of many of the artists to sexually arouse the viewer. Now that's always been the case in art. The contemporaries of most artists understood that, so a lot of great art was banned at the time it first appeared. Then, over the years, we came to pretend that that wasn't at least part of the motivation of the artist, and so the art became acceptable—as if, now that we could set up a fence and deny the arousal aspect of the work, we could appreciate its beauty. Yet the work is still arousing. And that whole progression from recognition of the erotic, rejection of it, and acceptance of it when it's come to be seen as nonerotic *precisely* imitates the process of everyday life. *We* see the art as pure, but only *they* and *them* on the other side of the fence get aroused by it. When, in fact, *we all* get aroused by it too. We just pretend we're not on the same side of the fence with the pornographic outsiders."

"Do it if you have to, but make sure you feel bad about it and make sure you don't tell anybody." I stated the historical theme italicized on the Lifestyles exhibition brochure.

"Exactly," he said. "And what I find so engaging about the lifestyle is that I think they're way beyond their time as far as that mindset goes—I think it's amazing how far-reaching the whole mindset of the lifestyle person is. It's so far-reaching it can almost look dangerous, because it's unproven that a society could function if everyone was like that, having such a frank appreciation of human arousal—and not just intellectually."

I told him I had a party for him to go to up in Washington State.

"Talk about pornography!" he said. "They completely reverse the intellectual parameters so that *concealment* is pornographic and openness is wholesome. I'm not even referring to physical behavior, disrobing, or actual sex. If you go to McGinley's Friday-night social, you'll see what I mean," he said, referring to the Lifestyle's "Sultry and Sexy Night" soiree coming up at the Fullerton Day's Inn. "They're very—quote —well behaved in public. But what they do is practice true democracy. It's a kind of democracy no one but they practice." He contemplated a couple of small pen and ink drawings in the portfolio he'd brought along, by a woman named Sarah Troop. One was called *Erotic Odyssey I*; the other *Erotic Odyssey II*. Both were swirls of couples connected mouths to middles and hands to passionate faces.

"You know, I always say there's nothing created, just discovered," he said. "These artists, like the people in the lifestyle, have discovered their sensuality—the same sensuality that's in all of us, but which we have to feel guilty about because of the control it gives the people who rule us, who tell us to build those fences inside us and between us so we can't get out. But what I see at Robert's and in this art is—they're not guilty! And what I can tell you is that I believe that that's the correct direction for humanity's sake. So it's a matter of discovering what's already inside and ripping down the fence around it. If the art I present does a part of that, I've done my job. They can do the rest."

———————

"Sultry and Sexy Night" was exactly that. One hundred and fifty patrons dressed appropriately, as did LSO's fourteen staff and some friendly volunteers who would constitute the core of the Care Team at the upcoming convention. The brochures at the door featured an illustration of a couple making love and the promise that this would be a "Sensual Night of Fun, Desire & Arousal."

"Got somebody I want you to meet," Bob said, taking my arm and turning me around as I entered the ballroom, which was filled with well tanned couples in glamorous partywear. "Old-time swingers from Little Rock. They're friends of the Clintons'," he chuckled, entertained at the connection. "They used to visit at the governor's mansion with Bill and Hillary; they go to his birthday parties in the White House." He led me back outside to the sixtysomething female volunteer who'd affixed my wristband at the cash box, and who'd known the president since he was a boy. You can guess my first question.

"They do not, they never did, never, ever," the quite young-looking C.J. Callanen pronounced while her elegantly handsome husband, George Irwin, showed around a scrapbook filled with photographs of him and C.J. making love with the guests at their parties in Santa Monica. "Bill doesn't know our lifestyle."

Even if they had no scoop on group sex in the White House, C.J. and George were an interesting couple in their own right. They'd been together some thirty-eight years, swinging every one of them. George was a one-time Methodist minister from Texas with the white mane and patrician features of a Hollywood actor—which was his current occupation. In his long and varied career he had done counterintelligence work for the U.S. Army, brokered big business deals—including a personal investment in the Whitewater land deal—and between 1988 and 1992 had been a stand-in for George Bush, standing at the mike before the president would make his speeches so that technicians could set the sound for a Texan's wavering drawl. George and C.J. knew a lot of people high up in straight American politics—Bush, the Clintons, Ross Perot—yet they were total mavericks in their private lives.

"I got involved in swinging between the beatnik generation and the hippie generation," C.J. told me, "but I was neither. I've been a rebel all my life—I've always marched to a different drummer—so has George. We've always done everything different—nothing's ever been the norm with us. Ever. Not my whole life. I was never a follower; if I couldn't lead it, then I wouldn't do it."

"What's your politics?" I asked. "Are you a libertarian?"

"No—most of my life I voted Republican, but I voted for Bill, and I'm gonna vote for him this year."

"Bill's a good man," George said, sitting on the table beside Geri McGinley, who had known the two for many years. "I just read an article charging him with killing fifty-eight people and how him and Hillary killed Ron Brown, and I thought, my God! Who do you want in there with those lies—Ross Perot?"

"That's probably the agenda," Geri said.

"Here ya go, George," Joyce's husband, Richard, said, handing over George's scrapbook. He laid it down open to eight sequential photos showing George and C.J. at play with a dozen people on the lawn and lounge chairs.

"Thanks," George said. "Tell you a funny story about Ross. " George turned to me. "C.J. and I did business with him back years ago. He's a moralist, right? People work for him wouldn't dare go out with a woman that wasn't their wife. That's God's way. Happens that a lot of my friends from my old days in the church are still ministers, so one of my friends was in the church society where Ross Perot's mother went to church. So Ross gave them enough money to pay off the mortgage and do some work around the church. So I asked my friend one time, how'd it all turn out? He says, 'George, I'll tell ya, there's more pictures'a Ross in that church now than there is'a Jesus Christ.' Ross Perot is a moralist for Ross Perot, like most'a his kind."

"Hi, George!" called the LSO employee Jenny Friend, walking by on spiked heels in a lycra dress that barely covered her bottom.

"Hey, sweetheart!" George waved. Then he called, "Jenny! you know why I like to say good-bye to you?"

"Why's that?"

"Because I like to watch you walk away."

"Well, then, why don't you follow?"

"Ga'head," George patted my shoulder. "I'm watchin' my heart these days."

Lifestyles employees do not mind when old friends crack sexist jokes about them at parties, so I felt no need to be offended. Besides, I sort of intellectually knew what George was talking about, since I'd sat talking with Jenny for an hour and a half in the interview room of LSO headquarters a few days before. In addition to being the director of research, Jenny was LSO's on-staff counseling psychologist and certified sex therapist who interviewed new couples wanting to join Club WideWorld. Now in her mid-forties, she had written her two master's theses on swingers, both at the University of Texas at Austin ten years earlier, but she was refused entrance into a Ph.D. program because the administration thought the topic inappropriate. In many ways, Jenny was like Jodie, in that she was a single mother in the lifestyle and had an uninhibited sex drive that was unconnected to any one man. She'd discovered this—or rather admitted it to herself—at twenty-eight when after four months of happiness with the first man she both loved and enjoyed physically, she'd found herself desiring more sex than he was giving her, as well as a variety of men to get it from. He'd called her a "sexaholic." So she went to see a pair of sex therapists, Michael Riskin and Anita Banker, who were once in the swinging lifestyle. They told her to reject the addiction label, that she liked sex, and either hadn't met the right partner or wasn't cut out for monogamous love. At which point she went to a wild club called Freedom Acres, in San Bernadino, which was as fastlane as New Horizons. It was a remodeled schoolhouse with a dance room and the equivalent of an Annex, although on an architecturally less awesome scale. During her first visit she had sex with a number of men in the mirrored rooms. "After that experience I came to accept that I was never going to fulfill my sexuality through monogamy," she told me with astonishing dignity back at LSO headquarters. While taking a course on human sexuality at U.C. Riverside, she met Edgar Butler who told her about Bob McGinley and the Lifestyles Organization. "It came as a complete surprise to me that there was an actual organization devoted to people like me," she said. She went down to McGinley's old headquarters and he hired her part time to arrange academic speakers for the conventions. Then, when the office expanded to its La Palma location, she was hired on full time. Now she moonlighted as a counselor at the

Riskin-Banker Psychotherapy Center. Both therapists were here at the dance tonight, in a shifting crowd of folks which included Luis and Theresa, Cathy and Dan Gardner, and Frank and Jennifer Lomas.

Frank greeted me with his usual extroverted warmth, and Jennifer asked if I was managing to get a handle on the full spectrum of the lifestyle in Southern California. I told her I was getting there. The previous weekend, at my request, Frank had taken me out to Freedom Acres, which Jennifer had decided to pass on since it wasn't her favored haunt. When I got back I'd mentioned casually to McGinley that, in contrast to his club, many of the rural patrons at Freedom Acres looked like the first swingers I'd ever seen at Vancouver Circles seven years before—that is "low rent," as I'd heard them called. The words caused McGinley to launch into a five-minute lecture about how every person was entitled to the full enjoyment of their sexuality, no matter what they looked like or what their education. He said he counseled obese people and people in wheelchairs, and he reiterated how adamantly he was opposed to shapism, classism, and bourgeois-bashing, the main weapons the media always used to humiliate swingers. He concluded by saying: "Nevertheless, I understand your point, if you're speaking purely from a matter of taste, rather than as a judgmental journalist."

Out on the dance floor, the seventy-five couples were doing the Slide with their usual exuberance—raising their skirts and Tarzan cloths, basically giving the outside world the finger, practicing the open brand of democracy that Luis had called my attention to.

"I'm really glad to hear you're doing some serious work on this lifestyle," Theresa De La Cruz shouted to me. She was a petitely pretty woman who, in contrast to most of the others, was covered demurely to her knees. Luis had told me that while he assessed art with his mind, Theresa assessed it with her heart. When I'd asked whether that proved effective in choosing erotic art, he'd told me that the other day she'd looked through sixteen hundred small paintings of vulvas and uncannily chosen one for the show that was the artist's favorite. "You know what I find most interesting that's happening with these situations?" Theresa said. "They're having a domino effect, where people that utterly reject it say, 'Well, I'll go once,' and they come here and meet people and they say, 'Well, if they're in it and they're normal—.'"

"People learn to let go when they're in a lifestyle sexual situation," Cathy Gardner said to me, standing beside her tall husband, with whom she was a partner in their brokerage firm. "Not that that's the only way to get to that place of freedom, but it appears that that's an effective way. When you're at middle age, remaining sexually open means remaining intellectually open. That was my point on *Geraldo*."

"I'll bet that went over well," I said.

Cathy and Dan, Frank and Jennifer, and Jenny Friend had all been on the talk-show circuit, which collectively included their appearances on *Donahue*, *Sally Jesse Raphael*, *Geraldo*, and a few others of that stripe. They subjected themselves to that insanity because they all passionately believed they should be out there showing the world that the lifestyle was populated by normal folks.

"It was like, 'Lynch 'em, kill 'em!'" Frank said. "'Sickos! Pathological freaks.' I really got scared for a second."

"What right do people have to call these people pathological?" Anita Banker asked. "What information do they have?"

"I guess they think they all have five or six guys a night," I said.

"So—what's wrong with that?" Anita laughed, and she wasn't joking at all. She and Michael Riskin were writing a book called *Simultaneous Orgasm and Other Joys of Sexual Intimacy*. In their convention workshops they treated open eroticism and the lifestyle as normal behavior for those who liked it. Michael had even worked as a sex surrogate for women before he'd become a therapist; that is, he'd been paid for having sex with females who wanted the experience. I hadn't even known there was such a thing as a male sex surrogate.

"The government doesn't want people feeling this free," Cathy said. "I go out and I say, 'Look, we have five kids, we're grandparents and we care about the future.' I never say the lifestyle is the end in itself, but it's a stepping stone to discovering yourself and a lot of mental freedom. That's spooky for the powers that be, especially when they see me up there on TV. I am mainstream America. And my mind-set is mainstream American. And I have done everything socially acceptable to what mainstream is. Yes, I have one husband. But yet I have found a way that I can satisfy my sexual desires and social needs by going through this door. I know that makes me very unmanageable from [their] point of view, but don't dare try and stop me."

"We're adamant about that," Frank said to me. "Anybody discriminates against us because of the lifestyle, we'll sue their ass."

About half an hour later Jean Henry and her partner Clark Ross came through the door with a couple of colleagues she was staying with in Los Angeles. The looks on her friends' faces betrayed no surprise at the crowd: it turned out that they too believed swinging deserved some attention from academia. I waved to Jean and we sat down at a table in the back and watched some of the rites on the dance floor. I asked Jean if she'd found any differences between the subculture at clubs on the Coast and in the South and Mid West. "I was just telling them that I haven't, it's actually pretty uniform," she said. "What's interesting is that the norm wherever you go in the subculture is to rebel against this one area of sexual prohibition, and leave everything else alone. They really honestly believe the prohibition's based on an old set of rules that have survived despite the fact that the conditions have changed so much."

"I suppose historically we've always been ruled by men who've made those prohibitions and then ignored them," her friend said.

"We still are and they still do," Jean laughed.

CHAPTER ELEVEN

Balls of Fire

In addition to the fun, educational opportunities and social camaraderie of the convention, we hope to cause you to think about our personal freedom as Americans, our extraordinary Bill of Rights, and those who would deny, limit or reinterpret either.

ROBERT MCGINLEY, *Lifestyles 1996*
Convention Guidebook

Working feverishly, the staff at the Town and Country tore down the bunting, put up the bows, and changed the parking lot marquee from WELCOME REPUBLICAN NATIONAL CONVENTION to WELCOME LIFESTYLES '96. As couples from around the world converged on the resort, four Teamsters officials from Northern California innocently decided to stop at the hotel's popular sports bar for a quick beer before heading to their own inn across the street. They pulled into a back lot, made their way through the still-empty cement canyons formed by the rows of luxury towers, and entered Charlie's lounge, where I happened to be eating dinner. Like macho union boys, they rumbled back chairs around a table on the opposite side of the room from some middle-aged people and leaned forward over crossed arms to strategize their next day's negotiations. When the beers arrived, one of them toasted success in the morrow, then stopped swallowing with the glass at his lips, foamy Miller brimming his black mustache. He put his glass down.

One by one the Teamsters followed his gaze to the table across the still-quiet room. They saw a raven-haired woman of about forty in a leopard-print dress leaning across a balding guy in a golf shirt and soul-kissing with a woman in a padded power push-up outfit. Behind this fellow an athletic-looking woman in a bustier was bending over and nibbling at his ear. Stage left at this subtle table drama, two guys were sandwich-dancing a heavyset woman of perhaps fifty, whose hands were wrapped fore and aft about the belly and back of her partners. Stage right, two women slouched in the arms of their husbands with their legs overlapping and resting in the laps of their opposite spouse's.

"Something's up," one of the Teamsters said, noticing that the folks were wearing shiny blue wristbands, and that other banded couples in their thirties and forties were now crowding into the bar. The beaming males of this set were dressed mostly in loud, tropical shirts, loafers or sneakers, shorts or jeans, but the ladies at their sides were clad like soap-opera stars. The middle-aged union officials began to catch frank female stares without even trying. Checking reality in each other's faces, they watched these couples from Pluto establish a rapport that seemed to advance the starting gate of social intercourse almost to the finish line. Combos of triads, quartets, and quintets formed, and when "Erotic City" started throbbing from the jukebox a covey of them, with the exuberance of teenagers, leaped into the Electric Slide, emitting peals and squeals of laughter. Taken together, the whole scene must have seemed to the Teamsters to be the most fevered example of heterosexual activity then cranking up on earth.

Shortly after, another partygoer and his sexily dressed wife strolled in and stood five feet from the Teamsters at the bar. He was Roger Stone, and he had just spent five days at the Republican convention as one of Bob Dole's main PR consultants, advising the right wing on how best to condemn the degraded morality of America. He was also one of the partners of the conservative Washington, D.C., firm Davis, Manifort and Stone, and had been an operative in the Republican Party since 1968. I don't mind telling you his name because it would not be me who would expose him (although I did take a couple of pictures of him around the pool). He was "outed" in the *National Enquirer*, the *Star*, *Esquire*, Associated Press, and *Newsweek*, the latter featuring a double-page portrait of the couple that gave you a good peek up the short dress of his wife, Nikki. I'm only mentioning him now because of the events that would follow this convention, events in which Stone could be said to have had a part to play by helping others condemn the kind of immorality he had been experiencing at the past four conventions. "Roger Stone is not who I'm talking about when I say we're mainstreaming the lifestyle," Bob McGinley told me. "People have the right to remain in the closet and shouldn't be punished if they're outed, but they shouldn't be fostering a society that makes it likely others suffer if they're outed. We don't need those kinds of headlines."

He meant the one in the *Star*: "Top Dole Aide in Sex-Orgies Scandal."

And the *National Enquirer*: "Top Dole Aide Caught in Group-Sex Ring."

And from Associated Press: "Dole Aide Quits in Sex Scandal."

And *Newsweek*: "Private Lives, Political Ends."

But those headlines would appear two weeks hence.

Now a passing young waitress guessed correctly at the union boys' bewilderment in the face of this shindig, and leaned down over her platter of beers. "How you guys doin'?"

"Who *are* these people?" one of them asked, with heart-breaking sincerity.

"If you can believe it, they're *swingers*, they're all *married*," she shouted above the roar. "It's their convention. They take over the hotel every year. Nice people, but *re-E-E-ally* friendly —so you guys watch yourselves!" she said protectively.

Swingers? the Teamsters wondered in unison. Didn't that go out with the sixties? Bob and Carol and Ted and Alice? Free love, open marriage, naked orgies? Since when did they hold *conventions*? Where the hell were *we* when it came back?

"We love you! We love you! You are already booked until 1999, and furthermore, we are going into the next century with you! *Long live the lifestyle!*" the vice-president of the Town and Country, Felipe Ortiz, declared to the full house of long-married Care Team couples assembled in the Tiki Hut halfway across the grounds. Loud cheers and applause erupted from the hundred teachers and physicians, construction workers and computer programmers—most of whom were wearing nothing more daring than green Lifestyles golf shirts and jeans. Among them were George and C.J., Cathy and Dan Gardner, plus the whole LSO staff, including Joyce and Richard, who would be heading the Care Team from Wednesday night to Sunday afternoon. Leslie had flown down that afternoon and I'd introduced her all around. ("He's so ugly and you're so beautiful," old George had said.)

"Okay, guys, we have a fair amount of material to cover here," McGinley announced, mounting the podium with the high-headed posture of a small general in charge of giant matters, "but first I want to take a moment to say that this convention wouldn't take place if it wasn't for you people. You guys are out there really making this place function. Not only are you helping to make this a great convention but, when you think about it, you're also affecting the lives of thousands of people. And that's part of what we're all about—to give people more joy in their relationships, more joy out of what they're doing, more joy out of life itself! I just want to thank you very, very much."

"And thank-*you*, Bob!" Joyce called. "Thank *every*body!"

The Care Team couples applauded, perhaps feeling a warm sense of community. For years they had read the published reports that labeled them banal fornicators who hadn't a clue about the difference between joy and pleasure. But they themselves believed they had a handle on the total picture, and that if the world viewed them in disbelief, confusion, and irritation it was only because they were threateningly normal.

"I want to introduce to you our head of security, Jerry Baker," McGinley continued, holding his hand out to the well-muscled African American who was the manager of Alternative Security Concepts, which would have a dozen equally well-muscled agents wandering the forty-six acres for the next four days. "Jerry is a symbol of our success because Jerry is kind of the reverse of a prison guard. A prison guard keeps people in, Jerry keeps people out."

"And Dr. McGinley is *not* joking," Jerry said, taking the mike. "And thank-you for allowing me to do that job for you. I can't tell you how many people try to sneak into this convention every year—and more often than not, they're the ones who cause the very few problems that we've ever had, not the guests. But with that in mind, I can tell you that members of the vice squad of San Diego will be attending as couples, undercover, making sure all people are obeying the laws of San Diego and California. All I can ask is for your help in discouraging activity that you know in your gut would make a police officer unhappy."

"You mean happy!" someone called.

"I know how to make a cop happy. Haven't had a ticket in five years."

"Hey! We got two cops right here!"

Two fellows stood up and bowed. "Go ahead, make us happy!"

A blond woman in her early sixties ran up and embraced both.

"No, no—joking aside, this is a point that can't be over-emphasized," McGinley said. "As you know, beginning tomorrow we have this whole resort at our disposal, but that does not mean we own the resort or that the resort is considered a private party in the eyes of the laws of the State of

California. There are people from the outside working here—they are considered the public. As a consequence, we will permit no public nudity, no sex in public, no doors left open while sex is taking place within the rooms."

There were moans and groans from the audience, even hisses.

"I might add, however, that when the doors are closed, all the rooms are clothing optional, and private parties are private parties!"

To this, the Care Team couples offered hosannas.

"Well, with that, I'm going to give the podium over to Joyce now," McGinley said. "This convention is also a lot of work, it's a fun kind of work, but it's got to be organized: we have three big dances, forty or so seminars, a luncheon, costume judging, the Erotic Arts show—you name it—and we want to make sure that everybody knows what everybody else is doing. As you know, we have Care Team captains, and each captain is responsible for a particular area and for the groups of you who'll work with them. So I'm going to ask Joyce to discuss your roles. Then, afterwards, if you haven't already been over there, the hotel has set up a tent and made other arrangements for us at Charlie's—just to make it a very social place for people to meet and talk and have drinks and whatever else, so you're all invited over there after this."

A big round of applause greeted General Joyce as she skipped to the podium.

"Okay, first," she said, "I think what I'd like to do is have everybody introduce themselves. A lot of people in this room don't know each other, many of you are from different parts of the country—so the first thing I want is for all you guys to stand up and show us who you're with and tell us where you're from."

This sparked a near riot of protest from the women, who gave Joyce the good-natured raspberry.

"Whaddya mean, *the guys?*"

"Let the *gals* stand up and show themselves!!"

"We dragged *them* here!" a popular Lifestyles employee by the name of Juanita shouted above the rest, to thunderous applause, leaving the female members of an HBO TV crew, who were here to do a ten-minute segment for *Real Sex*, feeling as if they had passed through Alice's mirror into a swinger's version of Wonderland.

After their first vision of high-octane swingers, the four Teamsters decided a few more beers were in order. Seven hours later two of them were still at the same table while their buddies played pool with the partygoers. By then they'd spoken with a good sampling of the marrieds who'd crammed into Charlie's for the Early Arrivals Social. "I gotta tell you, I'm amazed, but they're really great people," remarked Tyler, a specialist in uniting Teamsters locals of different cultures under one contract. The raucous ladies performing their polyamorous acts around him kept inviting themselves to his table for a chat—Tyler being as dark and handsome as Omar Sharif in his *Dr. Zhivago* days—but as soon as they realized he was a straight Joe married to a straight Jane for umpteen years, they relaxed and answered his queries without reservation. "The things they've been telling me and the way they talk—it's a whole other world I didn't even know existed. Like they love their husbands, but—." He furrowed his dark brows and laughed. "Well, they say they're monogamous: they don't have sex with someone without him being there. It's definitely not for me, but I can't get over there's no jealousy. No games, no pretension—"

"I don't know, I don't know," said his squinting colleague, Stuart, who moonlighted as a clinical psychologist for trial lawyers when they needed jurors' minds assessed. "There's something else just below that surface. How do I know these people aren't acting out? Why would a normal woman—"

"I didn't say it was *normal*," Tyler laughed. "But my preconception would be that it's a man's thing. But they're saying, 'Yeah, maybe my husband got me into it, but now that I'm into it I'm more enthusiastic than he is.' So you just sit back and question why a normal wife would behave like this—even if her husband said, 'Okay, let's spice up our marriage.'"

Stuart looked sourly on that. "For who?" he asked. "For *him* —not for her." He was certain these women weren't here for the sex. The difference between a man's sex drive and a woman's was the same as the difference between shooting a bullet and throwing a bullet. Maybe these women were deeply distressed.

Stuart looked sideways at a passing redhead, youngish for this crowd—no more than her late twenties—in a sweetheart dress and garter get-up that stretched taut her French-seamed stockings. Stuart swiveled his head to follow her image on his other side and inadvertently caught her backward glance. She turned, her hands fluttering down upon his shoulders, violating the swing-club etiquette of no-invite, no-touch.

"Uh, oh," Tyler laughed, then called me and my wife confidentially close, since Steely Dan was loud on the jukebox. "I think he's threatened by the whole thing," Tyler told us while Stuart archly questioned the intruder. "The flirting's going in the wrong direction; he can't get his mind around it."

"True, it *is* a different way of thinking," the woman was saying. "But if you look at these different cultures—"

"Okay, fine, fine: what I'm saying is that from where I'm sitting you're making yourselves into objects," Stuart enunciated. "Not my object, but every other guy's."

"Gee, we probably never thought of that," she said.

"So the simple question is, Why is it necessary to do that?"

"We're making ourselves into objects for our*selves*," she

shot back, as if she'd debated the point before. "Women *always* look at magazines and think, That's what I should look like, a sexual object. And what they're doing here is *ultra* indulging it, and feeling it's *natural*—as a *group*, not like I'm going to steal a husband. It's a game."

"Oh, I see," Stuart said. "Perfectly natural."

"Well—one thing—we don't cheat on each other like everyone else," she replied; then—petulantly: "*Huh?*"

"Hey," he said, putting his hands up. "Don't get personal. I just wandered in here."

She shook her head at this hopeless case and walked away. "I guess I questioned a few of her assumptions. *Pre*sumptions," he laughed.

The collegiate young waitress leaned a long way down and asked Stuart if he'd like another beer. "Well-l-l now, I don't know," he said, looking sidelong at her, suddenly suave as James Bond. "Do you think it'll ease the tension?"

"Oh, *that* he can handle!" Tyler said to Leslie. "Now that it's on his terms!"

It was about half an hour later, perhaps one-thirty in the morning, that someone on one of the high balconies of the West Tower that overlooked the entire resort sent up a rocket. It whistle-screamed into the black sky trailing silver sparks, and everyone in front of Charlie's turned and peered through the palms to follow its arc. Its light went out, there was a quarter second of silence, and then it exploded in a shower of silver balls, like the Big Bang spraying galaxies in the eyes of the swingers and on the calm, blue pool below.

"Eeee-*haaa!*"

"Something tells me that we're not in Kansas anymore, Toto!"

So began the 1996 Lifestyles convention: it had taken a year to put together but it had really been "23 years in the making." After the congestion of Los Angeles, the stuffiness of Dublin and Bonn, the isolation of New South Wales, or the insufferable political correctness of Toronto, Lifestyles '96 came as an enormous release for these thousands. It had always been this way at conventions, and no matter how big it had grown, Lifestyles remained vastly unpretentious, spectacularly intimate, with the vernacular transactions of the swing world available to all.

You registered and you were in, but you never disappeared, for your playcouple spouse was by definition always on your arm. Around the pools the convention was a sunlit party; at the dances it was a dark, rowdy, and electric disco; at the seminars and art show it was high-minded and studious; at the adult marketplace it was plain tasteless; at the big luncheon it was archly political, First Amendment stuff; and—day and night in the rooms—it was tender in threesomes and purely "orgastic" in groups. In other words, the convention was constantly in flux. You wandered from college class to Mardi Gras to porno booths to pajama parties to group-sex passion. When you heard the laughter of more than four or five behind closed doors, you knew what was going on; you could knock and you would probably not be refused a place of witness. You were surrounded by those who were intolerant of smugness, but kind to both the timid voyeur and the cackling exhibitionist.

To take up residence in the Town and Country between August 21 and 24 was to install oneself on a merry-go-round in a marital amusement park. "Lifestyles '96 is a time of liberation and enchantment," McGinley had bannered his ethos on the back of his beige convention booklet, this one with another nakedly embracing couple airbrushed on the front. "A time to rekindle the passion and to enhance the romance in your relationship. The PlayCouple Philosophy is alive and well at Lifestyles '96."

At noon Thursday, the best and worst opened simultaneously. Behind the pool, on the far side of the Rose Garden, Luis welcomed the public to his gallery in what was called the Council Rooms. He stood with a shy young artist named Karen Swildens before a dozen bronze sculptures, one of a headless female riding a stiff phallus, named *Passion*, another of a body with a phallus-head and arms reaching up and holding its testicles, called *Ecstasy*, a third called *Battle of the Sexes*—that is, phalluses dressed as knights and doing battle with sword and mace. "You have to get on a level between the thought and your response to the thought—art's the original response," Karen told the bikinied couples who were at the convention precisely in order to cultivate original response. "Art is communicating on that level."

"I actually call art the shorthand of language," Luis said. "It goes right past that mental rhetoric, right past the definitions, occurring before the words about the thing itself come to mind. In Ms. Swilden's work we see the juxtaposition of fantasies—the male-female style of the critical creature...."

What was most fascinating about Luis's long-handed hour's talk was that fifty swinging couples listened raptly to it all, strolling from canvas to collage to sculpture with elbows resting upon fists and eyeglass-stems held to their mouths. "What is the challenge here?" Luis asked before some graphically homoerotic works that he always included in his shows to emphasize the plurality in the name Life*styles*. "Quite simply, it is the challenge of Goya. He too fought against the dogma of denial."

The Good. The Bad. The Ugly. The art show was the good. The alleged bad went on in the rooms. What about the ugly?

If you walked left from the Council Rooms, crossed the

solar furnace of the Mission Patio into the cool convention center where registration was proceeding furiously, then turned
right into the Mission Ballroom, you entered the warehouse
world of commercial porn and erotica, done up in feathers and
boas, a suburban whorehouse trade show. This was what
Jennifer Lomas referred to as X-Town, tempered every third
or fourth booth by some redeeming concept like Lifestyles
Travel, or the Tom of Finland Foundation—a charity for gay
artists with AIDS—but otherwise flaunting kinks sold by
Leather Masters, Pleasure Piercing, and Silverscreen Video.
Still, it was also a place to buy the outfits worn as a matter of
course at the dances, offered at bargain-basement prices by
companies like Desire Fashions, Tanya's Clothing & Shoes for
Brave Women, The Lingerie Lady. "Dressing rooms to try on
clothes are located in each corner of the exhibit hall"—and,
just for fun, some of those changing let their new friends watch.

Outside, at two o'clock that day, a reggae band named
Fried Bananas jumped up and the barefoot guys and dolls in
their American-flag bikinis jumped with it. A blind woman
reggaed with her Seeing Eye Dog; a one-legged man did so
on a roller skate. "Are you in the lifestyle?" I asked the blind
woman. She reached out and felt my face and chest. "Now
I am."

With the rest of the world locked out, the couples knew
that everyone here was a swinger, or sympathetic to swinging
—they were *play*couples, at least. Heterosexual wives oiled
other wives while their husbands oiled them. Shapely toes
extended to shore from air mattresses, offered as sucking
candies, and complementary remarks were made on bottoms
you could have rested tea cups upon as they passed. Hundreds sunned and gossiped and cracked lewd farmer's jokes
and then looked up through the laughter and music and
tall, spindly cabbage palms to the green San Diego hills.
Everything seemed yellow and beige, white and green, cut

sharply by black shadows. "This is paradise," said a woman from Saint John, New Brunswick, for whom Lifestyles '96 was her first convention. "It must be what gays feel like when they come out."

The sun moved, the black shadows lengthened, and about 150 couples lifted themselves from the water or stepped away from the dance party and headed east for Regency Hall, just a few steps from Charlie's, where McGinley conducted an hour-long seminar for those new to the convention, or those who could use some inspiration to get a better bang out of this one. "General Orientation Session," McGinley's seminar was called. "How to Enjoy Lifestyles '96."

"We see the convention as a place for people to meet people," he told them, while the HBO and German TV cameras whirred. "To come and be the adult sexual people that you really are without a great deal of fear that someone's going to frown upon you." He explained that the convention was also about the education they would receive at the seminars, the fun at the dances, and the spiritual awareness that came from being open in a nonexploitive environment. "People in the lifestyle have a spiritual side," he said. "And this comes to the fore many times. Obviously, one is in weddings," he stated, inviting the couples to attend one he would perform that afternoon. "Another has to do with the other side of life—when we leave." Oddly enough, he then urged them to contemplate the funerals he officiated at, offering up evidence that playcouples established lifelong bonds that brought them to one another's graves, since, he said, the lifestyle added to the capacity for long-lasting emotion. He urged them to come to the luncheon on Friday and hear Dr. Edith Eger give the convention's keynote address. "You're going to be surprised. She and her entire family were sent to Auschwitz when the Germans invaded her country. She was due to go to the Olympics as a gymnast, I believe. And Dr. Mengele, the Angel of Death, found out that she was also a dancer and told her she was to dance to entertain them for their luncheons. So dancing is what saved her life, although her entire family was killed and cremated. Her talk is called 'A Dance for Life.' It's not a downer, not at all, it's very inspirational. It's designed to help put the past behind you, to enjoy your life. Which is something of value to almost every one of us. If you've gone through a divorce, or lost a loved one, or whatever human tragedy you've endured, you've asked yourself, 'How can I go on?' Dr. Eger has asked that question after experiencing the worst there is—and she has put all this behind her and gone on to have a great life."

A great life! People cried at the wedding, threw colored rice at the couple, who would share their celebrations that night at eight with the thousands who swarmed the Atlas Ballroom dressed as flappers and Arrow Men for the Roaring '20s Dance. "You want fights and drunks and jealous tears?" Cathy Gardner told me during a dance. "Go to a psychiatrists' convention." These folks, on the other hand, were pro-sex popsicles—and the lineups at the bar were always short, the swinging men taking care not to stimulate desire then lose the ability to perform, the swinging women generally liking to stay in control. Some were tall, some skinny, some fat, and some looked like they could have been leading men and women in Hollywood movies. Some were. They had their hours of foreplay, which, for at least half of them, led inevitably to hundreds of rooms being occupied by more than two. You took it for granted. You did not think it odd.

Considering how many hours these parties dragged on, it was amazing that so many couples were up bright and early each day to attend some of the forty seminars that were scheduled over the weekend. It was even more amazing that Jenny Friend arranged these seminars so they would be kicked off by "Better Sex Through Religion," whose leaders, Rick and Carol Truitt, took an Aristotelian approach to God-communion. Rick was a main-line Protestant minister with a doctorate in divinity and Carol was a social worker. "We both obviously come from a Christian perspective," they told the spouse exchangers, comparing the structure of Christian rules to a manmade mountain and the reality of God's relationship to humans as like the rain and rivers that washed that mountain away, or went around it. The mountain of religious commandments opposed organic growth; religious structure opposed natural movement; rules set boundaries to intimacy; doctrine was rigid while God's spirit was free. It was the purpose of traditional religion to control people, not free the spirit. "The rules have become so important that people live for the rules, not for God." God was playful, not angry. Look at the world! All contained within God's mind, like a play He'd imagined and performed through each one of us. Indeed, they said "think of that word—'play'." It was in *the* play, and *in* play, that we felt God most. "That's why the Lifestyles convention is such a great place," Carol said. "Marriage is important to us, and intimacy in marriage is gained through playfulness."

Then there were the academics. Butler never made it, but a social anthropologist named Leanna Wolfe spoke to a packed house on "The Dynamics of Polysexuality," her thesis being that by practicing monogamy we were "defying our ancestral polysexual programming." "So you may ask," she asked her audience, "at a biological level, what causes humans to have the desire to have multiple partners? Anybody have a sense of what this might be? Just 'cause it's fun?"

"Variety!" someone shouted.

"Variety, that's right. And what's that variety based on? Basically it has to do with species survival. The more we mix around the gene pool, the more likely that some very healthy specimens will be produced that in turn would pass those very healthy genes on to the next generation. And so males are driven to do this by inseminating as many females as they can. And females are also driven, in a similar way, but there is a little difference. Basically the female appetite has to do with ensuring the survival of her young. And, in the behavior of many primates which we anthropologists study, we find that when a male encounters a female he's never seen before and she has a young one with her, he knows that that young one isn't his, and his likely response will be to kill it. And then once she cycles into heat again, she'll be his, and the baby that results he would never touch. And so for a female to ensure the survival of her young, she has to give every male in her vicinity the impression that the young could be his. That's part of the biological rootedness of why we are drawn to multiple partners."

It was welcome news to the "aberrant" swingers. Dr. Susan Block was there to drive home the point with her celebratory lecture "The Bonobo Way." "Don't let anyone ever tell you you're bad because you're a swinger," she proclaimed. "Bonobos aren't bad, and they swing constantly. They are the prototype of the human swinger! They practice playful, recreational, nonreproductive sex, and they never kill each other! Plus, ladies, they are *not* male-dominated!"

At a luncheon, McGinley gave out a Lifestyles of America Award to the Jamaican resort Hedonism II. "I think it's only fitting," he said, "that Jan Queen present the award, because it's in large part because of the efforts of Lifestyles Tours and Travel, working with Hedonism II, that we have created one of the most spectacular resorts in the world that has accepted what we call the lifestyle community. And they've done a magnificent job at Hedonism."

Jan climbed to the stage dressed in a glitzy gown, looking like a presenter at the Academy Awards. "The annual Lifestyles award is presented to the club voted most popular resort by playcouples around the world for creating an environment of freedom for the mind, body, and soul, on this date, August 23, 1996," Jan said. "Thank-you, Hedonism II."

After that the MC, comedian Larry Clark, standing beside a nude model, invited everybody and the Hedonism folks to "swing at the parties upstairs afterwards." He then introduced Dr. Edith Eger. "She's here today to speak with us because it's not only important to have fun and frivolity, but also to learn important lessons in life. So if you will please join me in a big round of applause for Dr. Edith Eger."

A tiny, frail woman mounted the stairs, looked the naked model up and down, and then sang in a heavy Eastern-European accent: "Anything you can do I can do better!"

This broke the audience into riotous applause.

"I'm older than you, but I'm also wiser—so don't call me shrink, call me stretch."

More laughter and applause from the two thousand people eating their fried chicken.

"I'm sort of a combo between Dr. Ruth and Joan Rivers," Eger self-mockingly apologized. Then she cut the jokes. "I just really am very, very happy to be here. My little token to you is to talk about the dance of life, about how beautiful it is for you to take time out and come here and take stock of your life, where you have been, and where you are now. And of course, how you can live in the present, and to be able to integrate the past, so you would never be the prisoner or the hostage of the past. That's why I studied human behavior, and that's why I became a sexologist, because if you were sexually abused as a child, you were far more in prison than I was.

"You see, I knew who was the enemy," she went on with utter gravity, "so I became very, very involved in the area of how a person can be a survivor, rather than a victim, of any circumstance. This afternoon I'd like to take from you any form of victimization in order that you can feel empowered, and be able to enjoy every moment of your life.

"I must tell you," she said, "I was lying among the dead in 1945 when a young GI, maybe your father or grandfather, found me, and my hand was moving. So my life is postmortem every moment, it's precious—and, of course, freedom and health are things we don't seem to appreciate until we lose them. I like very much the humor, the love, the laughter, the permission to have all the pleasures in the world which you can enjoy. I really feel that your love is very contagious, so that I know that when I go home I'm going to bring with me the celebration of life. I think that you are able to have freedom of expression. Thomas Jefferson said all men are created equal— he did not say that all men are created the same. The same is not equality. I think all of us have the equal right to be treated with dignity. And, with that in mind, I honor you for your self-expression, and if I can be me, and you can be you, together we're going to be much stronger than me alone and you alone. God bless you, thank-you."

Afterward McGinley was ecstatic. "They got the message!"

Four hours later, the three-hundred-couple "Evening Of Caressive Intimacy" took place on the floor of the pink Regency Ballroom. It was led by a hypnotherapist, Rick Brown, a huge, shaven-headed man with an Amish beard, accompanied by a gorgeous stripper-model from Toronto named Jesse Hill, who would lie on a big table as he demonstrated his techniques upon her. Rick stated up-front what everybody at the convention acknowledged to be the case: for all its fame and notoriety as a public-sex convention, actual coitus and genital fondling happened behind the closed doors of rooms. Therefore: "The goal of this evening is caressive intimacy. No sexual contact, no penetration—we'll have none of that. It has to do with touching and expressing the feelings of the person you are with. This is not a sexual event, but it's very close to it. If you leave here and you're not turned on, I didn't do my job."

Nine-tenths of the affair consisted of nothing more than

soft music, hypnotically relaxing talk by Rick, and the oily caressing of toes, breasts, backs, and foreheads by six hundred naked partners sprawled upon the rug. Nevertheless, this one-hour massage workshop always concluded with a happening whose name was as notorious as its modus operandi. It was the "Car Wash," and it was so scorned and condemned by the media that magazines almost always felt it necessary to include double-page photographs of the naked participants so that readers could fully comprehend how terrible the experience was. Essentially it was this: the ballroom was separated into quadrants of about seventy-five couples each. Men and women then divided and formed two lines facing each other inches apart. These lines of facing people kept their hands at their sides—"This is not a group grope; anyone in line who raises their arms will be asked to leave"—and the couple at the end of the line raised *their* arms and twirled their way up the line between bodies, slithering against bellies and breasts like they were moving past brushes of a car wash. Then the next couple in line followed on up until everybody had a turn. I personally could never appreciate its sensual appeal—but it was definitely not, as *GQ* had called it, reminiscent "of those fine Tailhook parties," the abusive gauntlet female naval cadets had been made to go through as part of their hazing ritual some years ago. It was just harmless and silly swinger fun.

After these couples had danced their heels off till three in the morning at the Sci Fi Costume Ball, many of them again managed to wake up and attend yet another 9:30 A.M. spiritual seminar booked by Jenny Friend—this one a "Dynamic Meditation" service led by one Dr. Carlos Penafiel. There they sat in their loud shorts and shirts, hands upturned in their laps and picturing the light at their third eye, watching their breath while Dr. Penafiel reminded them that the God in that light was the same for all—friend or enemy, relative or stranger. They may have been thinking about afterward attending Jack

Lambie's seminar on "The Three-Way Experience," or a live demonstration of female ejaculation conducted by a porn star named Kerri Downs, or even Mistress Delilah's "The Loving Art of Domination." But these taxpayers constantly reminded you by either their giggles or straining sincerity that they were not inhabitants of a demimonde of sordid sexuality. They were just folks putting the icing on a cake they thought tasted pretty neat.

For all those who came to Lifestyles, however, there was one event that was really the top of the cake: the height from which all the other layers would be surveyed in memory. The seminars, luncheons, dances, poolside flirtations, and room parties were sweet steps to this most important night of Lifestyles each year—one for which some couples literally worked months preparing: the Erotic Masquerade Ball. You can go to Mardi Gras in New Orleans and Fasching in Munich. You can participate in the Gay Pride Day parade in San Francisco and the Dinah Shore golf tournament—the annual gathering of lesbians in Palm Springs. Nothing you experience there will match the Erotic Masquerade Ball at a Lifestyles convention. It is not that the peacock costumes playing peekaboo with sexual flags are any more gaudy at Lifestyles than at the other events. It is that the people wearing these costumes are models of heterosexual parenthood and middle-aged modesty back home.

————

Two hours before the official start of this glitzy sabbath Leslie and I were surprised to find ourselves placed at a table of honor at a full-attendance sit-down dinner—along with Luis and Theresa, Cathy and Dan, and the porn star Ona Zee and her boyfriend Frank Wiegers. About half the people in the room were in costume at this point, the other half in tuxes and just plain sexy outfits—which would have been costumes at

any other party. "This is food foreplay," Ona told me. At
McGinley's table sat Frank and Jennifer, Jan, and the Eden
Resort's Pascal Pellegrino. Bob jumped up to greet a costumed
couple who looked like they were getting on to eighty. He
called me over.

"I want you to meet some swell folks," he said, putting his
hand on my shoulder when I got to his table. "Terry, this is
Carmen and John Major—they just celebrated their fifty-fifth
wedding anniversary."

John was dressed like Wyatt Erp, with dildos for guns,
and Carmen was wearing a skintight, silver-spangled, cowgirl
outfit with her breasts poking through, fluorescent bangles
hanging from her nipples. A woman in a see-through sari with
a *bindi* on her forehead grabbed John around the waist and
pulled him backward to the dance floor. "How long you guys
been in the lifestyle?" I asked.

"We're newcomers!" Carmen replied. "Only about ten
years!" They'd both worked for the airlines, John as a mech-
anic, Carmen as a booking agent, she said. "What happened
was, after we retired we both became real cranky, our sex life
went from good to terrible. So two of our friends who were
swingers—we didn't even know—they suggested a club. Took
us about six months to get used to the dos and don'ts, then it
became all dos!"

"Do you come to the convention every year?"

"Oh yeah; we just missed last year. The first time. My
God! The people were wondering what the hell was going on
we didn't make it."

"Your costume is spectacular—you've got a body like a
young woman. Do you guys actually swing here?"

"Oh yeah, we always party. Every weekend. People always
ask us, what keeps us young. I say, 'Swinging.' It's this kind of
atmosphere that keeps us young. I said, 'Without this, I could
see me getting old.' I will never get old. It takes sex to keep us

young. No way will I ever give this up—the Lord gives me my health, and the Lord gives me my pleasure."

"Terry's writing a book about all this for Random House," Bob said.

"Ohh, about time someone did."

Amid the uproar of thousands talking at once a bare-breasted Cleopatra and G-stringed Pharaoh came up to Carmen.

"Oh, you look gorgeous, Carmen!"

"Well, you know me. This young fellow saw me on the dance floor, he came up to me, and said, 'I'd love to have you as my mother.' I said, 'No way! I'm the sexiest lady you'll meet here tonight. I'm not sitting on a porch sipping tea being your mother.'"

"Oh, you're bad, Carmen!"

"You better believe it! Sex keeps me young. 'No way in hell am I being your mother!' He asks me, 'How do you keep your shape?' So I said, 'I'm very active where and when it counts!' Without sex, what's life all about?"

"Some of the women here are going through menopause and are wondering whether their urge to be in the lifestyle will be lowered. Did you find that?" I asked.

"No. I'll tell you what. I got into it past menopause. It's like any game—if you still like to play, you play. So as far as that's concerned, I never worried about it."

"Do you have men your age?"

"Hell, I wouldn't go with older men. No! The young ones come to me. Young thirties. Yeah! You know why, they like older women because they're more experienced—they think it's our last hoorah, you know, it's like the virgin in reverse—they think, instead of it's her first time, it's her last time. And you know what happens—I wear *them* out! They go, 'Holy shit! Where do you get all the energy?' I mean, I wear them right out, they go, 'Oh God, I can't believe this woman!' I'm not one to bang! bang! bang!—no, no, I like to, you know, make *love*! Well, I gotta go to my table! Nice talkin' to you."

When I got back to my own table Cathy was telling a story to Leslie about somebody surprising her and Dan that morning with a gift of a sensual foot masseur. "He bit my toes, bit my ankle, bit the arches on my feet—I was so stimulated I didn't know how to cover it up! I never had anybody massage my feet and suck it up. That's supposed to wake you up. I was awake, all right."

"It sounds like sexual reflexology," Leslie laughed.

"Yeah, no kidding—I said to Dan, 'Women don't need to pay for it, but I bet this guy could make a living at this by calling it something else.' It was too fun."

"I want that," Ona the porn star said. "Did he bring any paraphernalia?"

"No, just one helluva pair of hands."

It was then I got the news from Joyce.

Every year the selecting of finalists in the Best Man's, Best Woman's, and Best Couple's categories was made by a panel of three or four judges in the immense, chandeliered lobby of the hotel. The judges assessed those people in each category who were willing to put themselves on active display for TV crews like HBO's. Joyce was in charge of choosing the judges and she usually balanced the panel with a straight-world intellectual, a porn star, an LSO volunteer, and someone connected to some aspect of the playcouple lifestyle. Last year the judges had included author David Alexander, a cop turned call girl named Norma Jean Almovadar, and the porn star Nina Hartley—who portrayed the publicly promiscuous blond wife who is shot dead by her husband in the film *Boogie Nights*. This year Joyce chose Pascal Pellegrino, Kerri Downs, LSO publicity director Steve Mason's wife Sheilah—and me.

"You'll do a good job," Bob told me. "Assess the costume, not necessarily the figure. Time, effort, originality are the criteria."

"Thanks for the privilege," I said. "I'll bear the weight with aplomb."

Around ten-thirty we four judges took our chairs at a table on a high platform just outside the doors to the ballroom, opposite a floodlit stage decorated in Day-Glo silk masks pinned to a shimmering metallic curtain. Back in the ballroom McGinley mounted the stage and interrupted the music, informing the thirty-five hundred dancers that the show would be starting shortly. "If you want to be in this judging and on television, please proceed to the lobby immediately."

It took the colorfully costumed conventioneers another half an hour or so to get in order around the stage for the judging. We finally got started sometime after eleven, about the time a car on official state busines pulled into the breezeway by the resort's grand entrance on the other side of the grounds. Two plainclothes agents, a male and a female from the Department of Alcoholic Beverage Control, stepped out. As they made their way to the Atlas Ballroom lobby, we began judging the women. Only four men had come forward in costume: a bare-assed motorcycle cop, a drag queen, a hooded executioner, and a bonobo chimpanzee.

"We got a ton of females," Sheilah Mason said to me. "They've been asking me all night, lining up for half an hour." They came on stage four at a time, pretty tame at first, as if the ones in commercially bought, mix-and-match attire had bunched together socially the way the least talented kids on a softball team congregate. There was a young woman I'd met at the pool, a hydrologist now dressed as a harem lady in gold lamé bra and belt, a red silk scarf trailing between her legs. She lifted the scarf for our benefit, turned around, bent over, and graced her hands between her legs and over her thong-bikinied rump. The others had their nakedness adorned in one Mardi Gras way or another, one with little battery-powered lights and roses. A lady on the left wore a leather bustier top, black army boots, and sheer beige stockings with no gusset; she carried a riding crop that she moved back and forth between her legs. A woman in her sixties was dressed in just white feathers and bananas, like Josephine Baker, posturing and voguing for favorable judgment. We had to pick the best two; later on we would winnow down the winners in each category to four finalists, which the audience would judge by an "applause-o-meter."

"Whenever you're ready!" Steve called to us.

"I'm not impressed with this batch," I said.

"Pascal says he likes the old gal in white," Sheilah told me.

"Yeah, I could go for her," Kerri said.

"You like the harem one, Terry?"

"Only as an erotic costume on a good-looking body—but it didn't take much effort," I said. "Besides, I don't like being bribed."

"Yeah."

"How about the one with the plume and feathers?" Sheilah asked. "Or the roses and the lights. That's cute."

"Come on, you guys!" Steve shouted. "Jesus—choose two!"

"Well, which one takes the most work to make?" I asked. "Let's go by that."

"None, really," Sheilah said.

"I like the one in white," Kerri said.

"Yeah, the one in white's kinda cute. My vote is the one in the white," Sheilah agreed.

"The harem girl's erotic." I second-guessed myself. "But the one in roses took more work."

"All right, the one in roses and the gal in white."

We relayed our choices to Steve, who relayed them to a tuxedoed Care Team leader on stage, who tapped our choices —to the crowd's approval.

"Well, that worked out pretty good," I said beaming. "I've never judged a costume contest."

Over at the security table run by Jerry Baker, the two sex

cops flashed their ID. The California statutes say that ABC inspectors are to be allowed entrance onto any licensed premises twenty-four hours a day without warrant or warning. The convention had been held at the Town and Country on nearly this scale and with exactly these activities in 1977, 1991, 1994, and 1995 without a single complaint from undercover police, the staff, or the resort's management—who had followed up every event with letters praising LSO for its smoothly run show. Baker wasn't nervous, and let the agents by, his eyes as usual scanning the crowd for any obvious misbehavior. The agents crossed through the lobby and entered the main ballroom, observing the events out in the lobby on a huge monitor towering over the dance floor.

Six or seven couples were on stage before me now. One was actually a triad consisting of a six-foot-tall, bronzed muscle lady in silver stacked heels, her solid bare breasts draped by thin gold chains and her pubis covered by a tiny gold triangle. Beside her stood a fellow in a baseball cap and wearing a sandwich board, which read: "Ladies, Attention! Get your official boob exam here! I am Fred, 'boob inspector' of San Diego. You must have a 'boob exam certificate' in order to visit my room tonight." On the muscle lady's other side stood a woman dressed like one of the Blues Brothers and holding a sign: "I am Carla, Assistant Boob Inspector of San Diego. Men! I will also examine and certify your penis on the side!!" Asked to step forward for the judge's inspection, the boob inspector Fred reached over and squeezed the muscle lady's left breast—an act that I would later read in a government manual violated Section 143.2, Subsection 3 of Title Four of the California Administrative Code, which deemed it "contrary to public welfare and morals" to "touch, caress or fondle the breasts" on a licensed premises.

On the left side of the stage, the harem girl and her Sheik of Araby husband stepped forward. Hamming for the cameras, the harem girl bent over in fluid dance movement and her sleek sheik rubbed her buttocks—another apparent threat to public welfare and morals, according to the Code.

One couple were dressed as a six-foot penis and a five-foot vagina. The fellow was an airline engineer, and he'd been working since January designing and fabricating these anatomically accurate renditions of male and female genitalia. In a way, they were self-parodying works of art. The penis wore a Superman S on his corpus cavernosum and a red cape trailing from the back of his glans; the vagina had the wife's head poking through the labia just above the clitoris. When they stepped forward, the wife embraced the penis, and the crowd roared as he shot a green stream of ribbon skyward.

"Oh, he came! He came!" I laughed, giving them my vote, not realizing they could have been accused of violating Section 143.4 of the California Administrative Code, which governed "Visual Displays," and which forbade, on a licensed premises, "visual reproductions depicting: (1) Acts or simulated acts of sexual intercourse, masturbation, sodomy, bestiality, oral copulation, flagellation or any sexual acts which are prohibited by law"; and "(4) Scenes wherein artificial devices or inanimate objects are employed to depict...any of the prohibited activities described above."

"This is the most successful convention we've ever had," Bob told me after the applause-o-meter judging, which awarded a Lifestyles holiday to the penis and vagina. "You know, we've already got over two hundred bookings for next year—and this one's not even over."

In that lobby and ballroom, thirty-five hundred mostly married mainstream people partied on till 4 A.M. Eight hours later, many without sleep, they got on airport buses and returned to their 437 cities around the world. They'd had the time of their lives, and the government was now going to put a stop to it.

CHAPTER TWELVE

The Erotic Rights of Swingers

The story of how the forces of censorship melted out of the woodwork to shut down the Sensual and Erotic Art Exhibition, and how the LSO fought them to a standstill and went on with the show, is a tale both satisfying in its conclusion and alarming in its implications.

DAVID GUTCHEON,
Art Collector International

Jim Otto was in a panicky state. He was the director of sales of the Town and Country and he had just received a letter from the Department of Alcoholic Beverage Control regarding the Erotic Masquerade Ball. Not only had an unnamed male "caressed and fondled the exposed breasts" of one female, but, according to the ABC agents, "a female, while straddling the male's lap, did simulate sexual intercourse." The agents maintained they'd seen eleven more acts of lewdness perpetrated by a few of the thousands in the lobby and Atlas Ballroom during and after the judging of the costumes.

It was October 2, 1996, and the ABC was putting the entire Atlas hotel chain on notice that a revocation of its California liquor license was possible—which if enacted would drive the corporation into bankruptcy. Jim Otto phoned McGinley with the news.

The same week Otto received his heartstopping missive, Agent Gilson Grey from the Long Beach Bureau of the ABC paid a visit to the Seaport Marina Hotel, where McGinley was to hold his Halloween Banquet and Ball at the end of the month. Grey met with the Seaport's controller and appraised him of "the problems" the Lifestyles Organization was causing down in San Diego. He handed him a copy of the California Administrative Code, Title 4, Sections 143.2–4, which regulated sexual conduct and attire in licensed establishments. The Long Beach ABC followed up its visit with a call: agents from the ABC would be attending the Lifestyles Halloween Ball "in force." As stated in the ABC's mandate, the bureaucracy had the power to revoke the liquor license of an establishment for any infraction of the "morals" rules—including something as minor as displaying "visual reproductions" of the genitals, say in a painting or a costume. The Seaport's very worried catering director phoned McGinley, and McGinley—now very worried himself—phoned Agent Gilson Grey, only to discover that Grey had no interest in discussing the matter with LSO; the ABC's sole concern was with liquor-license holders.

Sitting in his office beneath his framed photographs of fighter aircraft, McGinley pondered whether the moment he had anticipated had finally arrived. For almost a quarter of a century he had sponsored public events at mainstream hotels and had never given the government any legal pretext to stop him—at least a pretext that would stand up in court. An officer spotting an isolated incident at an LSO dance or convention would have had to testify that McGinley's Care Team and security guards were constantly on patrol to stop any couple who violated community standards, much as guards did at a rock concert or at a sporting event where beer was served. But something had suddenly changed in the government's attitude toward the Lifestyles Organization.

Taking the government's point of view McGinley reasoned that the growth in his organization in just the last year would have caused officials to try to stop that growth through punitive actions against his venues—without having to prove a thing in court. And he was certain that if they got away with excluding playcouples without due process there would be a long list of others whose self-expression they would also exclude. That hunch turned out to be so completely accurate that David Gutcheon, the executive editor of *Art Collector International*, would soon label the ABC "an over-funded, crypto-fascist shadow agency." The American Civil Liberties Union would declare the ABC "drunk with its own power." And the president of the board of directors of the UCLA law school, Robert Burke, would accuse the agency of practicing "state Gestapoism."

These words were not chosen lightly; they were meant to describe the ABC's "clear awareness that their activities [were] violations of free speech and due process," according to Gutcheon (whose nom de plume is Morris Fischbein). "Indeed, the way in which they conduct themselves offers every indication that their policies are *intended* to implement a behind-the-scenes chilling effect through the use of intimidation and the threat of financial devastation."

In accordance with that intention, the ABC refused to deal directly with the Lifestyles Organization, over which it had no legal power, and moved instead on LSO's venues, over which they had absolute power without having to bother about due process in court. McGinley pushed ahead with his contractually arranged Halloween dance in the face of the ABC's intimidation of Seaport's management. Six weeks afterward he received a letter from the law firm representing Atlas Hotels stating that the ABC had suspended the Town and Country's liquor license for five days and had informed Atlas it was keeping the resort on probation for three years. "Atlas simply cannot afford to risk its alcoholic beverage license by permitting further Lifestyles events on Atlas' premises," their lawyer, William Shearer, informed McGinley. Atlas was therefore summarily canceling all its contracts with LSO for the next three years and holding LSO responsible for "all loss it sustains in this matter." McGinley at first tried to negotiate, arguing that the Town and Country had competitively campaigned for LSO's business. He then sued for breach of contract. LSO had already taken in some twenty-two thousand dollars in advance bookings for the 1997 convention, and now McGinley had to find other accommodation for an expected four thousand attendees—with, he was sure, the ABC informing all prospective hotel hosts of the bad karma that would accrue if they held the playcouple gathering.

As reservations for Lifestyles '97 poured in from around the world, McGinley put the word out that he was looking for a new venue. Unaware of the ABC's machinations, the Palm Springs Convention and Visitors Bureau came actively courting by phone, fax, and mail. Virtually deserted in the 110-degree summer, but loaded with hotels and a grand convention center, Palm Springs collectively realized that the influx of $1.65 million Lifestyles always brought to a city would give the town a great boost in the off-season. McGinley thought Palm Springs would do fine, and in April Lifestyles signed a contract for its convention with several hotels—the Spa, the Marquis, the Hilton, and the Wyndham—as well as the convention center, which adjoined the Wyndham and which would hold the Masquerade Ball, the Erotic Arts show, and the Adult Marketplace. As the Wyndham would book the majority of playcouples, all the seminars would be held there, as well as the Car Wash.

The ABC decided this would be morally inadvisable. The ABC's district supervisor, Dave Gill, called a meeting on May 9 at the Wyndham for all parties concerned—except the LSO. McGinley showed up anyway, with a First Amendment lawyer from San Diego named Paul Murray, whom McGinley had met on a Lifestyles Tours and Travel holiday to the Eden Resort the month before my own visit. Murray and McGinley took seats on the dais right beside Gill, who, like McGinley's old nemesis, Cronin, was six feet tall and clean-cut. McGinley's life seemed to have come full circle.

Gill opened the meeting by saying the reason he had called the hotel owners together was because of the "incidents by Lifestyles in San Diego last year." He reminded the assembled hotel owners of the ABC's legal mandate, as stated in the California Constitution: "To deny, suspend or revoke any specific alcoholic beverages license if it shall determine for good cause that the granting or continuance of such license would be contrary to public welfare or morals." Gill made it clear that the ABC would revoke the license of any venue that fulfilled its contract with LSO, since the activities of the LSO convention —in particular the Erotic Arts show, the Car Wash, and the Adult Marketplace, to name just three—could be *expected* to violate public welfare and morals. Murray interrupted Gill to point out that no liquor would be served at these events, but Gill replied that that was immaterial under the law. All activities that took place on a licensed premises had to obey the California Administrative Code: no sex, no nudity, and no representations of sex or nudity.

Then he added a statement that struck terror into the hearts of every hotel owner in the room. The ABC rules of morality applied even to the sleeping rooms of guests, since they were on the premises of the license holders. Attendees at the hotels, by inference, could not have sex in their rooms, nor could they walk around in those rooms naked, since ABC agents were empowered to enforce the regulations in those areas of a licensed premises. A light went on in McGinley's mind: it suddenly became clear to him that one of the goals of all this intimidation was the regulation of the *private sexual behavior of citizens*.

After the meeting Murray wrote Gill's boss, the ABC's deputy director, Manuel Espinoza, relating the gist of Gill's amazing statements regarding the private rooms. "Mr. Gill has subsequently refused to engage in any further discussion," he wrote, "and has advised the hotels in question that allowing LSO, Ltd.'s convention to proceed would jeopardize their licenses." Twelve days after Gill's meeting, in fact, the Spa backed out of its contract with Lifestyles.

If there were any doubts in the minds of the hotel owners that the ABC meant to enforce its regulations in the private rooms of guests if the Lifestyles convention took place, they were put to rest when Espinoza gave his final word on the

subject to Murray. It is a truly wondrous document, and war-
rants quoting almost in full.

"The entire Palm Springs Convention Center complex is
licensed for the sale, service and consumption of alcoholic beverages. The same holds true for the Wyndham Hotel property.
The regulations apply at all times to both facilities regardless
of whether or not alcoholic beverage service is being provided
at a certain time or location within the licensed premises or
whether *the activity is private or public in nature.* [Italics mine.]
Any other interpretation would render the regulations mean-
ingless and unenforceable.... The regulations are clear that
licensees shall not permit 'any person' to engage in the prohibited activities on the licensed premises."

The implication was clear: hotel owners had better play
ball according to the ABC's moral rules, or they wouldn't play
ball at all. There was a right way and a wrong way to have sex
in a private room—and swinging sex was the wrong way.

Murray threw down the gauntlet in a return letter, alert-
ing Espinoza to the "Constitutional significance" of his perceived mandate. He went on for five pages, making a clear case
that the ABC was selectively going after LSO, and demanded
that he enforce the regulations regarding sex in private rooms
equally, everywhere, and immediately. "If in fact you have no
intention of conducting such enforcement we would like a
detailed explanation as to the distinction which you feel pre-
cludes these areas from enforcement.... Absent such a distinction we will have no alternative than to challenge Section 143.2
et seq. as unconstitutional as applied." It was the first time anyone had ever threatened to stand up to the ABC in court on
Constitutional grounds. In its forty-year history, the regulatory
body had never had a restraining order placed on it.

The havoc that the ABC was wreaking on the Lifestyles
Organization became clear when McGinley won the first of a
series of court battles he would wage against Atlas Hotels. The

judge ruled that Atlas had failed to prove that LSO's activities had necessitated the breaking of the contract and most significantly, that there was "no evidence to suggest that any activity complained of was committed by any individual whose conduct would make [LSO] liable thereof."

For McGinley, though, the judgment was a Pyrrhic victory. "Until the ABC stepped in, we had the greatest relationship with the Town and Country," he told me over the phone at the time. "The ABC got what they wanted in that battle. And that really burns me. They're running around the state doing exactly the same thing to other people who are too poor or too scared of exposure to stand up to them. But I'll tell you something. They have not won the war. I'm just putting my troops into the field."

———

McGinley was not exaggerating when he said the ABC was "running around the state doing exactly the same thing to other people." From the California government's point of view, sexual tolerance had gone too far in society, period. The government was on a moral crusade and swingers, as McGinley had predicted, were now just one group among many who numbered among the infidels. When a government—any government—feels itself standing as a righteous bulwark against sexual immorality, the public becomes the enemy and the government usually turns loose on society what the Palm Springs *Desert Sun* would later inaccurately call a "renegade agency." There was nothing "renegade" about the ABC. Invested with the power of economic life and death over every hotel, bar, nightclub, and restaurant in a state of thirty-two million people, the ABC had the specific mandate of keeping the public in moral line—which it did in massive shows of force shortly after the Lifestyles '96 Convention. The ABC raided

bars, nightclubs, and dances where gays, lesbians, blacks, his-
panics, poor people, and artists were all alleged to be getting
out of hand. Willy-nilly, the ABC revoked the liquor licenses
of these establishments and drove them out of business. Since
the ABC had no power over organizations that didn't hold a
license to sell alcohol, such as LSO and other swing clubs, they
effectively shut down the spots where their members liked to
assemble. In its raids the ABC employed both its own agents
and proxies in city vice squads, which the ABC directly
funded. The ABC received those funds from the State of
California, which in turn received them from the federal government in order for the state to initiate a fresh approach to
crime prevention. Raiding the clubs of people perceived to be
immoral was the fresh approach to crime prevention taken by
the right-wing administration of Governor Pete Wilson.

"These raids were being conducted in the name of pro-
tecting the morals and the family standards of the people of the
State of California," the UCLA-affiliated lawyer Bob Burke
told a meeting of swingers that I attended at the height of the
harassment. Burke, who had taken up the cudgel for the
California Bar and Tavern Guild, explained that we lived in a
time when the government was not allowed to regulate private
sexuality, and the raids were its way of surreptitiously doing
the regulating. Instead of firing or jailing people who had sex
unconventionally, as they'd once done with swingers and
homosexuals, they were now removing the liquor licenses of
the establishments where they recreated, sending a message to
these and other subcultures that they should behave more con-
ventionally. The crime-prevention theory behind the raids was
that immoral sexual behavior led to the breakdown in family
values and the breakdown in family values led to criminal
behavior. Since immoral people were known to congregate
in taverns, nightclubs, and at conventions, the ABC was the
perfect enforcement arm. Its mandate entrusted it both with

safeguarding "public welfare and morals" and preventing "moral turpitude" in licensed premises.

"When I started looking into this, I found that these strike forces were moving selectively," Burke told the swingers. "They would first start in areas where there were African-American bars and then about three or four weeks later they would drop all enforcement there and they would move over into areas of Latino bars and raid these groups, and then pull off from there. Then they'd go to gay and lesbian bars and dance clubs and they'd raid these. Then they'd go back to black bars.

"Most pointedly, of course, they never went into the more affluent, prestigious, or more comfortable areas of the city," Burke related. "You never saw them going into West L.A. or Beverly Hills or Pacific Palisades or any place else like that. They were not to be seen. You would never see them in any of the sports venues."

In other words, the government took for granted that poor people and unconventional types were more of a criminal threat to society than were the wealthy. Afraid of exposure if they protested, or having no money with which to protest, the poor and unconventional were without power in society. And so the ABC treated them as governments always treat the powerless. A dozen agents at a time would pour through the doors of a bar in a poor neighborhood and force patrons to line up against a wall with their hands up, sometimes for two hours. One of these raids on a Latino bar was captured on the establishment's video surveillance monitor. As with the Town and Country, in almost every instance of a raid some infraction was discovered and the liquor license was revoked or suspended. The charges did not have to be proved in court, since the ABC was the regulator. The only appeal a bar or dance hall had was to the ABC itself.

"It is so outrageous and such a violation of our First Amendment rights," Burke said, "that we can't sit back and say 'It doesn't concern me.' If this kind of state Gestapoism can happen here with an agency, it can very quickly move to other states."

The ABC also took the regulations against public eroticism and applied them in the most suspect ways when it suited their purposes, which brings into question some of their allegations against anonymous couples at Lifestyles '96. In effect, the ABC moved the goal posts so close together on the playing field that there was no room left for the people they didn't want to play. "The ABC...busted into an unassuming gay bar in Hollywood," David Gutcheon wrote in *Art Collector International*. "In the bar was a model of Michelangelo's *David*, the sublime classical masterpiece.... The Department of Alcoholic Beverage Control declared that this icon was a violation of Cal. Admin. Reg. 4-143,4, and they revoked the bar's liquor license. That's how high the stakes are. In California, *right now*, Michelangelo's *David* constitutes obscenity, and displaying it can cost you your business. As Dr. McGinley put it, 'If they can establish legal precedent, they could shut down our whole civilization.'"

Art Collector International is perhaps the last journal you would expect to find Robert McGinley cited in as an authority on the government's threat to "our whole civilization." But Gutcheon had come to recognize what Bob McGinley knew in his gut back when the war on swingers had first begun: when the media spend years condemning one form of legal sexual expression on moral grounds, it sends a message to rulers that community standards allow for the oppression of all forms of expression, except those which the government approves. And that includes artistic expression.

Back in May of 1997, reflecting on the ABC's oppression of his own organization, McGinley began to feel the same emotion that had narrowed his eyes to slits thirty years before. "You bastards. You have picked the wrong guy to do this to."

———

A vital lesson of war taught by Sun Tzu states: "Maneuver in the highest heights." As the troops on the Palm Springs battle-field began to move about and fire on one another, McGinley began to search for high ground on which to make a stand. For almost fifteen years the press had been on the side of law and order and morality, and against the lifestyle. Now, he believed, the media had to be shown what the effects of their support for the "moral authorities" had wrought: people who were doing no more than having *erotic fun* in public, but *explicit sexual fun* in private settings, were being persecuted. "This is a battle to the finish," he told me. "Really—I'm serious. Losing it will mean the end of lifestyle conventions and dances, gay and les-bian dances, black and Latino dances—the works. Who's going to hold an event if the ABC wins here? I have to convince the press of that. They have to know we're on the same side. They have to know that when the ABC attacks us, they're also attack-ing free expression—they're attacking the media."

On July 15, with the 1997 convention less than two weeks away, the ground for McGinley's final battle was chosen for him by the enemy. In a meeting with Jim Dunn, general man-ager of the Palm Springs Convention Center, the ABC insisted that it was dead serious about enforcing its mandate: there was no room for negotiation on the artistic merits of any one event. Not only were the Trade Fair and the Car Wash "in conflict with the statutes of the ABC," but, pointedly, so was the Erotic Arts show, and the convention center would lose its license if it went ahead and displayed the works (which, amazingly, the ABC had not even inspected for violations of its rules). Dunn wrote McGinley that day, saying that the art show would have to be either canceled or moved to "a tent located on a nearby vacant lot." The cost of the tent, born by McGinley, would be almost fifty-four thousand dollars. There were more than a hundred paintings in the Erotic Arts show, and they would almost certainly suffer damage in the heat.

McGinley now knew he had his high ground, and he knew the press and public would rally around him. The ABC was now attacking a highly protected form of free speech in North America: art. The public might not give a hoot about swingers, gays, lesbians, and poor people, but they would realize that once the government moved on art illegally, it would eventually move on everybody.

In that last week before the convention, with the hotels and convention center forced to try to back out of their contracts with LSO (which would have meant losing most of their tourist income for the summer), the world joined McGinley on his redoubt. The American Civil Liberties Union took LSO's case, putting its First Amendment specialists, Peter Eliasberg and Dan Takoji, in charge of the ABC file. The ACLU linked up with Paul Murray and Bob Burke and prepared to take the ABC to court to stop its harassment of LSO with a temporary restraining order. After that they hoped to win a permanent injunction that would defeat the ABC on its other fronts of attack against gays, lesbians, Latinos, and African Americans. The *Washington Post* assigned its veteran California correspondent, William Claiborne, to the story. The Palm Spring *Desert Sun* prepared a space on its front page for coverage of the showdown in court. The local affiliates of the major TV networks showed up at the convention with their vans—this was too juicy to miss. *Art Collector International*, distributed in first-class cabins on American Airlines, would leave absolutely no doubt about where the interests of the public stood on this issue: "The promise that shaved gorillas calling themselves peace officers *shall not* be empowered to implement their hit-it-with-a-stick social policy upon society at large is *the* promise of America."

As the first of the early-bird swingers were landing in the Palm Springs heat, California's deputy attorney general, Dana Cartozian, argued before the Los Angeles Federal Court that the Palm Springs Convention Center was in violation of state laws barring liquor-license holders from allowing exhibitions depicting nudity; therefore, the art show should be banned. If not, the ABC should be allowed to revoke the Convention Center's liquor license. The ABC fully anticipated a victory that day and from there it would have been an easy step to shut down the entire convention with the threat of suspending the liquor licenses of all the host hotels. It had good cause for optimism. The district judge hearing the case was Dickran Tevrizian who, according to the *Washington Post*, "has a reputation as a hard-line, anti-pornography jurist that grew when he raised a fuss over an anatomically correct statue—called the 'New World' and described by Tevrizian as a 'shrine to pedophiles'—that was erected outside his federal court building."

Bob McGinley did not attend the hearing, opting instead to hang tough with his cell phone in the Wyndham where he tended to the thousand-and-one details in the last twenty-four hours before the official opening of the convention. One of these included fighting the Wyndham's paranoid insistence that all people entering the pool area show their proof of majority regardless of whether they looked seventy years old. "These ABC Gestapos have got everyone so sick with fear, the whole state is shaking," he told me at the pool gate. "Every convenience-store owner, every bar, every hotel that sells beer and *Playboy* is waiting for the knock at the door." Because of that fear, for the first time since its appearance at Lifestyles conventions in the seventies, the Evening of Caressive Intimacy— including the Car Wash—would not go ahead: ABC agents had made it clear to the Wyndham that this sort of mass body rub was impermissible in the State of California, no matter what the judge decided about dirty pictures or dirty trade fair products.

"What happens if you do lose this, Bob?" I asked him. "Where are all the people going to go?"

"I can't even think about that," he said. "Right now, I'm just hoping Luis is in there doing his stuff."

In fact, right about then Luis was "reviewing the whole thing for the judge," as he would later tell me. Fortuitously, for the first time since 1990, Luis's responsibilities at the Los Angeles Music Society had prevented him from curating the 1997 show, which permitted him to testify before Judge Tevrizian as an expert witness. "One of the fundamental characteristics of today's erotic art is that it represents a movement of liberation," he submitted to the court, echoing the sentiments he had uttered to *Penthouse* eighteen months before. He emphasized the numerous women artists in the show and he could have been defending the interests of women like Jenny Friend and Jodie in his formal written submission: "For some women, erotic art is a rebellious attack on repressive institutions of family, marriage, and monogamous and compulsive heterosexuality; for others it is an important source of pleasure and liberation." It was a show for all, nonetheless. "Erotic art is an important outlet for artists who have led closeted lives, especially for gay artists."

At about three in the afternoon the call came through from Paul Murray. The judge ruled that the ABC was aggressively misusing its authority in order to suppress free speech. Tevrizian pronounced that although he personally had no taste for erotic art, "this is a heavy-handed tactic. ABC has no business revoking a liquor license for this type of activity." He slapped a restraining order on the ABC and told it to let the Lifestyles convention proceed without harassment.

"Hot dog! I told you!" McGinley came striding up to me in the lobby with his hand out and his face filled with a lifetime's worth of good news. "They picked the wrong guy! But this, my friend, is for everyone! They *can't* get away with this in our country. Now they know!"

———

The next day there was jubilation among the four thousand swingers in Palm Springs, most of whom had decided they would show up for this convention, banned or not. "I told Eddy, they ban us," a lady in her thirties from Portland told me as she stood in line to register, "we're gonna camp out on City Hall and party in the desert."

That night, at the Marquis Hotel's rooftop lounge, McGinley made an official announcement to the sexy throngs. "By now everybody in the world knows," he said. "We tried to keep it quiet, but if you've been watching television at all or reading the newspaper, we've been having a momentous battle with the California Alcohol Beverage Control board. And it's one thing we could not have walked away from: we felt that because what they were trying to do was so dangerous to any lifestyle, not just ours here at the convention—but to the gays and lesbians and Latinos they were oppressing—to *all* the citizens of California, that we felt obligated to charge ahead with it. We are the first citizen group that is forcing the ABC to actually obey the law, something they've never been asked to do before. Incredible!"

The crowd went wild with cheers and applause. Somebody gave the best vocal imitation of the Seventh Cavalry bugle charge I have ever heard in my life. "You get 'em Bob!"

I was standing beside Earl and Pia, the physician and nurse I'd met at New Horizons, who had just entered the lifestyle back at the "Lifestyle and You" seminar, but who in the last year had paddled up the rivers of the subculture to its most remote and steamy reaches. Over the winter they had gone all the way in and come all the way out to their grown kids, and were thinking—just thinking—that if public acceptance increased, they might like to come out generally. This victory was a good sign.

When the huzzahs died down, McGinley went on, soberly: "But—we have to obey the law, too. Now that we've cleared all the issues they brought before the court, we want you to have a heck of a lot of good old fashioned adult fun. But I want to caution you not to get carried away. I'm sorry to put it this way—but particularly the women—"

The crowd exploded into uproarious laughter. They were in on a joke the world hadn't yet caught onto—except, that is, when it was presented in the form of some glaringly erotic and self-confident ladies called the Spice Girls.

"Ain't nobody's business if I do!" Pia curled her hands around her mouth and called, a changed woman from the one who had folded her fantasies into little squares on her lap at New Horizons.

"Yeah, whose convention is this, anyway?" said Earl beside her.

The LSO's lawyer, Paul Murray, took the mike, smoothed the rebelliously long hair he wore over his suit collar, rolled his head back as if raising his nose through water to air he hadn't breathed in weeks, and inhaled a breath that could have filled the lungs of Moby Dick. For two months he hadn't had a day off. Word by word he proceeded to state what lifestylers believe is their ultimate due.

"What we are about," he said, then paused, surveying the line of spicy women in the front of the crowd, and their proud husbands holding them around, and the sides of the room packed with couples standing high-heeled and barefoot upon tables, and the back of the room crowded with people sitting on the bar, and the patio filled with couples leaning in. Murray raised a hand in the air, "What we are about," he said, "*is liberty!* Maybe this isn't the kind of liberty that everybody *thinks* of as liberty, but it is liberty. It's the right to express ourselves in the medium that we enjoy and understand. A medium that is offensive to other people and that possibly isn't afforded to other people because of their personal tastes or inhibitions. But it is our medium, our expression, and we want to preserve that right, and continue to be treated in the public press in the same unique and positive light we have just been treated, *which has never to my knowledge been so favorable and respectful.* And we want that to continue!"

He waited a long moment for the cavalry-charge bugle calls and the applause and the victory cheers to die down. He waited, in fact, for silence, and then again held his hand in the air.

"Now," he said. "I need your help. Dr. McGinley needs your help and this is what I am going to ask of you. *NO PUBLIC SEX!* Absolutely none! We are going to be watching because one couple, *one couple*, could undermine everything we've been fighting for months. I will make a confession to you right now. Are you ready?"

This time the crowd waited.

"I LOVE PUBLIC SEX!"

That released the crowd again, as hard to stop as an avalanche of beer barrels fallen off a truck on a steep hill. Murray didn't try and stop the racket. He just shouted over it.

"I like to watch it; I like to participate; I like to see it," he said, and order was restored, mostly out of curiosity, shared interest. "As a matter of fact," he said, "the ABC wrote a report about this convention last year and there were thirteen citations of public sex. And in my office we came up with a game: 'What number public sex do you want to be?' 'I want to be number nine.' Public sex is a wonderful thing and I think that's a big part of what all of us are. But you cannot do it. As much as you want to, you *can-n-not* do it!"

Fifteen minutes later, when the speech-making was over and the getting-to-know-you party had commenced, I sat down for a beer with Pia and Earl not far from the triads and tetrads grinding out on the dance floor and asked them what they thought of this—the enormous numbers, the California glitter crowd, the ABC victory haloing them all. Earl repeated almost verbatim what the New Brunswick woman had told me beside the pool at last year's convention. "It's like a gay person coming out."

"And it isn't even so much any actual physical thing," Pia said. She looked around at the crowd. "Obviously no one's having sex *all* the time. It's not having to hide who you are naturally—with women, with men, with your partner—being able to relax and share it and not be tortured by guilt about it."

"How long do you think it lasts for?" I asked. "In marriage —that happiness in release?"

"In sharing? Why not forever?" Earl said.

———————

On the night of the Masquerade Ball, Dr. Robert L. McGinley, Minister of the Earth Church of the Pacific, married a couple who couldn't have been more than in their mid-twenties. The wedding took place at the height of that wild last evening of this politically triumphant gathering of swingers—long after the packed news conferences and endless string of TV interviews in the lobby and at the pool and at the dinners. It was held, thanks to the victory over the forces of sexual concealment and secrecy, in the Palm Springs Convention Center Ballroom, where both Bob Hope and Ronald Reagan had been honored in the past.

The couple were Rachel and Michael, and he—tall, squarejawed, and very handsome—marched though the carnival crowd to the stage in a tux, flanked by a best man and friends also dressed in black and white. The veiled Rachel, on the other hand, wore a metallic, silver-sequined bikini, high heels, and a garter on her left thigh; she marched down the aisle with friends wearing matching bikinis of gold. They were embarking on a marriage in the playcouple lifestyle—young for that, but they were doing it—and these days they are featured on Lifestyles promotional literature for conventions.

"Let me have your attention, please," the tuxedoed McGinley called, hoarse after three days of shouting at dinners and dances and news conferences. "Rachel and Michael and all who are here! All come! Michael and Rachel! Let this be a day of gladness, thanksgiving, possibilities, and great good fortune for all!

"Michael and Rachel," he went on, as this year's batch of media camera crews wove and ducked to record the event, "we have come together this evening to demonstrate the wonder of love through the celebration of marriage! We all live in the hope of loving and giving love," McGinley stated in sincere belief. "Michael and Rachel, therefore, we give thanks—for sweet happiness. Their enthusiasm," he turned to the crowd, "their loving and their belief and destiny for love is inspiring! And their *great* expectation!" he said in wonderment, which must have caused a few members in those media crews to wonder what sort of bizarre expectations this couple had for their wedding night.

"For a marriage is a very happy place, a sheltered environment in which we can endlessly explore ourselves in the presence of another," McGinley went on. "We are so happy that Michael and Rachel and everyone know how much in love they are. And that they have found each other and that they're choosing this day, a very special day, to become for all time the accurate and beautiful reflection of each other's essence. We ask that the visions they have of one another be always informed by the spellbinding radiant power that first brought them together," he said, a little cornily, as was his occasional bent. "And we pray as they move to the hallowed ground that is marriage, that they may always hold one another in the light of all times in the love of all love.

"May I have the rings, please!" he called.

On my left and on my right, middle-aged women dressed in every conceivable girdle-and-lace outfit, most not too far in skimpiness from the bridesmaids on stage, wiped tears from their eyes. The men—naked cowboys with holsters, bare-assed buccaneers, and a lifeguard with a pith helmet that read "Let me save you!"—held their wives tight, smiling.

"Michael and Rachel," McGinley announced in the heightening silver glare of klieg lights, "now that you have heard of the magic of the mysteries of marriage, the way it will continue to broaden you, the spring and wisdom it will everlastingly have for you: Do you, Michael, want to marry Rachel, to have her and hold her above all and have her as your life's partner?"

"I do," said Michael.

"Do you, Rachel, want to marry Michael and have him and hold him above all and have him as your life's partner?" McGinley asked.

"I do."

"Having taken these vows before this assemblage and according to the laws of the State of California," said the man who had just battled that state to a standstill, "we are extremely pleased to pronounce you husband and wife."

Robert McGinley turned from the couple's kiss, threw his arm back, and, looking as if he had attained the highest peak of pleasure and happiness in his own life, declared: "May I have the honor of presenting to you Mr. and Mrs. Michael Barns!"

Mendelssohn's *Wedding March* came on in deafening organ fanfare and the couple and their train marched back through the crowd, to ecstatic cheers and shouts.

"Good luck!"

"Take care of each other!"

"*Mazel tov!*"

"I give these kids six months," the director of one of the media crews said to me as we watched the young couple go by.

"No," I told him. "Probably longer. In the lifestyle or out-side it, most everything's the same. The only thing that's different is the style. They think it's more fun their way."

CHAPTER THIRTEEN

The Future

We could have had sex but there weren't enough
people.

WOODY ALLEN, *Sleeper*

Eight months after that night of victory at the 1997 convention, Robert McGinley's voice was broadcast across Canada in nine separate CBC radio interviews, each in a city that had at least one swing club, many of them affiliated with NASCA. Two weeks before, on March 1, 1998, Montreal's Club L'Orage, one of fifteen lifestyle clubs in the city, had been raided by the police and twoscore solid citizens had been arrested and charged as "found-ins in a common bawdy house."

The raid made front-page headlines in the national and local press, but there was a different spin on the story than was usual when swingers were driven into the street with raincoats over their heads. What had startled the press this time, and had put McGinley on the radio, as well as on the front page of the *Globe and Mail*, was the reaction of the public. Rather than morally condemning orgiasts, everyday people expressed support for the swingers and outrage at the police. "On the city's most popular open-line talk shows," the Montreal *Gazette* reported, "the majority of the callers said the state has no business intervening in the orgies of the nation, so long as they involve consenting adults, do not include degrading or dehumanizing behavior and otherwise do not cause harm."

The public, it seemed, had adopted the principles of ethical hedonism: "Police have found themselves in the unexpected position of having to defend the raid."

In staid Ottawa, home to both government and the sophisticated Club Desire—a member of both NASCA and the Equal Opportunity Lifestyles Organization—a CBC radio host wondered (as McGinley had predicted the mainstream press would start wondering) what the heck was happening? Swingers?

"The word swinging just conjures up martini glasses and polyester, you know," the not unfriendly but nonplussed host, Ken Rockburn, commented.

McGinley set him straight. The best words to describe swingers were "in the lifestyle." And polyester was not the favored attire of most lifestylers. "Socioeconomically we're talking middle- to upper-middle class," he explained. "We're talking relatively high education levels. These are primarily married couples but not exclusively so. And obviously they have discretionary income to enable them to be involved in such activities. So we're really talking about the movers in Western society."

Yes—but what about having extramarital sex within the institution of monogamous marriage? That sounded a little different.

Not to McGinley. "They view swinging as a social activity. They view it similar to being involved in dancing, for example. Dancing is an activity of the couple that's not something that's going against their marriage at all."

Then Rockburn hit McGinley with the million-dollar question, the one that was hardly ever asked of him, except rhetorically. "Is there a long-term detrimental impact on a couple's relationship if they're involved in this activity over a prolonged period of time?"

McGinley referred Rockburn's audience to "Dr. Edgar W. Butler, chairperson of the Department of Sociology at the University of California at Riverside, who has done research on this and indeed has published in the area. And there are many others. We find that swinging relationships tend to be very solid ones."

———————

Since his battle with the ABC, McGinley had been having his say in just this manner. In the press there were none of the usual snarling adjectival phrases that for more than fifteen years had invariably followed his quotes in print. On the radio, talk-show hosts withheld their angry interruptions that at one time peppered every interview; in McGinley's previous experience the most civilized interviewers, without the least nod to politeness, would accuse him of being a sex profiteer in the face of plagues and psychological illness. The *Los Angeles Times*, the *Globe and Mail*, network radio, and television stations—always reflecting societal norms—now reflected the curiosity of their clientele. They interviewed "Dr. McGinley" straight up. They seemed to temporarily accept him as a spokesperson for people of a particular orientation.

There was also a new, human texture to this commentary. Newspaper reporters, induced by reader interest to open their eyes to the full range of the people at the events they attended, started going beyond searching out the most obvious examples of abnormality or duncehead IQs. Writers still often led their articles with these spectacular types, but they started including others as well. Most significantly, they were willing to let go unchallenged McGinley's claim which they perceived the public might now be willing to accept: Lifestylers, whatever you thought of their sex lives, came from the ranks of "the movers in our Western society."

Overall, it seemed, they detected a new tolerance among the bourgeoisie for swingers and they allowed themselves to relate the story that had been staring them in the face for years. Something was definitely happening that might not yet be mainstream but was flowing parallel to the mainstream; it was being fed by the mainstream through underground channels, and the swinging lifestyle just might, if the force of that flow ran its banks, actually merge with the main channel.

The big question, of course, is: Will it?

———

Twenty years ago Edgar Butler had predicted "that swinging, as an emerging alternative lifestyle, will continue to exist and probably grow substantially in the future." In his Ph.D. thesis McGinley had made the same argument. "All evidence points to swinging as a natural desire. It is not new, only its ready availability is new."

To date, those predictions have proved accurate: swinging continues to exist, and it has grown substantially. The annual Lifestyles convention is a mega-event. Miniconventions are taking place every Saturday night in the smallest towns, and new clubs are opening all the time. In Legion halls and hotels, normal people dress the same as at the big conventions, talk the same, and do the same things with one another on the dance floor and in the bedrooms. It is just possible that we are entering an era in which the playcouple lifestyle is going to take a big jump in popularity. I have several reasons for feeling that way.

The first is that there has been a sea change in the North American public's overall attitude to unconventional sexual behavior. It can be summed up in the oft-used phrase, "It's none of my business," and it augurs well that swingers may have less to fear now than ever before if they are "outed." In a study of middle-class Americans published in 1998, *One Nation, After All*, the sociologist Alan Wolfe deduced that, at least at the time he'd written his book, the media were completely out of touch with the new wave of public tolerance for the private sex lives of individuals—even public individuals, as demonstrated by the "leave him alone" reaction of most Americans when the media began endlessly repeating Special Prosecutor Kenneth Starr's detailed exposure of the consensual sexual activities of President Bill Clinton. They accepted that he was married and that he lied about having had sex with a White House intern. They were aware—and willing to admit they were aware—that their own sex lives were not as clean as the driven snow either. Sexual condemnation, once an automatic reaction even in the face of one's own personal sexual indulgence, was finally being assessed by common people as "no longer cool"—just as swinging had once been assessed. The *Gazette* could in all seriousness ask the question: "Do orgies fall within acceptable community standards?" The answer seemed to be: "Yes."

A second reason I believe the playcouple lifestyle will grow is because of the sexual, social, and economic empowerment of women. It is very difficult to describe to someone who has not been to a club or convention how "sexually liberated" women can behave in those environments. Many of them are self-confident, independent professionals who choose to emulate both the new and the old icons of movie stardom—without guilt, without fear, without heart-wrenching emotional attachment to their partners in bed, and without feeling they have sacrificed their love for their husbands and families by having a delightful sexual experience. Given everything we have been brought up to believe about "the relatively low female sex drive," and that that drive is predicated on a lasting bond, swinging women are a new breed to behold. They obviously enjoy their lifestyle within their marriages and in the larger subculture—where the kinds of expressions once reserved for men are permitted, and are safe for them to experience. They seem to truly prefer the lifestyle to standard monogamy, as it is taken for granted their husbands do. It is not a recommended "cure" for a couple's sexual problems, if they have any, and it probably doesn't offer any therapeutic "benefits." But for women it does offer social-sexual fun in marriages that can handle it and provided all the ethical and emotional rules are followed. Wives find out relatively quickly whether they can deal with spouse exchange, how their husbands react to their enjoyments, and what level of participation they are comfortable with in the lifestyle. Some remain soft swingers. Ninety percent move on to one of the other levels—right up to "hard core." Even those who engage at this level maintain that they enjoy this too, without ill effect.

The last reason I believe we are in for a jump in swinging is because of the commercial and electronic means swingers are now taking advantage of to get in touch with one another. Type "swinger" on the Internet and you will see that the old reviews that were swinger publications of the past have evolved esthetically—well, at least a bit—and have certainly grown in distribution. You don't even have to click on "NASCA" or "Lifestyles": innumerable swinger-contact links are up and running around the planet, many of them affiliated with LSO, and many of them independent of the organization (so watch yourself). Most of these links have sheaves of members' home pages—hot pink household displays with interactive communication, steamy text, baroque cartoons, and naked centerfolds inviting an e-mail. Twelve hours later, when you click off, you will swear that three-quarters of the world is covered in water and the other quarter in swingers. And they're all advertising themselves to the nonswinging millions.

It is in fact inevitable that more and more straight people will run across these ads—sexuality being of interest to many who peruse cyberspace—and many will feel safe enough in the virtual world to plug in and play. Thousands will certainly find their way to clubs no one suspected of being up and running within a fifteen-minute drive from home—these clubs tastefully but erotically advertised on the Net so as to encourage inquiries, with forms to fill out and appointments for screening interviews easily arranged.

And, of course, anyone on the Internet looking for swingers runs into LSO and its tours, conventions, clubs, dances, and philosophy—which have contributed to the growth of life-stylers in the nineties and will probably contribute to its growth in the future.

For this, oddly enough, McGinley finds himself criticized in the media for "commercializing" swinging, for keeping it "tightly organized," as if the media had no inkling of Love-boat holidays for straight couples—or, for that matter, the entire romance-based travel industry, the largest industry in the world as well as the most commercialized. As McGinley says, he provides a service—one that every year books hundreds of couples at a time to clubs in the hot places. Today playcouples are given the royal treatment in transit to their destinations by conveyors like Jamaica Airlines, and they are met at the airport by smiling representatives of national bureaucracies like the Jamaican Travel Board. Swinging makes people money, and that, I suppose, is another reason it will keep growing.

All these factors, coupled with the new, slightly more respectful attention of the media, seem to point to future "substantial growth" of the lifestyle. My feeling is there will almost certainly be a backlash to this growth; the raids will probably continue; some state or provincial government will reach a boiling point and act as if to save civilization itself from this detrimental, dangerous, and just plain tacky behavior. The weathervane media will probably sway whichever way the wind seems to be blowing at the time. If there is a single murder in a single swing club, it will probably make international headlines and the experts will be trotted out to say "I told you so." But playcouples will keep on playing, the swingers among them will keep on swinging, and lifestylers overall will keep on living in their own style.

In one form or another, people have been living that way for thousands of years.

Sources

Ackerman, Diane. *A Natural History of Love.* New York: Random House, 1994. Quoted from "Love and the Evolution of the Species." Broadcast on *Ideas*, CBC Radio, 14 February 1996.

Anand, Margo. *The Art of Sexual Ecstasy: The Path of Sacred Sexuality.* Los Angeles: Jeremy P. Tarcher, 1989.

Anapol, Deborah M. *Love Without Limits.* San Rafael: Intinet Resource Center, 1992.

Anka. "Unconventional Behavior." *Details*, November 1994.

Associated Press report, 13 September 1996.

Baker, Robin. *Sperm Wars: The Science of Sex.* New York: Basic Books, 1996.

Dartell, Gilbert. *Group Sex: A Scientist's Eyewitness Report on the American Way of Swinging.* New York: Peter H. Wyden, 1971.

Becker, Howard. *Outsiders: Studies in the Sociology of Deviance.* London: Free Press, 1963.

Block, Susan. Dr. Susan Block's Book Shop (Web page, cited 1996). drsusanblock.com.

Block, Susan. *Susan Block's Radio Sex TV.* Broadcast on HBO, 1996.

Block, Susan. *The Ten Commandments of Pleasure: Erotic Keys to a Healthy Sexual Life.* New York: St. Martin's, 1996.

Brecher, Edward M. *The Sex Researchers.* New York: Signet, 1971.

Broca, Lilian. Unearthing Angels (an exhibition of art on Lilith). Victoria: Fran Willis Gallery, 1997.

Bugliosi, Vincent, with Curt Gentry. *Helter Skelter: The True Story of the Manson Murders.* New York: W.W. Norton, 1994.

Butler, Edgar. *Traditional Marriage and Emerging Alternatives.* New York: Harper & Row, 1979.

Burkert, Walter. *Creation of the Sacred: Tracks of Biology in Early Religion.* Cambridge: Harvard University Press, 1996.

Chapple, Steve, and David Talbot. *Burning Desires: Sex in America.* New York: Doubleday, 1989.

Cooper, Matthew, and Mark Hosenball. "Private Lives, Political Ends." *Newsweek*, 23 September 1996.

Dale, Stan, and Val Beauchamp. *Fantasies Can Set You Free.* San Francisco: Celestial Arts, 1980.

Darwin, Charles. *The Descent of Man and Selection in Relation to Sex.* London: John Murray. Cited in Meredith Small. *Female Choices: Sexual Behavior of Female Primates.* Ithaca: Cornell University Press, 1993.

Darwin, Charles. *The Origin of Species by Means of Natural Selection.* London: John Murray. Cited in Meredith Small. *Female Choices: Sexual Behavior of Female Primates.* Ithaca: Cornell University Press, 1993.

De Waal, Frans, and Frans Lanting. *Bonobo: The Forgotten Ape.* Berkeley: University of California Press, 1997.

De Waal, Frans. "Bonobo Sex and Society." *Scientific American*, March 1995.

Dennett, Daniel C. "Appraising Grace." *The Sciences*, January/February 1997.

Dimont, Max I. *Jews, God and History*. New York: Signet, 1962.

"Discovery in Kazakhstan: Are These Women the Amazons of Legend?" Broadcast on *Quirks and Quarks*, CBC Radio, 15 March 1997.

Fillion, Kate. *Lip Service: The Truth About Women's Darker Side in Love, Sex, and Friendship*. Toronto: HarperCollins, 1996.

Fisher, Helen. *Anatomy of Love: A Natural History of Mating, Marriage, and Why We Stray*. New York: Fawcett Columbine, 1992.

Ford, Clellan S., and Frank A. Beach. *Patterns of Sexual Behavior*. New York: Harper & Brothers, 1951.

Fouchet, Max-Pol. *Erotic Sculptures of India*. Translated by Brian Rhys. London: George Allen and Unwin, 1959.

French, Marilyn. *Beyond Power: On Women, Men and Morals*. New York: Ballantine, 1985.

Friedl, Ernestine. "Sex the Invisible." *American Anthropologist* 96 (4) 1994. Cited in Timothy Taylor. *The Prehistory of Sex*. New York: Bantam, 1996.

Gandi, M.K. *An Autobiography or The Story of My Experiments With Truth* (translated from the original Gujarati by Mahadev Desai.) Ahmedabad: Navajivan Press, 1940.

Gilmartin, Brian. *The Gilmartin Report*. Secaucus: Citadel, 1978.

Globe and Mail, 12 March 1998.

Graves, Robert. "The Naked and the Nude." In *The Complete Poems*. Beryl Graves, and Dunstan Ward, eds. Manchester: Carcanet, 1995.

Gould, Terry. "A Dangerous State of Affairs." *V*, March 1989.

Gould, Terry. Registration desk survey questionnaire: 312 respondents (161 female; 151 male) of 3,500 attendees. August 1996.

Gutcheon, David (nom de plume Morris Fischbein). "The Politics of Erotica." *Art Collector International*, December 1997.

Haich, Elisabeth. *Sexual Energy and Yoga*. New York: ASI, 1972.

Hazelton, Lesley. *Israeli Women: The Reality Behind the Myths*. New York: Touchstone, 1977.

Heinlein, Robert. *Stranger in a Strange Land*. Berkley: Berkley Publishing, 1961.

Henican, Ellis. "Swinging Swings Back." *Penthouse*, November 1993.

Heyn, Dalma. "The Affair." *Cosmopolitan*, August 1995.

Holmberg, Allan R. *Nomads of the Long Bow: The Siriono of Eastern Bolivia*. Washington: Government Printing Office, 1950.

Hrdy, Sarah Blaffer. *The Langurs of Abu*. Cambridge: Harvard University Press, 1977.

Jewish Publication Society of America. *The Torah: The Five Books of Moses*. Philadelphia: Jewish Publication Society of America, 1962.

Jones, Steve, Robert Martin, and David Pilbeam, eds. *The Cambridge Encyclopedia of Human Evolution*. Cambridge: Cambridge University Press, 1992.

Junod, Tom. "The Last Swinger." *GQ*, April 1996.

Kerouac, Jack. *The Dharma Bums*. New York: Signet, 1958.

Kinsey, Alfred C. *Sexual Behavior in the Human Female*. Philadelphia: W.B. Saunders Co., 1953.

Klaw, Spencer. *Without Sin: The Life and Death of the Oneida Community.* New York: Penguin, 1993.

Kosinski, Jerzy. *Passion Play.* New York: Bantam, 1979.

Krishna, Gopi. *Kundalini: The Evolutionary Energy in Man.* Berkeley: Shambala, 1967.

Krishnamurti, J. *The First and Last Freedom.* San Francisco: Harper, 1975.

Kurtz, Irma. Agony Column. *Cosmopolitan,* December 1995.

Kurtz, Irma. Agony Column. *Cosmopolitan,* February 1998.

Lewis, Steven. More Bing FAQS/Bing's Home Page (Web site, cited 1996).

Liberated Christians (Web page, cited 1997). P.O. Box 32835, Phoenix Az, 85064-2835.

Los Angeles Times, 12 February 1998.

"Love and the Evolution of the Species." Broadcast on *Ideas,* CBC Radio, 14 February 1996.

Loving More, Spring 1996.

Loving More, Summer 1996.

Malinowski, Branislaw. *The Sexual Life of Savages.* Boston: Beacon Press, 1929.

Mason, Steve. "Playcouples: Reviving Romance in the Nineties." Anaheim: The Lifestyles Organization, 1993.

Masters, William A., with Virginia E. Johnson. *Human Sexual Response.* Boston: Little, Brown, 1966.

McGinley, Robert L. "Development and Structure of Swinging in the United States with Reference and Challenge to Published Reports." Ph.D. diss., Newport International University, 1979.

Michael, Robert T., John H. Gagnon, Edward O. Laumann, and Gina Kolata. *Sex in America: A Definitive Survey.* New York: Warner Books, 1995.

Mickey, Paul A., with William Proctor. *Sex with Confidence.* New York: William Morrow, 1988. Reprinted in David L. Bender, Bruno Leone, and Lisa Orr, eds. *Sexual Values: Opposing Viewpoints.* San Diego: Greenhaven, 1989.

Money, John. *The Destroying Angel: Sex, Fitness & Food in the Legacy of Degeneracy Theory, Graham Crackers, Kellogg's Corn Flakes & American Health History.* Buffalo: Prometheus, 1985.

(Montreal) Gazette, 7 March 1998.

NASCA International. *Etiquette in Swinging.* Anaheim: NASCA International (LSO, Ltd.), 1990.

NASCA International. *International Directory: Swing Clubs, Publications and Events.* Anaheim: NASCA International (LSO, Ltd.), 1996.

National Enquirer, 1 October 1996.

National Enquirer, 24 September 1996.

Nearing, Ryam. *Loving More: The Polyfidelity Primer.* Hawaii: Pep Publishing, 1992.

Newman, Judith. "Strange Bedfellows." *GQ,* October 1993.

Nietzsche, Friedrich. *Beyond Good and Evil.* Translated by R.J. Hollingdale. Penguin Classics. Middlesex: Penguin, 1973.

Nietzsche, Friedrich. *Twilight of the Idols.* Translated by Walter Kaufmann. Viking Portable Library. New York: Penguin, 1954.

Orff, Karl. *Carmina Burana.* Mainz: Schott Musik International, 1936.

Osborn, Lawrence. *The Poisoned Embrace.* London: Bloomsbury, 1993.

(Palm Springs) Desert Sun, 30 July 1997.

Partridge, Burgo. *A History of Orgies.* New York: Crown, 1960.

Pringle, Heather. "New Women of the Ice Age." *Discover*, April 1998.

Rapport, Samuel, and Helen Wright. *Anthropology.* New York: Washington Square Press, 1968.

Reifer, Susan. "Sensual and Erotic Art Exhibition." *Penthouse*, January 1996.

Ridley, Matt. *The Red Queen: Sex and the Evolution of Human Nature.* New York: Penguin, 1993.

Robinson, Jill. "Polanski's Inferno." *Vanity Fair*, April 1997.

Rothenberg, Randall. "The Age of Spin." *Esquire*, December 1996.

Sager, Mike. "Deviates in Love." *Esquire*, October 1992.

Shearer, William K. Letter to Robert McGinley, 17 December 1996.

Sherfey, Mary Jane. *The Nature and Evolution of Female Sexuality.* New York: Random House, 1972.

Slomiak, Mitch. "The Dark Side to Community." *Loving More*, Spring 1996.

Slomiak, Mitch. "The Dark Side to Community—Part II." *Loving More*, Summer 1996.

Small, Meredith. *Female Choices: Sexual Behavior of Female Primates.* Ithaca: Cornell University Press, 1993.

Smith, James R., and Lynn G. Smith. "Co-marital Sex and the Sexual Freedom Movement. *Journal of Sex Research* 6 (2). Reprinted in *Beyond Monogamy*. James R. Smith, and Lynn G. Smith, eds. Baltimore: Johns Hopkins University Press, 1974.

The Star, 1 October 1996.

The Star, 24 September 1996.

Symons, Donald. *The Evolution of Human Sexuality.* Oxford: Oxford University Press, 1981.

Talese, Gay. *Thy Neighbor's Wife.* New York: Ballantine, 1981.

Tannahill, Reay. *Sex in History.* Toronto: Scarborough House, 1992.

Taylor, Timothy. *The Prehistory of Sex: Four Million Years of Human Sexual Culture.* New York: Bantam, 1996.

Thera, Narada Maha. *The Buddha and His Teachings.* Singapore: Buddhist Meditation Centre, n.d.

Thomas, Patti, ed. *For Play: A Look at New Horizons.* Ohio: Emerald Bay Publishing, 1996.

Tiger, Lionel. *The Pursuit of Pleasure.* Boston: Little, Brown, 1992.

(Vancouver) Province, 19 March 1998.

Vancouver Sun, 15 May 1998.

Vancouver Sun, 26 October 1996.

Ward, Tim. *Arousing the Goddess.* Toronto: Somerville, 1996.

Washington Post, 2 August 1997.

"What Do Women Really Want?" Broadcast on The Learning Channel, 19 October 1997. Quotes in Chapter 7 from Patricia Gowaty, Sarah Blaffer Hrdy and Tom Shackelford are taken from this program.

"Why Sex?" Broadcast on *The Nature of Things*, CBC TV, 1996.

Wright, Robert. *The Moral Animal: Why We Are the Way We Are.* New York: Vintage, 1994.

Yogananda, Paramahansa. *Autobiography of a Yogi.* Los Angeles: Self-Realization Fellowship, 1940.

Young, Louisa. "Sex Convention." *Marie Claire*, May 1993

Young, Lucie. "The Swinger Convention." *Elle*, December 1995.

Acknowledgments

My effort to explain the lifestyle was made easier because of the assistance I received from five distinguished academics. All are cited in this book but I would like to specifically acknowledge their contributions. Dr. Josef Skala, currently professor emeritus on the faculty of medicine at the University of British Columbia, freely offered his time and knowledge as my medical advisor throughout this project. Dr. Jean Henry, currently developing doctoral programs at the University of Nevada, offered me her invaluable assessments of the couples she and I observed at several lifestyle gatherings. Dr. Edgar Butler, professor emeritus at the University of California, Riverside, shared with me his extensive knowledge of the lifestyle movement. The anthropologist and author Leanna Wolfe offered me her perspectives on the emergence of polyamory in the 1990s and directed me to source books which helped me immensely. Finally, Dr. Ted McIlvenna, president of the Institute for Advanced Study of Human Sexuality, gave me access to the resources of his institute and shared his research on lifestyle couples.

Without the cooperation of the lifestyle couples themselves, of course, there would have been no book. Some allowed me to use their real names; others asked that I use pseudonyms; all were open to my presence at their events and to answering my questions. I am very thankful to them for trusting that I would treat them with dignity.

An equal measure of thanks goes to Dr. Robert McGinley and the staff at the Lifestyles Organization. The access I had to LSO's day-to-day workings obviously contributed greatly to this book.

At the end of my research I wound up with over two

dozen cartons of notebooks, tapes, photo albums, documents, and textbooks. For her help in reviewing, summarizing and transcribing some of this mountain of material I would like to express my gratitude to my research assistant, Camilia Rabet.

Before I began this book I'd met very few colleagues who thought the lifestyle had important implications. Gary Bush, an Academy Award-nominated film director, was one of those few. In 1993 we teamed up to make a documentary film about the subject, and while we were not able to raise the funds to bring the project to fruition, Gary's many insights about the subculture have influenced my writing. For his gracious (and gratis) support of our proposed film, I thank entertainment lawyer Arthur Evrensel.

My literary agents, Perry Goldsmith and Robert Mackwood, were also among the first to recognize that the lifestyle required a broad explanation, and I am grateful for their encouragement in this project.

I am additionally grateful to the Canada Council for accepting my plan to handle the book and awarding me a short-term literary journalism grant.

In the end, it was Sarah Davies, my editor at Random House of Canada, who gave me the backing I needed to proceed with my approach to the subject. We both realized that an in-depth examination of the lifestyle would not be easy. Over the course of several drafts Sarah helped me find a form that communicated my research. Anne Collins, editorial director at Random House, offered invaluable advice on the final preparation of the manuscript.

I began this book with a dedication to my wife and I end with the same. Leslie never once expressed a doubt that I could explain the lifestyle high-mindedly. If I've come anywhere near to succeeding, it's because of her support.

Terry Gould
December, 1998

Index